NAPOLEON'S
MILITARY MACHINE

First published in January 2019

A catalogue record for this book is available from the British Library.

ISBN 978 1 78521 221 5

Library of Congress control no. 2018938904

Published by Haynes Publishing,
Sparkford, Yeovil, Somerset
BA22 7JJ, UK.
Tel: 01963 440635
Int. tel: +44 1963 440635
Website: www.haynes.com

Haynes North America Inc.,
859 Lawrence Drive, Newbury Park,
California 91320, USA.

Printed in Malaysia.

Diagrams and battle plan artwork by Elly Forty

The author would like to thank the following people for their help with this publication, particularly in collecting the photographic content: Duncan Miles (www.45eme.com), Wesley Miles, Alan Baldwin, Paul Dawson, Michael Mathews (www.brigade-napoleon.org) and Christine Sepers.

All images are credited within the captions, apart from the following pages: 6–7 PD/CC, 18–19 PD/CC, 38–39 Veleknez / Shutterstock, 64–65 and 82–83 Wesley Miles, 104–105 Duncan Miles, 122–23 Cesar Manso / AFP /Getty Images, p148–49 Ian Dagnall / Alamy Stock Photo.

Author's Note

I make every effort to ensure that the information in this book is accurate, yet I recognise that in complex topics some errors of fact or interpretation can slip through. If readers have any corrections or feedback, you are welcome to go to www.colour-blue.co.uk/author-zone, and use the feedback form provided. Please ensure that your comments are constructive, and made in the spirit of improving knowledge. Any corrections made will be listed there for the benefit of all readers, and will be made to the printed book on later reprint. The Author Zone will also contain additional information about the topic that readers might find interesting.

KEY TO BATTLE PLANS

BASIC SYMBOLS

Regiment	III
Brigade	X
Division	X X
Corps	X X X
Army	X X X X
Infantry	⊠
Cavalry	⊿
Cavalry Covering Force	• •⋅•

OTHER SYMBOLS

Troops on the march	→
Troops in position	▬
Troops in bivouac or reserve	◯
Troops displacing and direction	⊓⊓⊓
Troops in position under attack	⊞⊞⊞
Route of march	----→
Field works	∧∧∧

NAPOLEON'S MILITARY MACHINE

Operations Manual

CHRIS McNAB

CONTENTS

▼ *French cavalry, infantry and artillery (foreground) receive a charge from the Brandenburg Hussars during the battle of Leipzig, 16 October 1813. (FALKENSTEINFOTO / Alamy).*

▲ *A cavalry charge of French cuirassiers at Waterloo. (PD/CC)*

INTRODUCTION

Napoleon Bonaparte emerged onto the world stage in the 1790s as a talented and highly driven young military officer. In the space of just three years, his battlefield successes and political manoeuvring had made him the most powerful man in France, and a dominant force throughout much of Europe.

NAPOLEON AND THE FRENCH REVOLUTION

In his landmark 19th-century work *Heroes and Hero-Worship* (1840), the British historian Thomas Carlyle stated that: 'The history of the world is but the biography of great men.' Carlyle was one of the leading proponents of what became known as the 'Great Man Theory', the idea that powerful individuals, of singular talent, vision or character, were the driving force behind history.

Recently this theory has been reassessed; criticised, sometimes rightly, for ignoring the broader historical waves found in social and political movements, waves that prominent figures frequently ride to power. Yet there do seem to be undeniable occasions when a single individual has a disproportionate effect on the movements and outcomes of history, and surely Napoleon Bonaparte (1769–1821) is one of them. Such was the clarity and force of his military leadership, the dexterity of his political manoeuvring, and the loyalty he inspired amongst millions of French men and women, that it is difficult to interpret the history of Europe between c.1796 and 1815 without understanding this remarkable man.

An overview of the life of Napoleon, and that of the French Revolutionary and Napoleonic Wars, are necessary to understand the content that is to follow. Born Napoleone Buonaparte into a large family in Ajaccio, Corsica, the young Napoleon developed a strident Corsican nationalism, centred upon the figure of Pasquale di Paoli. The year before Napoleon was born, the French had invaded Corsica, and Paoli became a leading figure amongst the resistance.

Yet Napoleon's father, Carlo – previously a secretary and personal assistant to Paoli – found that commercial and social accommodation with the French was preferable to interminable strife, and thus began the Buonaparte family's gravitation into French high society.

EARLY MILITARY EXPERIENCE

At the age of nine, Napoleon moved to France, first studying in Autun, then at the military academy at Brienne-le-Château. A studious and ardent boy, Napoleon did well at his academic work, and progressed to the *École Militaire* in Paris in 1784. There he immersed himself in military studies, showing all the qualities of self-discipline and self-denial for which he would later become famous. On graduation in September 1785, Napoleon was commissioned a second lieutenant in *La Fère* artillery regiment.

Napoleon's early years in uniform were, truth be told, somewhat less than impressive. The young man was frequently absent (approved or otherwise) from his regiment while he sorted out the commercial and personal issues

▼ *Napoleon pictured at 23 years of age, as an officer in the Corsican Republican volunteers. (PD/CC)*

▼ *Napoleon's father, Carlo Buonaparte, quickly adapted to the French takeover of Corsica in the late 1760s. (PD/CC)*

DECLARATION OF THE RIGHTS OF THE MAN (1789)

The Declaration of the Rights of the Man and of the Citizen of 1789 is one of the founding political documents of the Western world. Drafted by General Marie-Joseph Lafayette, Thomas Jefferson (the influence of the US Declaration of Independence is clear) and Honoré Mirabeau, and enshrined by the National Constituent Assembly, it was a radical philosophical reframing of the relationship between the people and the state. Its Article 1 – 'Men are born and remain free and equal in rights. Social distinctions may be founded only upon the general good' – set a class-free individuality at the heart of the French identity, and established 'liberty, property, security, and resistance to oppression' (Article 2) as inalienable human properties. The remainder of the 17 articles set the groundwork for a free and just society, particularly in relation to the exercise of law and democratic governance. Over time, however, Napoleon subverted many of the articles in the Declaration, as he inched France from being a republic under elected legislatures to an empire under his sole authority. Article 3 is particularly relevant to his rise: 'The principle of all sovereignty resides essentially in the nation. No body nor individual may exercise any authority which does not proceed directly from the nation.' Napoleon, of course, would and did argue that his ultimate rule over France proceeded naturally from his deep belief in the Republican ideals and his intrinsic connection to the French people. In many ways, Napoleon felt that he *was* France.

▲ The Emperor Napoleon in His Study at the Tuileries *by Jacques-Louis David, Napoleon already demonstrating the affectation of placing his hand inside his tunic. (PD/CC)*

resulting from the early death of his father in 1785. Yet when he was with his regiment at Auxonne, attending the artillery school there, he worked hard to acquire the deep knowledge of gunnery that would serve him well in the future.

In 1789, France was convulsed by a revolution that came to define the country's modern history. As events played out in political and social upheaval, Napoleon adjusted himself to the new realities, evidently spying opportunities for advancement. Initially committed, albeit in a rather conflicted fashion, to Corsican nationalism, Napoleon largely embraced the Revolution's ideals, although he had an abiding distaste for mob disorder. Between 1789 and 1792, he served as the commander of a volunteer unit in Corsica, but his zeal in crushing riots by force brought him increased alienation from Paoli and, eventually, the Corsican nationalist project in general. Thus in June 1793, he and his family moved wholesale to France and from then on France would become Napoleon's first loyalty, both mentally and politically.

By the time that Napoleon completely turned his back on Corsica, France itself had descended into a major war. The French king, Louis XVI, was technically the head of a

constitutional monarchy, but real power now lay outside royal hands, a fact that was not lost upon the wider European powers. For many heads of state, the French Revolution was a seismic challenge to the God-ordained hierarchy that placed the monarchy at the summit of the social order and was the political foundation of imperial statehood. The perfectly realistic possibility that Revolutionary ideals could be exported from France struck a chill note among other European powers, who now began to align themselves against France. The Declaration of Pillnitz on 2 August 1791 saw King Frederick William II of Prussia and the Holy Roman Emperor Leopold II openly state their objective to return Louis to the throne, and an official Austro-Prussian alliance was concluded the following year. Thereafter the French Legislative Assembly (the main Revolutionary political body at this time, which was succeeded the following August by the National Convention) declared war on Austria and Prussia.

WAR OF THE FIRST COALITION (1792–97)

So began the War of the First Coalition, a prolonged and enormously destructive conflict that ran from 1792 to 1797. It was a dangerous phase for the French state. French forces had been undermined, particularly at officer levels and among the cavalry, by the emigration of many professional soldiers during the early phase of the Revolution.

WAR OF THE FIRST COALITION – COMBATANTS	
French	**Coalition**
France	Holy Roman Empire (Austria,
Spain (from 1796)	Prussia)
Batavian Republic (from	Great Britain
1795)	Army of Condé
various Italian Republics	Spain (until 1795)
Polish Legions (from 1797)	Dutch Republic
	Portugal
	Sardinia (until 1796)
	Naples
	various Italian states

Furthermore, they now faced the combined might of Prussia and Austria, to which Britain, Spain, Russia, the Netherlands, Naples and Tuscany eventually added their strength to form the First Coalition. The First Coalition forces, some 80,000 strong and headed by the Duke of Brunswick, got off to a powerful start, invading France and taking key fortress positions at Longwy and Verdun. Yet the existential threat now seemed to galvanise the French both ideologically and militarily. The Tuileries palace was stormed, Louis XVI imprisoned and France declared itself a republic. Then came the military fightback. On 20 September 1792, a 36,000-strong French force under General François Kellerman and General Charles Dumouriez pulled off a victory over Brunswick at Valmy. It was a seminal moment. Thereafter French forces enjoyed a string of battlefield successes across the Savoy, in the Low Countries and on the

◄ *A grand and regal portrait of the ill-fated Louis XVI, King of France and Navarre (1754–93), a king fatally undermined by financial and political mismanagement. (PD/CC)*

EDICT OF FRATERNITY

The Edict of Fraternity was essentially a revolutionary call to arms for the international community, an explicit statement that the overview of monarchs or tyrants was an endeavour that France would both applaud and assist. It stated:

> The National Convention declares in the name of the French nation that it will accord fraternity and assistance to all peoples who wish to recover their liberty. It charges the executive power to give the generals the necessary orders for bearing help to these peoples and defending citizens who are vexed for the cause of liberty. The present decree shall be translated and printed in all languages.

The provocation and threat to the European powers was evident in the language; the French were now aiming for international liberation (with, as would become apparent, many restrictive conditions) – not just the preservation of their own republic.

▲ *Volunteers sign up for military service during the* levée en masse *of 1793. The scale of conscription radically challenged the model of a standing army. (PD/CC)*

Rhine, pushing back the Coalition forces on several fronts. Brussels fell to French occupation. The fledgling republic had, for now, been saved, but the internal political and social turmoil was severe. The monarchy was abolished in the most demonstrative fashion, with the execution of Louis XVI on 21 January 1793. The Assembly had also issued its famous Edict of Fraternity on 19 November 1792, extending its sense of Enlightenment rights to the international community.

The year 1793 thus saw the Coalition unleash itself on the French with renewed vigour. A sequence of French defeats followed – at Neerwinden, Mainz, Condé and Valenciennes. British landings took place in Toulon. Royalist revolts flashed across French provinces. The French authorities now turned on themselves, unleashing the internecine Terror that saw thousands of its citizens imprisoned, tortured and murdered. Even the great Dumouriez, facing a suspicion of treachery following the loss of Brussels, saw the writing on the wall and defected to the Allies.

LEVÉE EN MASSE

Some responses, however, were more productive. Famously, on 23 August, the Committee of Public Safety – a potent supervisory organisation with broad powers, which had been formed the previous April – declared the *levée en masse*, in theory and partly in practice the conscription of the entire French populace for the war effort. Here, in effect, was the introduction of what we now term 'total war'. (It should be noted that in the spring of 1793 a *levée en 300,000* had been introduced as a first response, with the *levée en masse* simply extending the principle.) It was a groundbreaking approach to warfare, one that radically changed war in terms of ideology – in theory, at least, the French conscripts were fighting for their own republic, rather than for remote monarchical interests – but also in the sheer scale of warfare. By the end of 1794, France would have more than a million men in the field – an astonishing scale of expansion.

In 1794 the French Army renewed its offensive spirit, proven in a sequence of victories across Europe. These landmark events included Jean-Baptiste Jourdan's great triumphs at Fleurus (26 June) and Wattignies (15–16 October) and that of Joseph Souham at Tourcoing (18 May). Such was the scale of the French ascendancy that in 1794–95 Austria, Prussia, Spain and Holland all signed peace agreements.

▶ *The French commander General Jean-Baptiste Jourdan rears his horse and rallies his troops against Austrian–Dutch forces at the battle of Fleurus on 26 June 1794. (PD/CC)*

NAPOLEON'S RISE

Amid these thunderous events, one man was beginning his ascendancy. In 1793, Napoleon provided minor military service in helping to suppress local French revolts. He had also made some judicious choices when it came to friends, two of the most prominent being Augustin Robespierre, brother of the Revolutionary Maximilien Robespierre, and diplomat Antoine Christophe Saliceti.

It was partly through these sources of influence, but principally through his evident talent and motivation, that Napoleon took his first significant command, of the French artillery at the siege of Toulon (28 August–19 December 1793). Although the siege was under overall command of General Jacques Dugommier, Napoleon played a leading role over the French artillery batteries and the infantry who made final assaults on British and royalist positions. Napoleon also demonstrated, and not for the last time, his personal bravery and willingness to fight alongside his men, putting himself in the thick of the fighting sufficient enough to be bayoneted in the thigh by a British soldier during the fortress assaults on 16 December.

Napoleon's leadership and actions at Toulon gave him his first significant military victory, plus his promotion to the rank of brigadier general – and still only 24 years old. Now he was firmly on the political and military map of republican France. His stature increased accordingly the following year, when on 5 October (or, according to the new Revolutionary calendar, 13 Vendémiaire Year 4), Napoleon commanded cannon in the streets of Paris, using the guns to slash down the mob in defence of the Convention. Napoleon reputedly said that he used the 'whiff of grapeshot' to repel the crowds, although the attribution is probably apocryphal. Whatever the case, Napoleon had successfully demonstrated that he was someone loyal to the republic.

STRING OF VICTORIES

With the ear of the Convention, Napoleon took his first major theatre command, taking over as head of the Army of Italy in March 1796. It was this campaign, above all, that established Napoleon's reputation for military brilliance. The principal foes in the conflict were the Austrians and Piedmontese. Napoleon faced his enemies with a meagre force – a poorly equipped and neglected army of 37,000 men – but he set about revitalising its capability and its morale with an extraordinary dynamism. What came next was a rapid-fire string of French victories, delivered via a commander who used manoeuvre, speed, tempo and concentration of force with an almost unprecedented bravura. Napoleon swept his troops across northern Italy, through Nice, Savoy and Piedmont, defeating the Austrians at Milan, Arcola, Rivoli and, after a long siege, Mantua in February 1797, subsequently taking Venice and the Ionian islands. Napoleon's troops pushed far enough forward to be within sight of Vienna. The Austrians, unnerved by this now proximate threat and by the defeat of the previously insurmountable Archduke Charles by French offensives in northern Europe, sued for peace.

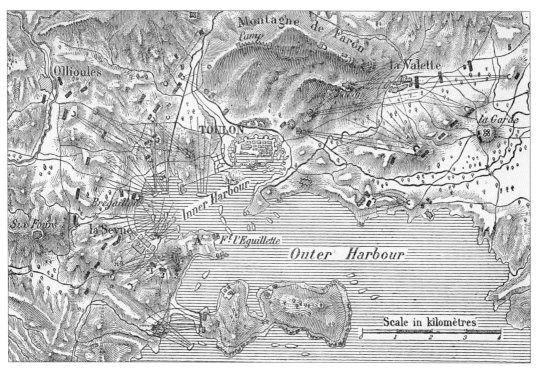

◄ *A map of the siege of Toulon in August– December 1793. It was at Toulon that Napoleon made an early impression as a leader, through his command of artillery resources. (PD/CC)*

What was notable about the Treaty of Campo Formio – the formal peace agreement between France and Austria – was that it was designed, negotiated and implemented almost unilaterally by Napoleon, without recourse to the Convention. For their part, the Convention watched this self-aggrandising behaviour with mounting disquiet, although such was now the popularity of Napoleon among both the military and the public, that they could do little to quash his ambition.

Napoleon was gathering momentum. In 1798, he took on his next command role, in charge of an expeditionary force against British interests in Egypt. By 1798, the war in Europe had largely, for now, been decided in France's favour, with most continental adversaries subdued. Britain, however, remained a stubborn thorn in the French side. While Britain itself was not a viable option for invasion, France looked to strike at Britain's colonial strongholds, specifically those in North Africa, where the French would also face resistance from the Ottoman Empire. Napoleon put his force of 40,000 men ashore in Egypt on 1 July, and again demonstrated martial brilliance, with Alexandria falling almost immediately on 2 July. He took his army south, beating off the Mameluke army of Murad Bey at the battle of the Pyramids on 21 July, before entering and occupying Cairo.

NAVAL DOWNFALL

But now the campaign turned for Napoleon, and for reasons largely beyond his control (which saved his reputation). The might of the Royal Navy ensured that Britain would remain largely immune from French invasion, and it also acted as a maritime bodyguard over Britain's extensive global empire. Even as France chalked up victories on land, so the British did likewise at sea – significant French naval defeats included Ushant on the Glorious First of June 1794, Cape St Vincent on 14 February 1797, and Camperdown on 11 October 1797. Seeing the threat in Egypt, Britain sent a fleet under Admiral Horatio Nelson, which on 1 August 1798 almost wiped out the French invasion fleet at anchor in Aboukir Bay. Napoleon's army was now effectively cut off from its maritime lifelines. Not that Napoleon gave in to passivity. Responding to the threat of a Turkish uprising in the region, Napoleon launched a pre-emptive campaign into Sinai, taking El Arish (14–15 February 1799), Jaffa (3–7 March) and besieging Acre. Here, however, was the high-water mark of his campaign in North Africa. With British transports landing Ottoman forces at Aboukir, and plague having killed many of his men, Napoleon retreated back to Aboukir, where he defeated the Turkish forces. The leader himself, seeing little future in the campaign and responding to military and political crises back in France, sailed back home on 22 August 1799, leaving the French survivors to fight on, leading some to see Napoleon committing an act of abandonment.

▶ Napoleon in Egypt *by Jean-Léon Gérôme. In Egypt, Napoleon was known for his sensitivity to local customs and religion; he studied Islam intensively prior to and during the Egyptian campaign. (PD/CC)*

▲ *Napoleon personally mans a cannon at the siege of Toulon, as seen in a 19th-century children's book. (Photo 12 / Alamy)*

WAR OF THE SECOND COALITION (1799–1802)

Even as French forces were fighting for survival in Egypt and Syria, in continental Europe the anti-French allies made another attempt to snuff out the nascent French Republic. The period from 1799 to 1802 was that of the War of the Second Coalition, with the principal members of that coalition being Austria, Russia, Great Britain, Naples, Portugal and Turkey.

This phase of the French Revolutionary Wars is critical to our history, for it saw Napoleon's ascent from being a sparkling new military commander to being the undisputed leader of France, and in perpetuity – an ironic achievement given the fact that the French Revolution was in many ways a reaction against hereditary and monarchical privilege.

THE EARLY BATTLES

The early battles of the War of the Second Coalition were confined to three main theatres – the Netherlands, Germany and Italy. In Germany and Italy in particular, 1799 saw the French take some heavy hits at the hands of the Austrians and Russians. Archduke Charles's drive into Germany resulted in the defeat of Jean-Baptiste Jourdan's army at Ostrach (21 March) and Stockbach (25 March) – these defeats leading to his resignation – while in Switzerland André Masséna was roundly beaten at the battle of Zurich (14 August). In northern Italy, matters were even more desperate for the French. The Austrian forces in this territory were supplemented by a large Russian army under the capable General Alexander Suvorov, who routed the French in a sequence of victories that effectively took back all the territory so hard won by Napoleon's army in 1796.

▼ *An Italian political cartoon, 1797, shows French Liberty being carried into the arms of Medusa. (PD/CC)*

WAR OF THE SECOND COALITION – COMBATANTS	
French	**Coalition**
France	Holy Roman Empire (Austria)
Spain	Great Britain/United Kingdom
Polish Legions	(from 1801)
Denmark–Norway	Russia
Batavian Republic	Portugal
Helvetic Republic	Naples
Cisalpine Republic	Grand Duchy of Tuscany
Roman Republic	Order of Saint John
Parthenopaean Republic	United States

French fortunes turned in the autumn of 1799, largely because of the inept lack of cooperation between the coalition allies, which meant that their campaigns lacked coordination and direction. The French reclaimed Zurich from Russian forces under General Alexander Korsakov on 25 September, a victory that led the tsar to dismiss Suvorov, who had been transferred from Italy to command forces in Switzerland, but had yet to arrive. An Anglo-Russian force was also defeated in the Netherlands, which resulted in the tsar withdrawing Russia from the coalition and the war in Holland being brought to an end by the Convention of Alkmaar on 18 October 1799.

▼ *A circular bronze medal commemorating the battle of Marengo, the medal designed by Bertrand Andrieu. (PD/CC)*

It was the evidence of French collapse, and particularly the news of Suvorov's victory at Novi (15 August) in Italy, that mainly drove Napoleon to abandon his Egyptian campaign and return to France. Napoleon not only saw a country in need of his military leadership, but also perceived a political window of opportunity, as the French republican government descended into factional infighting. Napoleon returned to a stormy Paris and built up canny alliances, aided by the ascent of his brother Lucien to president of the Council of the Five Hundred (the lower house of the legislature) on 25 October. On 9–10 November 1799, Napoleon drove a political and military coup (known as the Coup de 18 Brumaire) and established a new 'provisional executive' of three men, although the two others were quickly pushed into retirement and, on 25 December, Napoleon was declared as 'First Consul'. Bonaparte was now essentially the leader of France, and a new constitution was quickly ratified.

CRUCIAL VICTORY

Napoleon now took a firm hold on all the military campaigns. In 1800–01, northern Italy was once again taken back into French hands, with Napoleon leading the campaign on familiar ground with dash and aggression. A crucial victory was secured at Marengo in Piedmont on 14 June 1800, when his army – initially only 18,000 strong against an Austrian force of more than 30,000 – secured an exceptional

▲ *In this highly theatrical painting by Jean Broc, Napoleon is presented with the body of General Desaix, who was killed by a musket ball at the battle of Marengo. (PD/CC)*

victory, although only with the timely arrival of two French divisions under General Louis Desaix, who was killed leading the attack. The win at Marengo not only led to the collapse and surrender of Austrian forces in Italy, but also further cemented Napoleon's position as First Consul. In northern Europe, the Austrians also found themselves taking defeats as General Jean Victor Moreau pushed French forces through Bavaria and into Austria. At Hohenlinden on 3 December 1800, Moreau routed the Austrians, whose leadership now recognised that Vienna was under direct threat and that further resistance was pointless – other French forces were converging on Austria from Italy and Switzerland. They petitioned for peace, which was officially signed at Lunéville on 9 February 1801.

With the peace of Lunéville, the Second Coalition now effectively collapsed. Britain struggled on largely alone, principally wielding its sword through naval means, such as the raid on the French-allied Dutch fleet at Copenhagen on 2 April 1801. But such ongoing struggle seemed without strategic purpose and, on 27 March 1802, the Peace of Amiens was signed, bringing a momentary period – just 14 months – of peace to a war-torn continent.

NEW ERA

The French Revolutionary Wars ushered in a fresh philosophy of statehood, which was grounded – theoretically – in the hands of the people rather than a monarch. This political re-engineering had a direct military and strategic effect in the conflict, not least in the rapid expansion of the size of field armies, which now drew on more than just its regular forces.

Indeed, by August 1794 France had a field army that numbered possibly more than one million men-at-arms; at the very outset of the Revolution in 1789, the French Army had a total strength of just 170,000 men. It is partly this strength, combined with the leadership of commanders such as Napoleon, Moreau, Augereau, Jourdan and Masséna, and the increasing professionalism and *esprit de corps* of the soldiery itself, that explains how the new French state was able to resist and then dominate the collective might of Russia, Prussia, Austria, Britain and several other co-belligerents, each powerful in its own right.

But the Revolutionary period also provided the opportunity for military rethinking; sheer size alone could never guarantee victory. As shall be explained in detail in subsequent

chapters, the period from 1789 to 1802 saw numerous tactical innovations: the improved applications of artillery; the dramatically increased numbers of skirmishing troops; improvements in infantry battlefield formations; the formation of mixed-arms divisions and corps; and the ability for talented leaders to rise quickly to seniority, to name but a few.

One man in particular was at the vanguard of these advances – Napoleon. As a military commander, Napoleon

▼ *In James Gillray's political cartoon, Napoleon flies into a rage at the news of Nelson's destruction of the French fleet at the battle of the Nile. (PD/CC)*

had demonstrated martial daring, tactical sagacity, an intimate understanding of frontline soldiering, a grasp of the technicalities of warfare, a willingness to dispense with tradition and the ability to inspire tens of thousands of men to offer their unquestioning loyalty. But he was also politically opportunistic, and deeply devoted to attaining power and influence. Following the 18 Brumaire coup, his influence only increased.

On 2 August 1802, a plebiscite declared Napoleon Consul for Life – approval for this step was secured with more than 97 per cent of a public vote. Then, on 27 March 1804, the Senate voted on a motion 'inviting Napoleon Bonaparte to complete his work and render it as immortal as his glory'. Matters gathered pace and, on 18 May, Napoleon was declared Emperor of the French, with the modified constitution approved unanimously. A plebiscite on 2 August again brought near-total public approval for this step and, on

2 December a coronation of 'Napoléon Ier' was held at the cathedral of Notre Dame, Paris. From a republic, France had now become an empire, with Napoleon at its head.

The remainder of the book is largely focused on explaining the French armed forces from 1801 – when Napoleon secured his power over France – until the ultimate French defeat at Waterloo in 1815, although we will on several occasions return to an analysis of the Revolutionary military. In this journey, which will reach from minor practicalities of life on campaign through to major tactical decisions on the field of battle, we will see, arguably, the birth of modern warfare, partly impelled by the innovations of one of history's supreme military leaders.

▼ *Commissioned by Napoleon in 1804, Jacques-Louis David's imposing work depicts the consecration of Napoleon as emperor in the Cathedral of Notre-Dame de Paris. (PD/CC)*

1

NAPOLEON: THE MAN AND HIS COMMANDERS

From 1799 there was essentially one man at the helm of France's destiny – Napoleon Bonaparte. This dominance applied militarily as well as politically. Napoleon had some great commanders within his armed forces, but there was never any doubt about who was in charge.

WAR OF THE THIRD COALITION (1803–06)

Before probing deeper into Napoleon's command capabilities, we must complete the narrative of France's campaigns, taking them up to the final cataclysmic battle at Waterloo in 1815. By doing so, we see in striking fashion how France fared under Napoleon's imperial rule – a classic story of hubristic rise and fall.

The War of the Third Coalition began on 16 May 1803, with Britain's declaration of war on the French state, and its resumption of naval blockade activities. The Third Coalition would eventually include three of the greatest living empires – the British, Holy Roman and Russian – but by this time the alliance of nations was under no illusion that mere scale

▼ *An American map of the strategic situation in Europe in 1805, showing French forces redeploying to face the German states. (United States Military Academy/PD)*

WAR OF THE THIRD COALITION COMBATANTS	
French	**Coalition**
France	Holy Roman Empire
Spain	United Kingdom
Electorate of Bavaria	Russia
French-allied Italy	Naples and Sicily
Batavian Republic	Sweden
Württemberg	

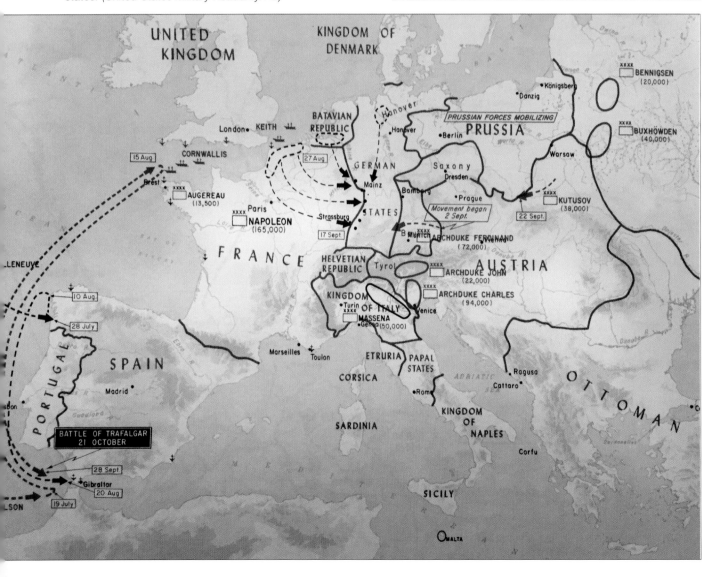

▲ *A portrait of Louis-Alexandre Berthier, Napoleon's Chief of Staff from 1796 to 1814 and a critical figure in Napoleon's command structure. (PD/CC)*

of forces was enough to defeat Napoleon. In 1803, Napoleon and his staff developed plans for an invasion of Britain, but further demonstrations of British naval supremacy, plus Napoleon's interference in naval planning (a subject of which he had limited understanding), meant that by 1805 such plans had largely been shelved.

WEAK LINK

As had occurred during Napoleon's Egyptian campaign, it was naval power that proved to be the weak link in the French strategic reach. In the battle of Cape Finisterre (22 July 1805), a British fleet under Admiral Robert Calder clashed with a Franco-Spanish force led by Admiral Pierre de Villeneuve and Admiral Frederico Gravina. The action was tactically inconclusive, but by forcing Villeneuve to sail down to Cadiz in south-western Spain, the Royal Navy scored a strategic victory by removing virtually all possibility of a French invasion of the British mainland, much to Napoleon's chagrin. On 21 October, a smarting Villeneuve then suffered the catastrophic defeat at Trafalgar, with the Franco-Spanish fleet eviscerated by Admiral Nelson's handling of a numerically smaller British fleet. The French Navy was on its knees.

REMODELLING THE FRENCH STATE

From 1801 to 1805, Napoleon was not purely focused on France's military renaissance, but also on remodelling the French state. He dramatically enhanced the power of the executive, at the expense of legislative bodies, and created a new series of ministries to govern the state and the growing empire, coordinated by a State Secretariat. A major new law-making body was the Conseil d'État (Council of State), formed by Napoleon in 1799 and acting much like a government cabinet, advising on the drafting of laws. Napoleon himself presided over this body of influential men. He also set about reworking the corpus of French law, assisted by a commissioned group of four hand-selected lawyers. By 1804 this process was complete in the 2,281 articles of the *Code Civil des Français* (Civil Code of France), later renamed the *Code Napoléon* (Napoleonic Code), a hugely significant political document that enshrined rights such as religious tolerance, property inheritance and equality before the law. Napoleon also reorganised governance down at regional and department levels, arranging it in a logical hierarchy to ensure that his dictates trickled down effectively through French society.

To our mind today, it seems clear that Napoleon was establishing a form of enlightened dictatorship. Yet it did bring about one key benefit – a pronounced speed and efficiency in decision-making, both military and political. Whereas many of the foreign powers struggled under the weight of complex factional debate, Napoleon could largely command by individual fiat, often meaning that he could outpace his opponents in operational tempo. Such command liberty would be extremely useful in what was to come.

▲ *A room in the farmhouse known as Ferme de Caillou, where Napoleon spent the night and briefed his officers before the battle of Waterloo. (David Coleman / Alamy)*

▶ *Napoleon was a prolific letter writer, producing literally thousands of missives both personal and professional. The letter here is to Eugène de Beauharnais, Viceroy of Italy and Napoleon's stepson, in 1812. The letter begins: 'My son, you have made a grave mistake in allowing the Rivoli to leave without a frigate and without clearing the seas.' (PD/CC)*

ULM AND AUSTERLITZ – FRANCE VICTORIOUS

Yet on land, matters were very different. Two major French victories defined the War of the Third Coalition – that during the Ulm campaign in September and October 1805, and at Austerlitz on 2–4 December. The former culminated in the surrender of an entire Austrian army under General Karl Mack von Lieberich on 20 October, which added 23,000 Austrian prisoners to around 35,000 already taken in the campaign. The campaign itself had again demonstrated the dynamic tactics of Napoleon and of talented subordinates such as Bernadotte, Ney, Marmont and Murat. The Austrians were consistently outmanoeuvred by the French advance. Austerlitz is for many the greatest of Napoleon's victories, from a long list. Exceptional and daring tactical manoeuvres enabled Napoleon to split a huge Austro-Russian army, about 80,000 strong, in the centre and then defeat the flanks, killing 16,000 of the enemy and capturing 20,000. By comparison, French casualties were about 9,000.

▼ *Napoleon receives the surrender of General Mack and his Austrian forces at Ulm, 20 October 1805. (PD/CC)*

WAR OF THE FOURTH COALITION (1806–07)

The victory at Austerlitz saw Austria compelled to sign the Treaty of Pressburg, but war was quick to reignite and, in October 1806, a Fourth Coalition took shape, which included Britain and Russia but now also brought Prussia into the orbit of the Allies, a decision by Prussia's King Frederick William III which proved to be a terrible strategic error for this venerable and most martial of states.

WAR OF THE FOURTH COALITION COMBATANTS	
French	**Coalition**
France	Holy Roman Empire
Spain	United Kingdom
Confederation of the Rhine (Bavaria, Württemberg, Saxony)	Russia
	Sicily
Kingdom of Italy, Naples	Sweden
Etruria	
Holland	
Switzerland	
Polish Legions	

▼ *Napoleon gives instructions to an attentive General Nicolas Oudinot at the battle of Friedland, 1807. (PD/CC)*

Napoleon made a rapid invasion, launched on 8 October, with a total of 180,000 men in four immense columns. For this campaign, Napoleon had arranged his corps into what was called the *bataillon-carré* (battalion square), in which the corps manoeuvred in a mutually supporting diamond pattern, able to turn and fight in almost any direction (see Chapter 6). The Prussian forces, under elderly traditionalists such as the Duke of Brunswick and Field Marshal Richard Mollendorf, were outpaced and outmanoeuvred and, despite some French lapses in coordinated movement, were routed by Napoleon at Jena, and at Auerstädt by his commander Davout.

BATTLE OF FRIEDLAND AND TREATY OF TILSIT

King Frederick and his surviving men fled to Russia, where they joined a large Russian force under General Levin Bennigsen, who directed a counteroffensive against the victorious French. On 8 February 1807, in appalling

▲ *On the eve of the battle of Borodino, Napoleon presents to his staff officers a portrait of the infant king of Rome, his son Napoléon François Bonaparte. (PD/CC)*

weather, the two sides met at Preussiches–Eylau, and fought an engagement that produced nothing but extremely heavy losses on both sides; for once, Napoleon's tactical manoeuvres failed to entrap the enemy force. But on 14 June, capitalising on Russian errors, Napoleon engaged the Russians at Friedland, where he trapped the army with the River Alle to its back, and left 20,000 men dead.

Following this victory, Prussia and Russia were compelled to sign the Treaty of Tilsit on 7–9 July 1807. Prussia lost much territory to France, including its Polish possessions (which became the Duchy of Warsaw) and all the lands between the Rhine and the Elbe; it was also occupied by French troops in lieu of payment of a huge indemnity. Russia, meanwhile, was compelled to swap sides, joining the French in a reluctant alliance against Britain, who now stood largely alone.

THE SPANISH ULCER

Most of Europe was now either subjugated by France, or in alliance with it. But from this point, cracks began to appear in this French supremacy, partly because Napoleon's enemies were now starting to get the measure of this new way of war.

From 1807 to 1809, Britain was Napoleon's primary focus. He had not been successful in suppressing British maritime commercial traffic, and British countermoves had affected French trade with North America. Napoleon identified Portugal as a particularly weak link in what was called the 'Continental System' (the system by which France stopped British imports). Through the Treaty of Fontainbleau with Spain – a secret agreement to the partition of Portugal – Napoleon moved French forces under Junot into the Spanish mainland, which Junot used as a jumping-off point for an invasion of Portugal in November–December 1807. Junot's advance went well, with Lisbon occupied on 1 December, but thereafter matters started to go awry for the French. Manipulative diplomacy by Napoleon resulted in alienating the Spanish, and in Napoleon forcing King Charles IV and his son Ferdinand to abdicate, replacing the king with none other than Napoleon's own brother Joseph, who was at the time king of Naples. By May 1808, revolt and insurrection were rippling through Spain, capitalised on by the British, who sent military forces under Arthur Wellesley, 1st Duke of Wellington, and later Sir John Moore. A series of British victories in the theatre forced Napoleon to intervene personally, temporarily restoring French authority. Yet Napoleon had opened another front in his war, one that would be a grim drain on men, money and energy until 1814. He referred to the situation as the 'Spanish ulcer'.

WAR OF THE FIFTH COALITION (1809)

Napoleon was not to stay so far south for long. On 9 April 1809 Austria returned to the picture, incentivised by French problems in the Peninsular War and invading Bavaria with a large army. This was the beginning of the War of the Fifth Coalition, with the main players in this conflict being Austria and Britain.

WAR OF THE FIFTH COALITION COMBATANTS	
French	**Coalition**
France	United Kingdom
Confederation of the Rhine	Austria
(Bavaria, Württemberg,	Hungary
Saxony, Westphalia)	Spain
Kingdom of Italy, Naples	Sardinia
Holland	Black Brunswickers
Switzerland	Tyrol
Polish Legions	

THE DEFEAT OF AUSTRIA

It was apparent from the outset that the Austrians had improved their game since the previous disastrous clashes, particularly in innovations relating to making battlefield formations more manoeuvrable. Napoleon, responding to what he saw were emerging threats, led the French Army to victory at Abensberg–Eckmühl (20–22 April) and Landshut (21 April), although the Austrian commander, Archduke Charles, managed to extract many Austrian troops skilfully from encirclement. Then, on 21–22 May, Napoleon suffered arguably his first major defeat, at the battle of Aspern–Essling. Napoleon, intent on crossing the River Danube and defeating Charles before he could receive reinforcements from Italy, from 19 May sent forces across via the Lobau floodplain near Vienna. On 21 May, however, Charles attacked the still weak bridgehead, established around the villages of Aspern and Essling, with a strength that Napoleon had severely underestimated. The battle became one of exceptional ferocity as reinforcements poured into the area. The villages changed hands on multiple occasions, and eventually Napoleon was compelled to pull his troops back over the river.

Although the battle was not a conclusive Austrian victory, in that Charles was unable to pursue and destroy his opponents, the fact remained that on this occasion Napoleon's ambitions had been thwarted by a talented opponent. But Napoleon was nothing if not resilient. On 4–5 July he made an unopposed crossing of the Danube and then engaged Charles's forces in the two-day battle at Wagram on 5–6 July. This time Napoleon was victorious – emphatically so – in an immense engagement that saw combined casualties of up to 80,000 men. Within days Austria was forced to accept tactical and strategic defeat, and Austria sued for peace, which was concluded at the Treaty of Schönbrunn on 14 October.

Wagram signalled the high point of Napoleon's ambitions, adding large swathes of Austrian territory to France's already swollen empire. It would be three years before Napoleon launched his *Grande Armée* on another brutal adventure, although the Peninsular War remained an intense ongoing action. The British, again under Wellesley, alongside Spanish and Portuguese forces, began to chalk up victories, or at least stalemates, such as at Fuentes de Oñoro (3–5 May 1811), Albuera (16 May 1811) and Badajoz (16 March–6 April 1812). For Napoleon, the Spanish ulcer was still seeping.

◄ *Soldiers of the Imperial Gendarmerie, who tended to provide security and VIP escort duties. (PD/CC)*

► *A portrait of Marshal Jean-de-Dieu Soult, whose military career spanned from the Revolutionary Wars to Waterloo. (PD/CC)*

THE RUSSIAN CAMPAIGN

Much like Hitler's experience more than a century later, it was Napoleon's decision to invade Russia in 1812 that triggered his decline in fortunes. Since the Treaty of Tilsit, Russia had been a restive ally, and rumours that the tsar might once again turn on France intensified in Napoleon's ear from around 1810. By 1812, mistrust on both sides was expressing itself in mobilisation for war.

The French invasion of Russia that Napoleon launched on 24 June 1812 was magisterial in ambition. To show how much times had changed, the French Army also included significant numbers of Prussian and Austrian troops; in fact, fewer than 50 per cent of the entire French force was actually native to France. Napoleon's Russian campaign was unlike anything he had ever fought before, however, both in terms of the scale of the forces he had to manage – something that ultimately he could not do – and the expanse of territory he had to conquer.

The story of this campaign has gone down in legend. Pushing eastwards in terrible weather, Napoleon's strategy of trapping the Russians in encirclement operations failed. The Russians withdrew deeper and deeper into the endless landscape, stretching Napoleon's lines of communications and logistics. (By the time the army reached Vilnius on 28 June, 10,000 supply horses alone had died.) Battle was finally joined in the epic clash at Borodino on 7 September, just 75 miles (120km) from Moscow, where Napoleon faced a Russian army

ADVANCE TO AND RETREAT FROM MOSCOW

This exceptional artwork was created in 1869 by innovative French civil engineer Charles Joseph Minard, a pioneer of what we would today call infographics. It forms a visual representation of the *Grande Armée*'s advance to and tragic retreat from Moscow, while also (at the bottom) showing the drop in temperatures during the retreat phase. The main description at the top reads in English as follows:

Figurative Map of the successive losses in men of the French Army in the Russian campaign 1812–1813.

Drawn by M. Minard, Inspector General of Bridges and Roads (retired). Paris, November 20, 1869.

The numbers of men present are represented by the widths of the coloured zones at a rate of one millimetre for every ten thousand men; they are further written across the zones. The red designates the men who enter Russia, the black those who leave it. – The information which has served to draw up the map has been extracted from the works of M. M. Thiers, de Ségur, de Fezensac, de Chambray and the unpublished diary of Jacob, the pharmacist of the Army since October 28th. In order to better judge with the eye the diminution of the army, I have assumed that the troops of Prince Jérôme and of Marshal Davout, who had been detached at Minsk and Mogilev and have rejoined near Orsha and Vitebsk, had always marched with the army.

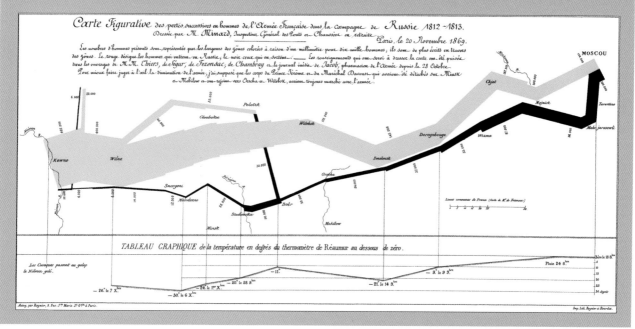

under General Kutusov. It was a shockingly brutal battle, one in which a fatigued Napoleon showed little tactical flair, and although the Russians were eventually put into retreat, the French suffered as many as 50,000 casualties.

The weary *Grande Armée* trudged on and entered Moscow unopposed on 14 September. Yet they found little of the expected, and desperately needed, food and supplies there. Furthermore, fires started by the Russians devastated two-thirds of the city, leaving much of it useless for the occupying army. As the French troops began to descend into lawlessness, Napoleon even reached out to Tsar Alexander for possible peace terms, but was rebuffed. Thus on 19 October, the French began their retreat back to the west, just as the Russian winter began its iron descent. The retreat was horrific in the extreme. Losing men constantly to Russian harassing forces, the French were also massacred by arctic extremes of weather, with men freezing or starving to death in their tens of thousands. By the time the skeletal remnants of the *Grande Armée* reached safety at the end of November, about 400,000 dead lay behind them. The *Grande Armée* was no more.

The Russian campaign dealt a near-terminal blow to Napoleon's ambitions and reputation. At home, he lost much of his mystique, not aided by a harsh economic recession that resulted in deprivation and rioting. There was an attempted coup by General Claude de Malet back in Paris, an event that caused Napoleon to leave his retreating army and flee home by sled. Furthermore, the wider European states smelled blood and sensed weakness. In June 1812, a Sixth Coalition had been formed, one that by March 1813 – when it struck against France – included Prussia, Russia, Austria, Britain, Portugal and several other states. Europe was out to crush the 'Corsican swine', as he was widely called, once and for all.

▲ *French troops erect a meagre bivouac during the retreat from Moscow in 1812, burning the spokes from gun wheels as fuel. (PD/CC)*

▼ *Marshal Jean-Baptiste Bernadotte survived the Napoleonic years and became king of Sweden in 1818. (PD/CC)*

THE SIXTH COALITION (1813–14)

Following the emphatic defeat in Russia, anti-French Europe sensed the opportunity to finish off its tottering foe. The coalition that gathered for this attempt in 1813 was vast in its scale, numbering more than one million men-at-arms, aided by the defection of Prussia from the French cause to that of Napoleon's enemies.

WAR OF THE SIXTH COALITION COMBATANTS	
French	**Coalition**
France	United Kingdom
Kingdom of Italy, Naples	Austria
Confederation of the Rhine	Prussia
(fragmented after battle of	Russia
Leipzig)	Spain
Switzerland	Sicily, Sardinia
Polish Legions	After Leipzig: Bavaria,
Denmark and Norway	Württemberg, Baden and
	United Netherlands

What would surprise the Coalition commanders was the speed at which Napoleon pulled together a major land army. By scraping the bottom of the French barrel, and through exigencies such as transferring troops from the Peninsula to northern Europe, he pulled together some 650,000 imperial French troops, who admittedly included 15- and 16-year-old conscripts. (They were known as 'Marie-Louises', named after Napoleon's second wife, the Duchess of Parma, whom he had married in 1810.) By bringing in c. 300,000 allies, heavily from the Confederation of the Rhine, Napoleon managed to generate a force of about 900,000 men.

▼ *A parade of the Italian military forces in 1812. Many Italian states were French allies. (PD/CC)*

NAPOLEON'S FIGHTBACK

After an initial French retreat back across the River Elbe, Napoleon went on the offensive towards Leipzig and Dresden. On the German battleground, a taste of what was to come was delivered in Napoleon's victory over the Russians and Prussians at Lützen on 2 May. However, the heavy casualties inflicted upon the French forces meant that they were unable to conduct an effective pursuit – some of the flexibility and dynamism of Napoleon's army was bleeding out. Continuing the drive, however, Napoleon next confronted the Prussians and Russians at Bautzen in Saxony on 20–21 May, once again taking charge of the battlefield but failing to permit the bulk of the enemy to escape. Furthermore, like Lützen, the battle of Bautzen was a Pyrrhic victory – the French lost about 20,000 men compared to Coalition losses of around 14,000.

An armistice after Bautzen gave all sides a breather until nearly mid August, although not so much in the Peninsular War, where British forces under the Duke of Wellington were continuing to inflict defeats upon the French. Once Central European hostilities resumed, the landmark action was fought at Dresden on 26–27 August 1813, in which Napoleon's army – outnumbered more than two to one by Austrian, Russian and Prussian formations – battered down the enemy, this time with an emphatic victory (around 38,000 enemy casualties for 10,000 French) that showed some of Napoleon's older brilliance for splitting and defeating larger enemies. His subordinates, however, were less fortunate around this time. Oudinot was defeated at Grossberren on 23 August, Marshal Étienne MacDonald at the Katzbach on 26 August (a clash of some 200,000 troops), and General Dominique Vandamme's French force was halved at Kulm on 29–30 August.

The war dragged on with a relentless counterpoint of victory and defeat on both sides, but steadily Napoleon realised that he was unable to defeat the Allied forces separately, so drew them into a single battle at Leipzig on 16–19 October 1813. Leipzig – the 'Battle of the Nations' – was the largest single battle in history prior to World War I, involving more than 600,000 troops and 2,200 artillery pieces. The outcome was Napoleon's emphatic defeat, and the *Grande Armée*'s retreat back to France.

EXILE AND RETURN

Napoleon remained defiant; he was confident in his ability to pull victory from the jaws of defeat. He rejected the Allied peace offers, and continued to fight on with his terribly overstretched forces. In the first two months of 1814, three huge Allied armies invaded France, converging on Paris. The same year saw the final British victory of Wellington over the French in the Peninsular War.

NAPOLEON'S ABDICATION – 6 APRIL 1814

'The Allied powers having declared that the Emperor Napoleon is the sole obstacle to the re-establishment of a general peace in Europe, the Emperor Napoleon, faithful to his oath, declares that he renounces, for himself and his heirs, the throne of France and Italy; and that there is no personal sacrifice, not even that of life itself, which he is not willing to make for the interests of France.'

Napoleon's defence was little short of astonishing. Switching between the threats individually, he won multiple additional victories, but was unable to prevent either his subordinates being overwhelmed or the Allied forces reaching and then, on 31 March, occupying Paris. Napoleon realised that the time

▼ *Napoleon's original tomb on the island of St Helena before his body was moved to Paris. (Lisa Strachan / Shutterstock)*

had come to accept defeat, and he abdicated on 6 April. An unconditional surrender was signed on 11 April, ratified in the Treaty of Fontainbleau, which, among other things, took France's territorial extent back to that of 1792. Louis XVIII was also installed as king – the monarchy had returned. As for Napoleon, he was effectively exiled to the island of Elba, although the treaty permitted him to rule over the island as a principality, with a guard of 600 men. He left France on 29 May – of note, this was the day that the love of his life and former wife, Josephine, died of pneumonia at the age of 50.

THE HUNDRED DAYS AND WATERLOO

It is in keeping with the remarkable nature of Napoleon that his exile to Elba was not the end of his military or imperial career. The new Bourbon regime brought back mismanagement, social conflict and nepotism, alienating large sections of the armed forces who had recently been fighting hard for France. The victorious Allied powers struggled to find an agreement for peace in Europe. Spotting an opportunity, and deeply bored with his life on Elba, Napoleon escaped and sailed with his guard to southern France, intent on reclaiming his throne. Thus began the Hundred Days campaign. Once back in France, Napoleon again took charge of the French Army, whose loyalty was largely undiminished and who were keen to turn their backs on the royalist regime. Napoleon recognised, however, that he did not have the capability to defeat the combined British, Russian, Austrian and Prussian force of some 800,000 men that the Allies began to mobilise against him. Thus he opted to make an incisive strike into the Low Countries against an Anglo-German army led by Wellington and, on the Prussian side, by Field Marshal Gebhard Leberecht von Blücher. The outcome was a true landmark in European military history – the battle of Waterloo, fought on 18 June 1815, two days after the brutal and related battle of Quatre-Bras. Waterloo was a close-run engagement, with Napoleon unleashing his men on the Allies with all his customary aggression. Yet the British held on while the French depleted their energy and men, and with swelling Prussian reinforcements, Wellington and Blücher finally crushed Napoleon once and for all.

FINAL DOWNFALL

Napoleon's imperial career was now truly at an end. He abdicated again on 21 June, and this time the Allies made sure that his expulsion was irrevocable, sending him to the distant, mid-Atlantic outpost of St Helena. There he stayed, doubtless painting the immense seascape views with memories of his past adventures, until he died on 5 May 1821.

PERSONAL CHARACTERISTICS

Napoleon was a true warrior intellectual. From his earliest days of education and military service in France in the 1790s, he was noted for his near-insatiable consumption of books, with his social life taking second place to spending hours in his room reading. He had an abiding interest in great military thinkers, and an equal passion for digesting classical works of statecraft and philosophy.

▲ Napoleon dictates some late-night instructions to his headquarters staff. (North Wind Picture Archives / Alamy)

▼ A recreation of Napoleon studying war maps. The reality was often more organised. (North Wind Picture Archives / Alamy)

CAPACITY FOR RECALL

Napoleon's controlled hunger for intellectual pursuits rarely wavered, and there were few subjects on which he could not hold forth with some degree of authority. He was helped in his learning through possession of a formidable memory. The contribution of this faculty to Napoleon's abilities as a commander cannot be highlighted enough. At the tactical and administrative levels, Napoleon would continually demonstrate recollection of almost every conversation with superiors and inferiors, recalling the details with unnerving clarity should there be later disagreements or failures. Everyone who made a commitment to do something, or who was given a direct order, regardless of how minor it was, would be held to account by Napoleon's memory should their paths cross again.

But Napoleon's memory was not purely an instrument of terrorising administration. In fact, it was central to the loyalty that he built up amongst both his officers and also the regular men. Napoleon not only mentally logged details of procedures and orders, he also remembered the faces and personal details of most of those he encountered throughout his career. This impressive faculty could border on the unnerving. For example, in 1810, Napoleon was introduced to three deputies of the Valais and not only remembered having met one of them before, but also asked about the man's two daughters. After the encounter, the deputy told his colleagues that he had only met Napoleon for a matter of minutes outside his home, a full 10 years earlier, during the advance to Marengo. 'Problems with the artillery forced him to stop for a moment in front of my house. He petted my two children, mounted his horse, and since then I had not seen him again.'[1]

WORK ETHIC

Although such a powerful memory might seem to be potentially demoralising for ordinary mortals, when combined with Napoleon's herculean capacity for hard work it was a tremendous force for efficiency when on campaign. Napoleon would work virtually around the clock, setting a pace that even the most indefatigable of subordinates would struggle to match. On the question of hours of sleep required, he is famously quoted as saying: 'Six for a man, seven for a woman, eight for a fool.' During campaigns, even six hours would have been a luxury, with the emperor basically surviving on snatched naps for weeks at a time. In one

---

1 Roberts 2014: 137

▶ *Napoleon was known for his ability to engage easily with the common soldier. Here he stops at an evening mealtime bivouac to converse with the rank-and-file soldiers, who offer him one of their potatoes. (Niday Picture Library / Alamy)*

night alone in 1809, Napoleon's stoic Chief of Staff, Louis-Alexandre Berthier, had to rise to attend various meetings and dictations of his superior no fewer than 17 times. This relentless energy, which excluded nothing from its attention – from great campaign strategies through to logistical points such as the provision of footwear for soldiers – produced an enormous output of orders and directives. In one nine-month period in 1796, for example, he created more than 800 letters and dispatches.[2] Only later in the Napoleonic Wars, as history started to crush rather than support his ambitions, did his energy lag at times, seeing him slump into intellectual torpor and low spirits, from which he had to drag himself.

MORALE BUILDING

Napoleon extended his affections down to the lower ranks. He would often stop to talk with familiar veterans, and was also known for allowing men to vent their grumbles openly, which he seemed to note with sincerity. The needs of the campaign notwithstanding, he would sit for hours with privates and NCOs around camp fires, thrashing out their issues with openness on both sides. Speaking with men of the 17th Demi-Brigade he once said: 'Do not hide any of your needs from me, and be free to speak any complaints you have about your superiors. I am here to give justice to everyone, and the weakest of you deserve my protection.' Napoleon's men referred to him affectionately as *le petit caporal* – the little corporal – identifying him with the rank and file, rather than a high-ranking elite. Such a categorisation, combined with elevated respect for his strategic and tactical skills, bought tremendous loyalty. If Napoleon heard of any individual exploiting or abusing his men, he would root that person out and have him very publicly punished.

PASSION AND FURY

Napoleon was indeed a master of both individual and unit psychology, knowing when to give praise and when to unleash his wrath, which could be furious indeed. He was known to lash out physically, kicking or punching his subordinates when they had displeased him. On one occasion, when Napoleon flew into a rage, he even grabbed the throat of his most trusted right-hand man, Berthier, and beat his head against a wall. Yet those around him, and even the mass of his soldiery, feared his words more than his fists or boots. For those units that performed heroically in battle, Napoleon's words seemed to lift them to the heavens. During the Italian campaign, for example, Napoleon wrote in a bulletin after the second battle of Lonato on 3–4 August 1796: 'I was tranquil. The brave 32nd Demi-Brigade was there.' Such words made a unit feel part of Napoleon's personal elite, as when in 1807 he spoke to the 44th Line infantry, saying that 'your three battalions count as six in my eyes', prompting the shout in return: 'And we shall prove it.' He could also deliver devastating tirades. Also from the Italian campaign, on 7 November 1796 Napoleon addressed two demi-brigades, the 39th and 85th, that had failed to live up to his high expectations at the siege of Mantua:

> Soldiers: I am not satisfied with you; you have shown neither bravery, discipline, nor perseverance; no position could rally you; you abandoned yourselves to a panic-terror; you suffered yourselves to be driven from situations where a handful of brave men might have stopped an army. Soldiers of the 39th and 85th, you are not French soldiers. Quartermaster-general, let it be inscribed on their colours, '*They no longer form part of the Army of Italy!*'

NAPOLEON'S PROCLAMATION TO THE ARMY OF ITALY, MAY 1796

Soldiers: You have in fifteen days won six victories, taken twenty-one stand of colours, fifty-five pieces of cannon, and several fortresses, and overrun the richest part of Piedmont; you have made 15,000 prisoners, and killed or wounded upwards of 10,000 men. Hitherto you have been fighting for barren rocks, made memorable by your valour, though useless to your country, but your exploits now equal those of the armies of Holland and the Rhine. You were utterly destitute, and you have supplied all your wants. You have gained battles without cannon, passed rivers without bridges, performed forced marches without shoes, and bivouacked without strong liquors, and often without bread. None but Republican phalanxes, the soldiers of liberty, could have endured what you have done; thanks to you, soldiers, for your perseverance! Your grateful country owes its safety to you; and if the taking of Toulon was an earnest of the immortal campaign of 1794, your present victories foretell one more glorious. The two armies which lately attacked you in full confidence, now fly before you in consternation; the perverse men who laughed at your distress, and inwardly rejoiced at the triumph of your enemies, are now confounded and trembling. But, soldiers, you have yet done nothing, for there still remains much to do. Neither Turin nor Milan are yours; the ashes of the conquerors of Tarquin are still trodden underfoot by the assassins of Basseville. It is said that there are some among you whose courage is shaken, and who would prefer returning to the summits of the Alps and Apennines. No, I cannot believe it. The victors of Montenotte, Millesimo, Dego, and Mondovi are eager to extend the glory of the French name!

Such words, even though they sound irreparably harsh to our ears, were usually perfectly judged to galvanise a formation into raising its game and winning back the approval of Napoleon.

RUTHLESS COMMAND

Taking the broadest view, Napoleon seemed to combine a genuine interest in the wellbeing of his soldiers with well-judged levels of distance. We certainly must not, however, let his consideration for his troops mask his ruthlessness. This is the man, after all, who once remarked: 'A man like me troubles himself little about the lives of a million men.' There is much to be considered in how Napoleon defined

▼ *Napoleon and his staff review the Chasseurs à Cheval de la Garde Impériale (Horse Chasseurs of the Imperial Guard) in this painting by François Flameng. (PD/CC)*

'A man like me . . .' Certainly, from the outset he seemed to have a particularly strong sense of destiny. During his early campaigns in Italy, his unilateral negotiation of major peace treaties, often without prior consultation with the Directory, the body governing France at the time, showed that he considered himself above tawdry politicians and lawyers. Once he had attained supreme power, he also tolerated no deviation from his commands by his marshals, however experienced or talented they were.

Napoleon once said: 'Destiny urges me to a goal of which I am ignorant. Until that goal is attained I am invulnerable, unassailable. When Destiny has accomplished her purpose in me, a fly may suffice to destroy me.' In this grandiloquent passage, Napoleon sees himself as being almost carried to greatness by a semi-divine power. Yet he also had the maturity to recognise that great men could eventually fall.

IMPERIAL STAFF

Napoleon's specific 'art of war' is examined fully in Chapter 6. Here, however, we shall explore the system through which he was able to express his martial will – his Imperial Staff and the commanders who led his armies into battle. One point needs to be made at the outset: from his first consulship onwards, there was never any doubt about who was in charge.

Given the size of both his army and the campaigns that he fought, it was inevitable that Napoleon's staff would grow to a prodigious size: by 1812, the total staff system surrounding Napoleon consisted of 3,500 officers and some 10,000 other support personnel.[3] On campaign, Napoleon's immediate entourage would likely number 1,500 individuals, a sprawling system that was almost exclusively designed simply to deliver the will of the emperor. Because of Napoleon's initially inexhaustible work ethic, his outstanding memory, and his command of detail, he was able to do this for many years. What he did not want were commanders going off and expressing their own independence, although there were many occasions where he benefited from their initiative.

Napoleon's Imperial Headquarters was divided into two principal sections: the *Maison Militaire de l'Empereur* (Emperor's Military Household) and the *Grand-Quartier-Générale* (Army General Headquarters). In addition, there was the General Commissary of Army Stores, a separate organisation – albeit one that was utterly intertwined with

---

3 Haythornwaite 2017: 14

▲ *An artist's impression of Napoleon giving orders to Berthier in the field, c. 1803. (PD/CC)*

▼ *Louis Albert Guislan Bacler d'Albe, as head of the* Bureau Topographique, *accompanied Napoleon on all his campaigns from 1804, producing the detailed battle maps on which the emperor relied. (NMUIM / Alamy)*

▶ *Roustam Raza, also known as Roustan or Rustam (1783–1845), was Napoleon's trusted Mameluke body-guard and valet, but refused to go into exile with Napoleon on Elba. (PD/CC)*

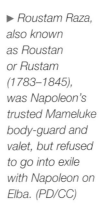

the activities of the Imperial Headquarters – responsible for campaign supply and provisioning.

THE MAISON

Napoleon's overall command within the *Maison* (as it is usually abbreviated) was assisted by a body of aides-de-camp (ADCs) – usually general-rank officers who distributed orders to army field commanders and conducted reconnaissance – and 12 more junior orderly officers, who performed various special missions on behalf of the emperor. The command powerhouse of the *Maison*, however, was the Cabinet, which itself consisted of three sections. First, there was the *Secrétariat* (Secretariat), essentially a hand-picked group of assistants who supported the emperor closely in his command work and his day-to-day practicalities. Next came the *Service d'Espionage* or *Bureau de Renseignements* (Intelligence Service), which collected battlefield and strategic intelligence, mainly passing the details over to the Army General Headquarters. Finally, there was the *Bureau Topographique* (Topographic Bureau). Despite its rather bland bureaucratic name, this section was of great importance to Napoleon's leadership. Headed by the indefatigable Louis-Albert Bacler d'Albe, the *Bureau Topographique* kept Napoleon presented with large-scale up-to-date maps of the theatre of operations, showing the position of all known units, allied and enemy. This information lay at the heart of the Napoleon's strategic and tactical judgements, so d'Albe's thorough work was central to French war-making.

◄ Aides-de-camp of Marshal Joachim-Napoléon Murat: a colonel in full dress (left) and a squadron leader in undress to the right. (PD/CC)

Another cornerstone of the *Maison* was Napoleon's Civil Household, a large (roughly 800 persons by 1806) group of largely civilian staff who looked after Napoleon's various personal needs, but also facilitated the practicalities of command. It included domestic staff, cooks, maintenance men, bodyguards – the most famous and devoted of the latter was a Mameluke, Roustam – butlers, court physicians and assorted others. The most senior position in the Civil Household was the Grand Marshal of the Palace, held by General Géraud Duroc, 1st Duke of Frioul, from 1804 until 1813. Duroc was essentially the head of the Civil Household, responsible for its smooth running and its finances and administration. The other major senior post was that of Grand Equerry, with General Armand-Augustin-Louis, Marquis of Caulaincourt and Duke of Vicenza, the incumbent. He oversaw Napoleon's equestrian transportation and associated equipment. Given Napoleon's propensity to dash about the theatre of operations, ruining numerous horses along the way, de Caulaincourt's position was a demanding one.

GRAND-QUARTIER-GÉNÉRALE

The *Maison* was essentially the civil part of Napoleon's imperial court, while the *Grand-Quartier-Générale* contained much of its military function and was headed by Louis-Alexandre Berthier, Napoleon's Chief of Staff, and a central figure in Napoleonic history. Berthier's central talent was the taking, or interpreting, of Napoleon's strategic or tactical directions and translating these into accurate and meticulously detailed written field orders, produced in large volumes and at great speed. In this role he took very personal responsibility, checking the work of his own cabinet constantly, although they provided invaluable support. This cabinet was known as the *Bureau du major général* – Berthier was also ranked a major-general in the army – and was subdivided into four offices: Troop Movements, Secretariat, Accountancy, and Intelligence. The Troop Movements office, headed by the dynamic and sharp Captain Salamon, was particularly important, as it was a vast repository of knowledge about the composition and commanders of all major units and their location on the battlefield. Salamon also had the onerous responsibility for organising the mass movement of forces on campaign, with all the attendant complexities.

Assisting Berthier professionally and personally were the personnel of the *État-major particulier* (Private Military Staff), which mainly consisted of high-ranking military officers, plus a number of aides-de-camp. The main utility of the officer group was to provide Berthier with trusted individuals who could undertake military and diplomatic missions in support of the distribution and execution of Napoleon's orders.

The final major element of the Army General Headquarters was the *État-major général* (Army General Staff) itself. This was a large organisation, headed by the First Assistant Major-

LOUIS-ALEXANDRE BERTHIER (1753–1815)

Of Marshal Louis-Alexandre Berthier, Napoleon once said: 'Nature has evidently designed many for a subordinate situation; and among these is Berthier. As Chief of Staff he had no superior; but he was not fit to command 500 men.' Beyond its undeniably superior tone, the judgement is largely accurate. Berthier had entered military service as an engineer, and his real gift was a phenomenal confidence in administration and organisation – talents that made him invaluable to pedantic and meticulous leaders such as Napoleon. Berthier first served Napoleon as part of the Army of Italy in the 1790s, but Napoleon recognised his qualities, and, as well as Chief of Staff, Berthier was also Minister of War from 1800 to 1807. Forays into field army command in 1809 were not successful, and he thereafter stuck with his management role, ensuring that Napoleon's wishes were effectively transferred to the commanders and the armies in the field. Napoleon leaned on him heavily, reducing the man to periods of despair through incessant overwork. Following Napoleon's abdication in 1813 and the restoration of the Bourbons, Berthier once more switched his allegiance to the royalists, an alignment he maintained in 1815. On 1 June 1815 he died falling from a window in Bamberg; whether by accident, suicide or murder is not known.

▶ *A portrait of Louis-Alexandre Berthier, the authority of his pose and setting reflecting his importance to the Emperor, although such importance did not always bring respect from Napoleon. (PD/CC)*

General and divided into three specific bureaux, or sections, each commanded by an adjutant-commandant ranked colonel. The three sections had the following responsibilities:

1st section: Administration relating to troop movements; transmission of orders
2nd section: Arranged accommodation for headquarters staff, plus handled matters relating to security/ police forces, requisitions of supplies and hospitals
3rd section: Responsible for conscripts, prisoners of war, deserters, legal issues

Above, in outline, we see the powerhouse of Napoleon's war-making. Without his capable staff, prepared to sacrifice both waking and sleeping hours to their emperor, Napoleon would have been unable to command such a vast army. In fact, at its largest, the French Army was almost ungovernable, even with a huge imperial court at Napoleon's disposal. Part of the problem was that there was ultimately no devolution of command. Despite the legion of talent at his disposal, Napoleon remained emphatically in charge.

▼ *Napoleonic staff had to possess real skill and speed with quill and ink. During campaigns, individual staff might write dozens of directives every night. (Yakim Art / Shutterstock)*

NAPOLEON'S MARSHALS

The honour of *Maréchal d'Empire* (Marshal of the Empire) was first bestowed by Napoleon in 1804. He made six further promotions between 1807 and 1815, by which time he had granted the title 26 times. It was not technically a rank, although it carried a rank indicator – a fourth silver star – and was only awarded to general officers who had demonstrated exceptional service.

The title was more of a civil honour, and actually harked back to the *Maréchal de France*, which had been granted in France from 1185 until it was abolished during the Revolution in 1793. Napoleon's resurrection of the title in 1804 reflected his desire to reward excellence and to acknowledge and promote loyalty among his most talented commanders. Men who had been granted the title of marshal generally held the highest and most auspicious commands in the *Grande Armée*.

MERITOCRACY

What was particularly powerful about the status of marshal was that it was truly meritocratic, as indeed was the whole command structure of the French Army. Napoleon's famous quotation, 'Every private in the French Army carries a field-marshal's baton in his knapsack', had a definite ring of truth about it, enabling every soldier to imagine, with wildly varying degrees of plausibility, that one day the most lofty command might be attained. Jean-Baptiste Bernadotte, for example, joined the French Army as a private in 1780 but became marshal in the First Promotion in 1804. (This was far from the summit of his ascent; he later became the king of Sweden and Norway from 1818 to 1844.) Other marshals who rose from low rank or humble origins include Pierre Augereau (son of a Parisian fruit seller), Joachim Murat (a farmer's son), Jean Lannes (another farmer's son) and Michel Ney (son of a

◄ *Marshal Joachim Murat rose to high position undoubtedly by merit, although assisted by the fact that he war married to Napoleon's younger sister, Caroline. (PD/CC)*

MARÉCHALS D'EMPIRE (MARSHALS OF THE EMPIRE)

- Louis-Alexandre Berthier, Prince of Neufchâtel and of Wagram, Duke of Valangin (1753–1815), Marshal of the Empire in 1804
- Joachim Murat, Prince of the Empire, Grand Duke of Clèves and Berg, King of Naples (1767–1815), Marshal of the Empire in 1804
- Bon Adrien Jeannot de Moncey, Duke of Conégliano (1754–1842), Marshal of the Empire in 1804
- Jean-Baptiste Jourdan, Count Jourdan (1762–1833), Marshal of the Empire in 1804
- André Masséna, Duke of Rivoli, Prince of Essling (1758–1817), Marshal of the Empire in 1804
- Charles Pierre François Augereau, Duke of Castiglione (1757–1816), Marshal of the Empire in 1804
- Jean-Baptiste Jules Bernadotte, Prince of Pontecorvo, King of Sweden and Norway, Marshal of the Empire in 1804
- Guillaume Brune, Count Brune (1763–1815), Marshal of the Empire in 1804
- Jean-de-Dieu Soult, Duke of Dalmatia (1769–1851), Marshal of the Empire in 1804, Marshal General of France in 1847
- Jean Lannes, Duke of Montebello (1769–1809), Marshal of the Empire in 1804
- Édouard Mortier, Duke of Treviso (1768–1835), Marshal of the Empire in 1804
- Michel Ney, Duke of Elchingen, Prince of Moscow (1769–1815), Marshal of the Empire in 1804

master barrel-maker). There were certainly plenty of nobles within the pantheon of marshals, but while their position at birth may have provided them with early opportunities, blue blood had to be backed up with demonstrations of military tenacity and competence.

The degree to which the marshals were loyal to their emperor varies on a case-by-case basis. Certainly, Napoleon's autocratic leadership style did not necessarily breed unquestioning loyalty, although there were many marshals who stood devotedly by the side of their emperor throughout the war, even during the ill-fated Hundred Days. The year 1813 was the acid test of many a marshal's allegiance if not to the empire, then at least to Republican ideals, although we must, of course, allow for the influence of sheer pragmatism over principle. Berthier was not the only marshal to rededicate himself to the Bourbon monarchy on their restoration; others include Dominique Perignon and Nicolas Oudinot. We also see some marshals clearly conflicted. The great Jean-Baptiste Jourdan, for example, allied himself with the Bourbons following the 1813 abdication, then led a small army for Napoleon during the Hundred Days War, before going back to royal service after Waterloo. In a double irony, he also sat on the court that tried another of Napoleon's marshals, Ney, for treason, following Ney's admittedly disastrous service for Napoleon at Waterloo.

While there were many talented marshals, without whom Napoleon would not have been able to build his empire, there seems little doubt that the eyes of France's soldiers were turned towards their emperor. Napoleon possessed an undoubted talent for inspiring those around him.

Although Napoleon gave his high-ranking subordinates no leeway when it came to designing strategy, he left it to them to control the tactical battlefield movements at unit level. The success of the French Army should not be solely equated with the person of Napoleon himself, however influential he certainly was. Without the direction and innovation of his marshals, generals and field commanders, Napoleon would have been unlikely to reach the levels of power that he did.

▲ *Having been a sergeant in the pre-Revolution Royal Guard, François Joseph Lefebvre became a marshal and one of Napoleon's most ardent supporters. (PD/CC)*

- Louis-Nicolas Davout, Duke of Auerstädt, Prince of Eckmühl (1770–1823), Marshal of the Empire in 1804
- Jean-Baptiste Bessières, Duke of Istria (1768–1813), Marshal of the Empire in 1804
- François Christophe de Kellermann, Duke of Valmy (1737–1820), Marshal of the Empire in 1804 (Honorary)
- François Joseph Lefebvre, Duke of Danzig (1755–1820), Marshal of the Empire in 1804 (Honorary)
- Catherine-Dominique de Pérignon, Marquis of Grenade (1754–1818), Marshal of the Empire in 1804 (Honorary)
- Jean-Mathieu-Philibert Sérurier, Count Sérurier (1742–1819), Marshal of the Empire in 1804 (Honorary)
- Claude Victor, Duke of Belluno (1764–1841), Marshal of the Empire in 1807
- Jacques MacDonald, Duke of Taranto (1765–1840), Marshal of the Empire in 1809
- Nicolas Oudinot, Duke of Reggio (1767–1847), Marshal of the Empire in 1809
- Auguste Marmont, Duke of Ragusa (1774–1852), Marshal of the Empire in 1809
- Louis-Gabriel Suchet, Duke of Albufera (1770–1826), Marshal of the Empire in 1811
- Laurent de Gouvion Saint-Cyr, Marquis of Gouvion Saint-Cyr (1764–1830), Marshal of the Empire in 1812
- Prince Józef Antoni Poniatowski (1763–1813), Marshal of the Empire in 1813
- Emmanuel de Grouchy, Marquis of Grouchy (1766–1847), Marshal of the Empire in 1815

2

NAPOLEON'S INFANTRY

In the early days of the French Revolutionary Wars, the regular professional infantry of the French Army was supplemented by a vast new army of volunteers and conscripts, individually of poor quality and inadequately equipped in almost every way. Nevertheless, in a fervent mass, the infantry became a war-winning machine. Under Napoleon, the infantry was further enlarged and refined until it became one of the greatest forces in military history.

LINE INFANTRY

Taking the broadest of categorisations, the French infantry was split into two distinct elements – line infantry and light infantry. Line infantry was composed of soldiers who formed the principal ranks on the battlefield; they were essentially the 'mass' of the army. Light infantry, by contrast, had a tactically freer role, being applied to skirmishing, reconnaissance, screening and pursuit purposes.

As we shall see, the strict distinction between line and light infantry became a little blurred over the course of the Napoleonic Wars, but there remained conceptual differences, as well as practical ones.

REVOLUTIONARY FORMATIONS

At the very beginning of the Revolutionary Wars, France was able to draw upon the professional and formerly royalist line infantry formations – a total of 79 French and 23 foreign regiments. Each regiment consisted of two battalions, and each battalion of five companies (four fusilier companies and one of grenadiers). In addition, the French state could draw upon an assortment of provincial militia, of variable quality but containing some experienced troops in the form of ex-servicemen. The burgeoning wars of the 1790s, however, placed an inexhaustible demand on the French state for military manpower, necessitating a nationwide programme of

▼ *A grenadier of the Old Guard, affectionately referred to by the French Army as* grognards *(grumblers). (PD/CC)*

volunteerism and recruitment, as noted in the Introduction. This mass recruitment plus internal reorganisation produced two new strains of line infantry. The provincial militia was disbanded in 1791 and its forces became the National Guard, distinguished by its blue uniforms, as opposed to the white of the regular army (see below). Other reforms of 1791 included the removal of regimental honorific titles – now regarded as badges of royalist elitism – and the use of a simple numerical system, and the reorganisation of the battalion strength into eight fusilier and one grenadier company. To the regular and National Guard regiments were added the swarms of men recruited under the *levée en masse*, who were arranged into a hotchpotch of units and formations.

DEMI-BRIGADES

Although the size of the line infantry certainly expanded – some 750 new battalions were created between 1791 and 1793 – the quality of the infantry overall left much to be desired. The volunteer and conscript units in particular were prone to battlefield breakdown and desertion. In 1793 the Committee of Public Safety decreed a major organisational change for the line infantry, enacted in 1794. This was known as the *amalgame*. The venerable title of 'regiment' was abolished in favour of a three-battalion demi-brigade, with one of the battalions drawn from the regular army to bolster the other two battalions of volunteer formations. Some 426 volunteer battalions were therefore combined with 213 regular battalions, and the remaining 299 volunteer battalions either disbanded or used to establish reserve battalions.[1] Total on-paper establishment of the new demi-brigade was 2,437 men and four 6pdr cannons in the regimental artillery.

The rationale behind the demi-brigades is open to question, but the fact remained that they enabled the French state to survive and thrive in a hostile world. Further human resources were channelled into the infantry through Jourdan's conscription law of 5 September 1798, which made all men aged 20–25 eligible for call-up. The resulting manpower was used to form numbers of auxiliary battalions, which were eventually incorporated into the demi-brigades.

In September 1803, with Napoleon supreme in the French political and military leadership, the infantry saw a return to the use of the 'regiment' title, with 'demi-brigade' now being applied to provincial formations only. The new regiments each had three or four battalions, although in 1806 the four-battalion regiments often had one regiment removed and

---

1 Haythornwaite 2017: 27

▲ *A fusilier-grenadier of the Imperial Guard, as depicted in a series of famous artworks by Bellange. He wears the black shako introduced from 1806. (PD/CC)*

▲ *A grenadier (left) and* voltigeur *(right) of the line infantry, their roles indicated by the colour of their epaulettes, collars and cuffs, sword knots and shako adornments. (PD/CC)*

▼ *A re-enactment of Napoleonic French infantry lines gives an accurate sense of the compression of men into parallel ranks. (Wesley Miles)*

used to form the kernel of a new regiment or demi-brigade. With a clear hint of return to pre-Revolutionary traditionalism, Napoleon also brought back the rank of major, which had been abolished. Further significant changes were to come for the infantry the following year. On 20 September 1804, it was decreed that one company of fusiliers was to be converted into a company of *voltigeur* light infantry, an indicator of how important the light troops were becoming in Napoleon's tactical thinking. Four years later, in 1808, regimental organisation was set at four combat battalions and one depot battalion, totalling (at least on paper) 108 officers and 3,862 other ranks. Each battalion was divided into six companies: four fusilier, one grenadier and one *voltigeur*. The grenadier company also included four sappers.

FUSILIERS

Fusil is the French word for a type of flintlock musket, and fusiliers were the basic musket-armed soldiers of the line infantry. Fusiliers stood distinct from elite companies of troops, and were thus often branded as 'centre companies', meaning that they took the centre positions in battlefield formations. The elite companies (grenadiers and *voltigeurs*) occupied the flanks, which were more prestigious owing to the decisive role they could play in the outcome of the battle.

SAPPERS

Although their origins lay in the digging of 'saps' (trenches applied to undermine a building or structure, typically during a siege), by the Napoleonic era sappers were specialist assault troops, issued with heavy axes to demolish enemy defences or other obstacles. Their status prior to the Napoleonic decree of 1808 (when they became part of the official establishment of grenadier companies) was varied, with their numbers fluctuating according to both wartime demands and peacetime thinking. Under Napoleon, however, they took a prestigious position, reflected in the fact that they would typically lead a regiment on parade. Sappers were instantly recognisable by their long leather aprons, plus their thick-set and robust frames – only particularly solid men were selected for sapper service. In addition to an axe, they were also equipped with a bayonet and a musketoon, a short-barrelled musket that acted much like a modern combat shotgun, delivering close-quarters firepower.

▼ *A depiction of a sapper, showing the distinctive bearskin, leather apron and pick. (PD/CC)*

GRENADIERS

French grenadiers had their origins in the 17th century, under the reign of Louis XIV, and were formally introduced into the army in 1667 through the reforms of the then Inspector-General, the witheringly severe Lieutenant-Colonel Jean Martinet. The original purpose of the grenadier was to attack enemy positions with grenades. Although this role effectively disappeared by the late 18th century, the grenadiers remained as soldiers of elite standing, known for their bravery, physical endurance and ferocity in battle. Grenadiers were specially selected from the ranks of fusiliers, with the chosen men being of good character with a solid service record. Once in the grenadiers, soldiers would receive appreciable benefits, including higher pay, first position in the distribution of rations, and freedom from many menial duties.

▼ *A French Guard badge, depicting a white flaming hand grenade. Grenadier grenade badges were red. (Shutterstock)*

RESTORATION INFANTRY AND THE HUNDRED DAYS

Following Napoleon's abdication in 1814, the line infantry reverted back to royalist control. It was by now a somewhat emaciated service, ravaged by constant war. The restored monarchy reduced the number of line infantry regiments to 90, each of three battalions, although most of the regiments did not have sufficient men to establish the third battalion. On his return Napoleon attempted to undo the royalist reforms, decreeing that the infantry regiments should form a provisional establishment of five battalions, something that almost no regiment was able to achieve.

This all paints a picture of an orderly evolution in line infantry, but in reality there was much practical fluidity within Napoleon's orders of battle. Provisional regiments would flare into being for specific campaign purposes, often formed from depot companies. Battalions would be detached from their parent regiments and sent to bolster other regiments, or create fresh regiments of their own. Elite battalions in particular were in high demand, sometimes combined with other elites (such as grenadiers) to form new formations. As always, what mattered most to Napoleon was results on the battlefield, not rigid adherence to formulae.

LIGHT INFANTRY

The growth of the light infantry was a most significant trend of French military development during the Revolutionary and Napoleonic Wars. This is reflected in the fact that at the beginning of this period there were just 12 battalions of light infantry, which swelled to 35 battalions at its peak.

Napoleon found that light infantry was particularly suited to his brand of warfare. Not only could they disrupt the enemy prior to the clash of main lines, but they also performed the valuable role of screening the deployment of main forces from the eyes of their opponents.

CATEGORIES OF LIGHT INFANTRY

Within the category of 'light infantry' (*infanterie légère*) were a collection of types – *chasseur*, *voltigeur*, *carabinier* and *tirailleur*. The historical and practical distinctions between each category were often more conceptual than actual, but some distinctions can be made.

The carabinier troops were initially expert marksmen, although unlike the British the French rarely ever used rifled muskets. It is challenging to distinguish this role from that of the *voltigeur*. The *voltigeur* was given a higher pay than many other soldiers and like the *chasseur*, the *voltigeur* was a short man, under 5ft 3in (1.6m tall).[2]

The *carabinier* troops were initially expert marksmen, likely armed with rifled muskets instead of the usual smoothbores. They wore the bearskin cap, but to separate them out from the grenadiers these caps did not display the latter's brass plaque on the front. The *tirailleur* were another species of light infantry skirmishers, concentrated in the Young Guard of the Imperial Guard. There were 16 regiments of *tirailleur* by 1814. These were disbanded during the Restoration, and Napoleon raised eight regiments during his Hundred Days campaign.

Light infantry, in the form of 12 battalions of *chasseurs à pied*, had been a formal part of the army since 1788, with each battalion consisting of four companies but raised to eight companies in 1791. In the same year, each company of *chasseurs* was allocated six *carabiniers* in its ranks. *Carabiniers* had originally been formed in the *chasseurs* in lieu of elite grenadier companies, but by 1794 they had their own dedicated companies.

---

2   Crowdy 2015: 35 notes that: 'There were two reasons for this selection process. Firstly, short soldiers (of which there were plenty) could never qualify for service in the grenadiers, but they could aspire for service in the voltigeurs. Secondly, Bardin [Colonel Bardin, a French military reformer] estimated this measure increased the pool of those eligible for conscription by about 40,000 men.'

◥ *A* voltigeur *and* carabinier *of the light infantry march alongside one another, c.1809. (PD/CC)*

▶ *Long hat plumes were more common during the early imperial period. (Alamy)*

GROWTH OF LIGHT INFANTRY

Between 1794 and 1804, the light infantry grew steadily, both in terms of the numbers of battalions and regiments formed and in the complement of personnel allocated to each company. There were also numerous irregular provincial corps organised, but although some of these units were sizeable formations – the *Légion des Allobroges*, for example, had a total of 14 companies of light infantry, plus three companies of dragoons and one of artillery, mostly composed of Swiss, Piedmontese and Savoyard volunteers – many of them disappeared after a brief existence.

As mentioned above, *voltigeurs* were introduced into the formal structure of the line infantry, through the reforms of 1804. This change was significant, because it also indicated how the light infantry was steadily becoming less separate from the regular line infantry. Indeed, in the later years of the Napoleonic Wars the tactical distinctions between light and line could be less clear, as regular line battalions and companies might be called upon to perform the functions of light infantry in battle, and received training to do so. In terms of military culture, however, the light infantry always retained a certain *esprit de corps*, priding themselves on their mobility, dash and courage.

▶ *A Napoleonic Guard* tirailleur *(left) and* voltigeur *(right)by Bellange. On campaign the long plumes would be rolled and packed away to protect them. (PD/CC)*

▲ *A group of French Guard grenadier re-enactors; note the red grenadier badge on the bearskins. (Shutterstock)*

IMPERIAL GUARD

Napoleon's Imperial Guard was initially just a small, elite Consular Guard, formed in 1799. It grew under Napoleon to be an army in its own right, swelling to about 110,000 men by 1813. It was a true multi-arms force, containing all the elements needed for battle – infantry, cavalry, artillery, logistics and specialist troops – but also one with a direct sense of loyalty to Napoleon himself.

ORGANISATION OF THE IMPERIAL GUARD

Grenadiers and *chasseurs à pied* formed the kernel of the Consular Guard, but the size and status of the Guard grew under Napoleon. In May 1804, Napoleon rebranded the Consular Guard the Imperial Guard, and thus began the accelerated expansion of the Guard forces.

Over time, the Guard was famously divided into three elements: the Old Guard, Middle Guard and Young Guard. The Old Guard were the original soldiers of the Guard, known with some affection as *les grognards,* 'the grumblers'. The nickname was due to the fact that Napoleon came to regard the troops of the Old Guard as his most stalwart men, committed to battle only when needed to save the day or to tip the action in France's favour and the old soldiers grumbled about this and other matters; their long service and status gave them a special licence to express opinions. The titles Young Guard and Middle Guard came later, in 1809 and 1811 respectively, and in rough terms were used to denote the length of service. This division was far from watertight, as, for example, you would often find officers with long military careers serving in the Young Guard, finding more opportunities for promotion there, and officers of Guard *voltigeurs* and *tirailleurs* might take the status of Old Guard after about six years in uniform.

The organisation and development of the Imperial Guard was complex (see Further Reading for recommended titles), and the Guard formations were expensive entities to maintain. This latter factor, plus the supposed elite status, raised eyebrows amongst many non-Guard commanders and the wider mass of soldiery. A modern analogy might be the questioning of the rationale of the US Marine Corps by some in the United States, who argue that the functions of the USMC should be absorbed within (or are already actually performed by) the far larger US Army.

This issue was addressed directly by Louis de Bourienne, Napoleon's personal secretary, in his *Memoirs*. His views very likely reflect those of the emperor himself. He stated:

> The men composing [the Imperial Guard] were invariably taken from the old and distinguished soldiers of other regiments. There have always been two opinions among French officers on the wisdom of this proceeding, some complaining of the weakening of the regimental *esprit de*

▶ *A M. Burg, an Old Guard grenadier, one of the last surviving veterans of Napoleon's army, photographed here in c.1858 wearing full dress uniform. (PD/CC)*

▲ *A French soldier in the ranks of infantry in 1813 bites the end off a cartridge, ready to prime the pan. gunpowder ingestion could lead to sickness. (Pictorial Press Ltd / Alamy)*

◤ *French chasseurs of the Imperial Guard, the man on the left being of sergeant rank. The soldier on the right is in full dress, the man on the left in undress. (PD/CC)*

corps caused among the ordinary regiments, which were thus trained to look on the Guard as a superior body, and the bad effect of withdrawing so many old and good soldiers who should have leavened the mass of recruits. On the other hand, the Imperial Guard became an enormous reserve for use on the decisive point, and its very approach raised the spirits of the other troops acting on that point, where they then knew the great effort was to be made. Also, there was less jealousy aroused by keeping the Guard in reserve than there would have been if an ordinary corps had been selected for each occasion. Gradually increased, in 1814 the Guard was 112,482 strong.[3]

De Bourienne's point about moderating 'jealousy aroused by keeping the Guard in reserve' is likely warranted, and not merely an act of justification. Napoleon heaped praise on those units and formations who distinguished themselves in battle, and thus being kept in reserve, away from the front, rarely led to satisfaction amongst those men held to the rear.

3 De Bourienne 1905: 816

FOREIGN CORPS

Although on the ideological level the Napoleonic army might appear quintessentially French, in terms of actual frontline personnel the French forces could be heavily international in composition. In fact, by 1812 about half of the total military manpower available to Napoleon were foreigners, serving either as mercenaries, foreigners who had enlisted in French regiments, in foreign units under French service, or in units from French-allied states. The list of nationalities under Napoleon's direction is expansive, and includes Swiss, Germans (from numerous states), Poles, Italians, Spaniards, Austrians, Prussians, Portuguese, Croatians, Hessians, Danes, Greeks, Egyptians and Irish. The biggest contributors were the Italians, Spanish and the German states. The Army of the Kingdom of Italy, by 1812, had some 90,000 men in uniform allied to France, led by Napoleon's stepson Eugène de Beauharnais. They included the Royal Guard (a mixed cavalry and infantry force), seven line and five light infantry regiments, six regiments of cavalry, two artillery battalions, plus two artillery train and two equipment battalions. Spain provided extensive land and naval support to Napoleon's cause, although often of poor quality; both army and navy were wracked by corruption and chronic under investment. The German states, by contrast, had units and formations of the highest order, known for discipline and fighting courage. When the *Grande Armée* went into Russia in 1812, it included an impressive 174 units of German origin.

▶ *Napoleon haranguing Marmont's 2nd corps on the bridge over the Lech at Augsburg, 12 October 1805. (Getty Images)*

Yet there were numerous other smaller contributors. Switzerland, for example, provided four numbered infantry regiments plus two prestigious battalions (the Valais Battalion and Neuchâtel Battalion). These four regiments alone fought in 69 battles between 1805 and 1815 and suffered heavily for it. The main Swiss motivation for fighting for the French was commercial – they served as mercenaries, hence the contemporary saying 'No money, no Swiss' – but their bravery and sheer professionalism made them a very welcome addition to any commander's force portfolio. Similarly, the Poles, whose four regiments of troops (three infantry and one cavalry) gradually formed the Vistula Legion. The Polish regiments fought under the French banner from 1807 until 1814, but suffered terribly in the process, virtually being wiped out during the Russian campaign of 1812 and at the battle of Leipzig in October 1813.

The contribution of foreign corps to Napoleon's campaigns and battles was inestimable. At the battle of Borodino alone, 25 per cent of all 'French' troops were foreigners, principally Poles (15 per cent), Westphalians (7 per cent) and Italians (5 per cent). Keeping this in mind, we realise that the Napoleonic Wars were truly an international struggle, and not just a case of France standing alone against the rest of Europe.

▶ *A mid 19th-century depiction of Polish troops from the Legion of the Vistula, one of the larger Polish formations in Napoleon's service. (PD/CC)*

INFANTRY WEAPONS

By today's standards, the firearms of the Napoleonic era were crude devices indeed, known for their poor accuracy, unreliability and slow rates of fire. In response, however, the armies of this era implemented procedures that compensated for the limitations, such that small arms were able to make a proper tactical contribution to the outcome of a battle.

MUSKETS

The battlefield utility of the Napoleonic French soldier was defined by his two weapons – the Model 1777 musket and its accompanying bayonet. These two weapons were almost the only means a soldier had of imposing some form of influence over and destruction upon the enemy, hence they are worth our detailed consideration.

The Model 1777 was the final major variant in a series of .69in (17.5mm) flintlock muskets that were the standard French infantry weapons for more than a century, from 1717 until 1840, with 7.7 million of all types produced. Collectively they are known popularly as the 'Charleville musket', after one of its armouries at Charleville-Mézières in the French Ardennes, and there were several other centres of production. During its time in service, the *modéle de 1777 corrigé en l'an IX* ('The Model of 1777 modified in the year IX'), to give it its full name, provided respectable service to hundreds of thousands of French infantry.

Long and heavy by modern standards, the Model 1777 was a carefully considered weapon. The barrel, which constituted the majority of the gun's length, ensured that it delivered a decent muzzle velocity of about 1,000ft/sec (328m/sec), although this figure was variable depending on factors such as the operator's loading technique and the quality of the powder. The calibre, .69in, was actually smaller than rivals such as the .75in (19mm) ball of the British Land Pattern musket, but it was still capable of inflicting a truly nasty injury; at ranges of under 100 yards/metres, tests

have shown it driving up to 28in (71cm) into ballistic gelatin blocks. By opting for a smaller calibre, furthermore, the French ordnance authorities also reduced the weight of the ammunition, which meant more rounds could be carried for the same weight as a British soldier's cartridges.

Flintlock mechanism

The Model 1777, like virtually all firearms of this period, was a flintlock musket. The flintlock mechanism consisted of a spring-loaded hammer that gripped a piece of flint in a set of screw jaws. Forward of the hammer was the gun's pan, which, when primed, contained a small amount of gunpowder, covered and held in place by a spring-loaded frizzen, which featured an angled striking face for the flint. The gun was fully loaded when the pan was primed, and powder, ball and wadding had been loaded into the musket's chamber, via the muzzle. On firing, the cocked hammer was released by the trigger; the flint struck the frizzen, generating a shower of sparks at the same time as it pushed the frizzen off the pan, exposing the powder to the sparks and starting the process of ignition. The flame from the priming powder flashed down a vent hole into the chamber, setting off the main charge and firing the gun.

The flintlock worked, but it was far from reliable by modern standards. Misfires were extremely common, at a rate of roughly one per six or seven shots, although for expertly maintained weapons the rates could be much lower, in the region of one in 26.[4] Causes of misfires were:

- Damp or wet powder
- Priming powder lost from the pan
- Poorly adjusted lock springs (rare)
- Dirty or improperly tensioned frizzen (rare)
- Flint not secured properly in the hammer jaws (a piece of lead or leather formed a grip surface between the jaws and the flint)
- Flint worn, therefore not producing sparks (the firer had, on occasion, to sharpen the flint edge with a small knapping hammer)
- Fouling in the vent hole.

Particularly in inclement weather, the rate of misfires could become so significant that they forced a change in tactics to a bayonet charge, as occurred at the battle of Ligny on 16 June 1815.

▼ *Re-encators hold their muskets in the present arms position (présentez vous armes), prior to working through the loading procedure. (Shutterstock)*

MODEL 1777 MUSKET

Calibre:	.69in (17.5mm)
Length:	49in (124cm)
Barrel length:	43in (110cm)
Weight:	9lb 10½oz (4.38kg)
Action:	Flintlock

Accuracy

Smoothbore muskets were almost invariably inaccurate weapons. The lack of rifling meant that the projectile had no spin stabilisation, but this was just one of several factors afflicting accuracy. The fit between bore and ball could be less than precise, particularly if there had been errors in the ball casting process, or if the ball had been damaged in storage, resulting in the ball not exiting in a clean, linear fashion from the muzzle. The act of ramming could also inflict damage on the ball. You could add the severe problems of fouling, with the barrel, pan and vent hole becoming progressively choked up with powder residue. Not only could these affect the weapon's accuracy, but they also retarded the rate at which the soldier could reload, as it was harder, and therefore slower, to ram a ball down a heavily fouled bore.

All these influences, combined with the most rudimentary of sights and also poor training among many soldiers, meant that musketry in the Napoleonic Wars was a rather wild affair. Various trials and tests, conducted by both the French

▼ *A close-up of the Model 1777 flintlock mechanism. Here the hammer is in the half-cock position and the frizzen is raised to exposed the priming pan. (Duncan Miles)*

▲ *The Model 1777 musket was the standard infantry arm of Napoleon's army, with some shorter patterns available for some light infantry and cavalry. (Royal Amrouries)*

▼ *The muzzle end of the musket, with the flared tip of the steel ramrod clearly visible beneath the muzzle, emerging from its storage pipe. (PD/CC)*

and their enemies, suggested that at a range of 100 yards/ metres, some 40–50 per cent of shots fired would miss even a target as big as a massed rank of infantry. Beyond 165 yards (150m) and the miss rates climbed to about 60 per cent. For this reason, musketry engagement was most effective at ranges of under 100 yards/metres. Of course, the limitations of an individual musket were somewhat levelled out by the area effects of mass musketry volley fire, with volume of shot compensating for technological deficiencies. A single fusilier battalion, presented in a three-rank line with a front of about 200 yards (180m), was capable of firing anywhere between 1,000 and 2,000 rounds per minute. This blast of fire did much to compensate for inaccuracy, although we could rarely say that any Napoleonic battle was decided by musket fire.

RIFLED WEAPONS

Shorter carbine versions of the *An IX* were also produced for use by light cavalry officers and some light infantry, mainly officers and senior NCOs of the *voltigeurs*, with both smoothbore and rifled versions. Rifled weapons were rare in the French army, less so in the hands of their British opponents. Rifling transformed the musket into a weapon with genuine accuracy over range, with the properly trained rifle-armed soldier able to hit a selected individual human target at ranges in excess of 200 yards/metres. Furthermore, the rifling meant that the barrel length could be reduced without concomitant reduction in accuracy, (The barrel length of a 1793 cavalry carbine was just 16in/406mm.)

The problem, however, lay in the loading procedures. Because a musket ball had to be tightly engraved into the lands and grooves of the rifled bore, the ball had to be an exceptionally snug fit in the barrel. The *carabine d'infanterie Modele An XII*, for example (known as the 'Versailles carbine'

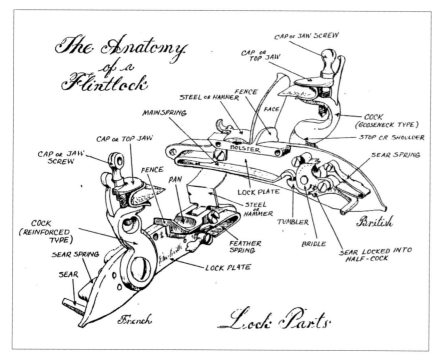

▲ A comparative diagram showing the French (left) and British (right) lock parts on flintlock weapons. Note the difference in hammer/cock shape. (PD/CC)

▲ The lock mechanism of the 1777 musket, here shown with the flint on its upper impact point on the frizzen. (Duncan Miles)

MUSKET LOADING AND FIRING PROCEDURE, EARLY 19TH CENTURY

1. Hold the musket well supported against the torso, keeping the gun level. Draw the hammer back to its half-cock position, then push the frizzen forward, exposing the pan.

2. Take a cartridge out from the cartridge pouch, and hold it between thumb and the two forefingers. Tear off the top of the cartridge with the teeth, exposing the powder inside.

3. Pour a small amount of powder into the pan and then snap the frizzen back down to hold the powder in place.

4. Up-end the gun and lower the stock until the butt plate is resting on the ground, with the muzzle in front of your chest.

5. Pour the remaining powder down the barrel, then push the empty paper cartridge (which contains the ball, and which now serves as wadding) into the muzzle of the musket. With the right hand, remove the ramrod from its pipe socket and ram the powder and wadding firmly down, seating them in the chamber on top of the powder. Withdraw the ramrod and return to its socket.

6. Shoulder the musket and draw the hammer back to the full cock position. Aim and fire.

▲ The charge of powder is poured down the barrel, the top of the cartridge having been torn off. (Francesco de Marco / Shutterstock)

▲ The ramrod is withdrawn from its storage pipe, ready for impacting ball, powder and paper in the chamber. (Francesco de Marco / Shutterstock)

▲ The hammer of the flintlock is drawn back to its full-cock position, with the frizzen closed down over the pan. (Francesco de Marco / Shutterstock)

▲ *This photo of Prussian or Saxon re-enactors clearly shows how lock smoke could affect the vision of man operating the musket. (Shutterstock)*

▼ *A French An IX 1777 musket produced in 1814, by the manufacturer Mutzig. (INTERFOTO / Alamy)*

after its place of production), had a calibre of ⁷⁄₁₆in (13.5mm), but the ball itself was ⁹⁄₁₆in (14.4mm). The disparity here was overcome by 'forced loading', i.e., the ball was actually hammered down the barrel by striking the top of the ramrod with a mallet, with the ball deforming into the rifling as it was tapped down. Needless to say, this process was slow compared to a smoothbore musket, especially as rifled weapons were even more prone to fouling. The reloading rate for a rifled musket could be slower by a factor of three when compared to the smoothbore, which meant that it was used infrequently, and certainly didn't carry the battlefield authority of the massed smoothbore musket.

PISTOLS

Flintlock pistols were weapons of last resort, with little in the way of accuracy over 5½–11 yards (5–10m). They were also a somewhat expensive luxury, hence they were not used by many – mainly cavalrymen, some infantry officers and men of the eagle guard. For offensive purposes, cavalry units tended to use both carbines and pistols in the same way; the cavalry would wheel in front of the ranks of enemy infantry, discharging their weapons into the mass of humanity on the way past. But pistols were also drawn in close melee, particularly when the mounted cavalryman was trying to keep swarming enemy infantry away from his mount, or as close-in defence if he had been dismounted.

▶ *A French officer's flintlock pistol made in France, c.1805–10 by Fillon, a Parisian gunsmith. (PD/CC)*

The most popular and prolific of the military-issue pistols was the *pistolet modèle An XIII*, manufactured between 1806 and 1814, with more than 300,000 produced. (The other main cavalry model was the earlier, heavier, *An IX*, made from 1801.) Total length was 13¾in (352mm) and weight was 2¾lb (1.27kg) – heavy by modern standards but aiding accuracy through better stability in a one-handed grip.

BAYONETS

The bayonet was an essential addition to the *An IX* musket (the carbines generally couldn't take a bayonet, nor had little tactical reason to do so). Following successive exchanges of musket fire between infantry, a charge with fixed bayonets might be the only way to take ground or to fracture an obstinate formation. Bayonets also had the vital function of providing a means of defence against enemy cavalry attacks – even the most ferociously ridden horse had little incentive to pile into a glistening row of bayonet spikes. This being said, it is now commonly understood that bayonets made a very limited contribution to the final casualty counts of any battle. Dominique-Jean Larrey, Chief Surgeon to the Imperial Guard

▲ M. Mauban, who served in the 8th Dragoon Regiment in 1815, displays his cavalry sabre. (PD/CC)

and inventor of a battlefield ambulance service, conducted a study of one melee fought in Russia and found that of 119 men injured, only five (4 per cent of the total) actually sustained wounds from bayonets; the remaining 96 per cent were injured by musket or artillery fire. Other studies revealed similar or even lower figures for bayonet effectiveness.

Yet this was not to say that the bayonet had little application for the infantryman. Sometimes it had a very literal utility, such as being used to conduct rudimentary equipment repairs, punch holes in leather, or even – in versions manufactured with poor-quality metal – bent into fishing hooks. In infantry battle, however, the bayonet undoubtedly added a psychological effect, one that could decide the clash between two opposing units without the forces actually locking into hand-to-hand combat.

Sometimes a purposeful advance alone could throw an enemy into retreat, as observed by an anonymous British officer writing about the battle of Salamanca. Here he describes the effect of a stoic French advance, which almost certainly included fixed bayonets:

> The French regiment formed close column with the grenadiers in front and closed the battalions. . . . They then advanced up the hill in the most beautiful order without firing a shot . . . when about 30 paces distant our men began to waver, being still firing. . . . The ensigns advanced

MUSKETRY KIT

The most visible piece of musketry kit was the sizeable cartridge pouch on the right buttock. The cartridge pouch, or *giberne*, was actually a stiff wooden box spacious enough to hold 35 prepared cartridges plus a small bottle of oil. The box was in turn covered by blackened cow hide, with a large flap overlapping the top and protecting the contents from the elements. The whole pouch was supported on a leather shoulder strap belt and held firmly against the buttock with a further strap. (This latter restraint, called a *martingale*, was essential to prevent the box moving as the soldier withdrew the paper cartridges.) The interior of the wooden box was divided into three sections. In the central section there was a wooden block, drilled with six holes – five of these held cartridges, while the sixth held the oil container. (Oil would be applied regularly to the lock and trigger mechanisms and the frizzen hinge, and would be used to clean and protect both the outer metalwork and the gun's bore.) Each of the two other compartments held 15 cartridges.

Various tools were important for keeping the musket in optimal condition, and for effecting repairs when necessary. The standard gun kit included a *tire-balle* (ball extractor), a spiked device fitted to the end of a ramrod and used to extract a musket ball that had become stuck in the bore. The *tourne-vis* (turn-screw) was an implement used for loosening or tightening the various screws on the musket, such as the hammer jaws holding the flint, while the *épinglette* (literally

'pin') was a thin tool used for unblocking an obstructed vent hole. Each infantryman carried several spare flints, each of these properly knapped by a *tailleur de pierre* (stone cutter) into the most efficient shape for generating sparks. An inert wooden or horn flint, used for training drills, was also part of the kit. Further items included spare leads or leather patches for holding the flint in the hammer jaws.

▼ The French infantryman's giberne, seen here fitted to its banderolle leather shoulder belt, contained cartridges and musketry tools and was worn on the right hip. (M. Mathews)

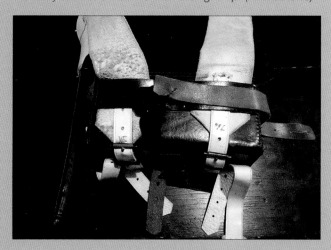

two paces in front and planted the colours on the edge of the hill and officers stepped out to encourage the men to meet them. They stopped with an apparent determination to stand firm, the enemy continued to advance at a steady pace and when quite close the Fusiliers gave way: - the French followed down the hill on our side.

In fact, bayonet fights between mass ranks of infantry on open battlefields seem extremely rare. Although there certainly are incidents of such clashes – localised examples are found at Eylau (1807), Borodino (1812), Salamanca (1812) and Ligny (1815), amongst others – in most cases, bayonet fights appear to have taken place between relatively small units of men, caught in a melee in broken or urban terrain, or while assaulting a defensive position. General Jomini indeed once declared that 'I have seen melees of infantry in defiles and in villages, where the heads of columns came in actual collision and thrust each other with the bayonet; but I never saw such a thing on a regular field of battle.'

By the Revolutionary Wars, the days of the plug bayonet had long passed. Most infantry initially would have used the M1777 socket bayonet, with the blade fitted at an angle to a tubular metal socket that fitted over the end of the barrel, locking into place via a rotating captive locking ring. The muzzle remained open, which meant that the musket could still be loaded and fired with the bayonet fitted, the angle of the blade in relation to the muzzle meaning that loading rates were not reduced. The primary bayonet of the Napoleonic Wars was the *An IX*, introduced in 1800. Total length of the triangular-profile blade was about 17¾in (450mm) with variations and the socket measured 2½in (66mm). Fitted to the end of a musket that was already more than a yard/metre long, the bayonet gave the infantry substantial reach in a close-quarters defence or melee.

SWORDS

Prior to the French Revolution, the long, thin épée sword had been standard issue to all French fusiliers, while grenadiers received chunky and rather unwieldy sabres. In 1767 both were replaced and standardised with the *sabre-briquet*, which was shorter, flat-bladed and of simpler construction, with a straight stirrup hilt. The new sabre was no longer a universal weapon – in line regiments, only NCOs, musicians, grenadiers and men of *voltigeur* companies carried the sabre, while in the light infantry the sabre was a standard-issue

weapon. (Light infantry, because of their mobile skirmishing role and their focus on more accurate individual shooting, did not generally carry bayonets, hence the sword provided them with a tool for close-quarters combat.) French officers would use the straight sword or épée, a light, thin thrusting sword with a blade about 27½in (70cm) long, although officers often swapped these out for sabres, wishing to imitate the dash of their cavalry comrades.

An updated version of the *sabre-briquet* was produced from 1800, which featured a one-piece cast hilt, a ribbed grip and a lengthened blade. The *sabre-briquet* would go through three subsequent variations during the Napoleonic era, with various changes to the hilt and the length of the grip; the variants were designated IX, XI and XIII, although the introduction of a new model of sword did not mean the others went out of service. Typical specifications for a *sabre-briquet* would be a blade length of just under 23½in (60cm), an overall length of 29in (74cm) and a weight of 2lb (905g).

An order of 1807 officially removed the *sabre-briquet* from the hands of the *voltigeurs* – an order apparently widely ignored – and light infantry remained the key non-cavalry combat user of sabres during the Napoleonic Wars. The degree to which they were swung in battle itself is uncertain and little recorded. Certainly officers, on occasions of pricked honour, applied their swords in duel fighting, but on the battlefield most of the sword-fighting was delivered by the cavalry, not the infantry. Among the humble ranks of infantry, therefore, swords were frequently repurposed for utilitarian tasks, such as cutting vegetation or for hanging utensils.

▼ *This re-enactor illustrates the layout of the infantryman's personal equipment. Note the positions of the* giberne *and the* sabre, *the latter for a cross-handed draw. (PD/CC)*

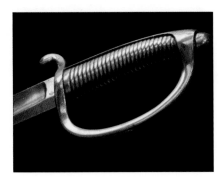

◄ *The sabre-briquet had a cast hilt, with a curled guard piece that could trap and twist enemy sword blades. (PD/CC)'*

INFANTRY EQUIPMENT

Napoleonic soldiers were beasts of burden. Calculations of weight carried by individual soldiers vary from about 53lb (24kg) for a regular fusilier up to about 73lb (33kg) for a sapper, although these figures do not include personal gear. The ideal healthy weight for a man 5ft 7in (1.7m) tall is about 135lb (61kg), but men in the Napoleonic era were often undernourished and underweight.

Physical loads for someone in Napoleon's army, therefore, would typically be in the region of 30–50 per cent of body mass. We see such weights being carried in today's modern professional armies, but those are achieved with all the benefits of ergonomic, nutritional and physiological research. The soldiers of the early 19th century had little but brute force and a dogged endurance to keep them going.

Below is a concise run-through of the kit and equipment typically carried by a Napoleonic soldier. The specific items would have fallen under the categories of *grand équipement*, which referred to equipment supplied directly by the government without personal deductions from the soldier's pay, and *petite équipement* (particularly clothing), which required direct pay deductions. Note also that the content lists would have been highly subject to the vagaries of the supply system and military manufacturing, plus would have changed naturally through the inevitable processes of loss, damage and acquisition in the field.

▼ *Two views of the giberne, an exterior view (left) showing the leather exterior, and an internal image showing the wooden slots for five cartridges and one oil phial. (M. Mathews)*

LOAD-CARRYING EQUIPMENT

The Napoleonic infantryman basically had two systems for the personal transportation of equipment – a *haversac* (haversack), worn on the back, and a loose *sac à distribution* (distribution sack). The former was the main piece of load-carrying equipment. It was constructed from animal hide, with the hair presented outwards to aid with waterproofing, and featured a top flap fastened by three buckled straps. Inside, the haversack was lined with canvas. Additional straps were provided on the top of the haversack, used to tie on additional items, such as a rolled-up greatcoat.

Two basic shapes and sizes of the haversack were produced. From the beginning of the Revolutionary Wars until 1812 the haversack was roughly 12in (30cm) deep by 17in (43cm) wide. The new regulation of 1812 flattened the haversack – its depth was now 4¼ in (11cm) – but made it squarer and wider, with a width of 19in (49cm) and a height of 12½ in (32cm). The impetus behind the new design was to make it less obtrusive when soldiers were pressed up against one another in close ranks. Yet, although strap adjustments now meant it sat higher up on the back, the new design actually made volley fire from ranks more difficult;

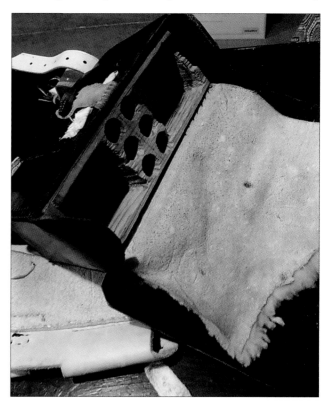

▶ *The hair of the hide used to make the haversack provided some degree of waterproofing. (Shutterstock)*

it was harder for the second and third ranks to level their muskets around the haversacks in front of them. In addition, the loaded haversack had a worse centre of gravity for the bearer, leading to bad backs and painful shoulders.

The *sac à distribution* was a large hemp bag measuring nearly 60in (150cm) long and 27½ in (70cm) wide, carried simply by slinging it over one shoulder. It was a general-purpose sack for holding assorted squad rations and equipment, but it also found value as a crude sleeping bag. When not in use, the *sac à distribution* was generally folded up tightly and stored in the haversack or rolled up and tied to the top of the main pack.

While the general mass of infantry carried their equipment themselves, officers enjoyed the luxury of having their equipment transported separately in a more spacious case or portmanteau. This was transported with the regimental baggage train and managed by the officer's orderlies.

Most soldiers had a non-regulation water container holding about 2 pints (1 litre) of water. This was made either of metal or, typically seen later in the wars, was a simple glass bottle protected by a wicker outer frame. The canteens were supported by a leather strap, usually worn over the right shoulder so that the canteen rested against the left hip. (The cartridge pouch had pride of place on the right hip.)

PERSONAL GROOMING

Many of the remaining pieces of kit were related either to personal grooming or to care of the uniform. Hair products

▶ *A presentation of infantry equipment, including a hide haversack, tin water container, shako, musket and a white leather giberne for cartridges and musket tools. (M. Mathews)*

▲ *This depiction of Napoleon on the evening before Austerlitz shows the emperor consulting his maps while his troops sleep on the ground, on top of fir bows to provide insulation from ground chill. (Photo 12 / Alamy)*

such as pomade, grease and powder were common, especially among those soldiers who wore the traditional *queue* (long plait). Short-cut hair became more common with the introduction of the shako from 1806, and Napoleon himself sported short-cropped hair from 1800, which gave him the additional nickname *petit tondu* ('little crop'). In fact, the wearing of short hair was not given official permission until 25 September 1815,[5] although it gradually became evident that short hair had hygienic benefits, particularly in the control of head lice. Furthermore, the various unguents and potions applied to hair tended to cause skin complaints, as they prevented perspiration from the scalp.

Uniform-related equipment included a wide range of devices and substances used for repairing inevitable damage and for sharpening appearance. Obviously, campaign uniform bore a dramatically different appearance from garrison uniform. On campaign, uniform colours became muted through exposure to the elements and through infusion of dirt; cloth over the knees and elbows quickly wore through; fur or hair became matted. While such deterioration could not be prevented altogether, the infantryman's kit enabled him to perform basic repairs and restorations.

PERSONAL EFFECTS

Each infantryman would of course carry a variety of non-regulation personal effects. Given the general poverty prevalent in any army of the 18th and 19th centuries, the high levels of deductions from pay, and also the general

COOKING VESSELS AND BASIC UTENSILS

The most visible of the French infantryman's cooking utensils was the metal *gamelle* mess tin, which hung from his haversack on a metal ring. Prepared food, especially soups and broths, would be poured into the *gamelle* for eating, and the tin could also be used for warming foods over a fire if necessary. Cooking, however, was usually performed in the larger *marmite*, a lidded metal pot featuring a sizeable lid that in turn could be upended and repurposed as a saucepan. The *marmite* was accompanied by a variety of smaller pots and pan for cooking, plus a water can for collecting cooking water.

GROOMING KIT

The infantryman's kit included the following:

- Clothes beater, strip of hide attached to a wooden handle, used to beat clothes. Each squad would carry two of these devices, known as *martinets*
- 3 × brushes, for cleaning the coat, shoes and leather items
- 1 × copper brush plus Tripoli powder (a fine powdered porous rock used as a polishing abrasive)
- 1 × metal-polishing kit
- 1 × clothing repair kit
- 1 × leather punch
- 1 × button polishing stick
- 1 × bag of wire wool
- Spanish whitener and pipe clay for cleaning up white straps
- 1 × *astic,* a wooden tool used for waxing cartridge pouches

unwillingness to add extra loads to the kit, these artefacts tended to be limited in number and light in substance. Such restrictions did not apply to officers, of course, who could, within reason, add all manner of personal luxuries to the baggage train – although Napoleon frowned upon excessive self-indulgence.

Typical personal items in an infantryman's kit would be a small pocket knife, a simple drinking cup and, for personal hygiene, a small toilet box containing items such as a comb, hair brush, shaving kit, nail file, and wooden picks for teeth cleaning (or, more rarely, an actual toothbrush). For the purposes of entertainment, a pack of playing cards (displaying either the traditional royal symbols or emblems approved by the Republican government) could while away many an hour, and small musical instruments were popular, especially flutes and whistles. (Drummers could use their issue instruments to provide a thumping accompaniment to the melody.) Most soldiers indulged in smoking of one form or another, hence pipe, pipe kit and tobacco were common, as were snuff boxes.

▲ A Napoleonic re-enactors' tented camp, with the cook fires located logically at regular intervals. Formal tented camps became a relative rarity in the imperial period. (Shutterstock)

◄ A re-enactor wearing a cuirass breastplate and bonnet. (Shutterstock)

▼ Muskets were often stored leaning against each other with interlocking bayonets. (M. Mathews)

INFANTRY UNIFORMS

The subject of Napoleonic army uniforms is one of great complexity, subtlety and exceptions, and only a brief overview can be provided here. The actual uniforms worn by soldiers in the field could be a long way from the official statute, depending on numerous factors of manufacture, distribution, practicality, availability and regimental identity.

This situation was particularly true in the 1790s, when the Revolutionary army was blighted with chronic shortages of clothing and equipment. The volunteer forces in particular could head out on campaign with an appearance more akin to ragged vagrants than polished soldiers, some wearing frayed civilian clothing items and walking barefoot.

JACKETS, VESTS AND OVERCOATS

As a point of departure, it is necessary to define the core items that composed French infantry uniform from 1792 to 1815. With these understood, it is easier to picture the evolution of uniforms generally during this period. For much of this time, the defining item of infantry dress was the *habit*, a long tail-coat that, through its facing colours, piping, insignia etc., defined the regimental belonging and arm-of-service of the wearer. During the Revolutionary Wars, the colour of the *habit* stated the difference between regular army troops and volunteer/National Guard units. The former wore traditional white coats while the latter adopted the Revolutionary dark blue with scarlet collar and cuffs and white lapels and piping. The visual distinction resulted in the regular army troops being known as *les blancs*, while the National Guard were

▼ *Line infantry re-enactors draw their musket ramrods for loading. Note how the uniform colours reflect French national colours. (Alan Balding)*

les bleus. Later, as will be seen, all infantry uniforms were standardised to the Revolutionary colours. Furthermore, in 1812 the *habit* was replaced by the *habit-veste*, a short coatee that had greater battlefield practicality (light infantry often wore coatees prior to 1812).

Beneath the *habit* or *habit-veste*, the soldier would wear a *veste* or *gilet*, which was essentially a close-fitting, long-sleeved vest. The *veste* flared out over the hips to form a *basque*, while the *gilet* was shorter and without a *basque*; the *gilet* tended to be worn by light infantry, but it become universal amongst the infantry in January 1812. The *gilet* and *veste* provided layering for additional warmth. For protection against the worst of the weather, however, the *capote* (greatcoat) was worn. This was initially issued mainly to sentries or to men destined for winter campaigns, but from April 1806, its use spread out among the military field armies generally (not depot, reserve or garrison troops). The greatcoat was a relatively rough-and-ready item, produced in thick cloth in a variety of muted colours, with beige, grey, blue and brown the most common.

BREECHES, TROUSERS, GAITERS AND FOOTWEAR

On the legs, the traditional military dress was a pair of *culottes* (breeches), made from linen and reaching down from the waist to the top of the calf, where they were buttoned in place. Traditionalism did not mask their inherent impracticality

▲ *French infantry of the Young Guard in loose skirmishing ranks engage enemy cavalry forces. (Fine Art Images/ Heritage Images/Getty)*

▲ *With adoption of the shako by the line infantry in 1806, short hair became popular. (James R Gibson / Alamy)*

on campaign, however. Being quite tight fitting, particularly around the lower leg, they were not items conducive to kneeling in comfort; the calf fastenings rode up high around the knee, and split seams were common. Therefore, in the late 1790s and early 1800s there was a gradual shift towards wearing the *pantalon* (trousers). This development took its momentum from the political associations of trousers with Republicanism, rather than the aristocratic elitism connoted by breeches or *culottes* (hence the application of the term *sans-culottes* – literally 'without breeches' – to early Revolutionary soldiers), plus the popularity of trousers amongst light troops and as general fatigue wear. Finally, in 1812, breeches were replaced altogether with trousers.

Gaiters (*gu tres*) provided the covering between shoe and breeches, and came in three different versions: black canvas for general service and warm-weather campaigning; black wool for cold-weather conditions; and white canvas for the parade ground. Much like breeches, gaiters were high on traditionalism and low on practicality. The 20–24 small buttons running up the side of the leg were a minor logistical burden in their own right, and were frequently lost or snagged on vegetation. They also capably collected dirt. They attached to the breeches by two small buttons and a strap, but although secure, this fitting further served to hamper mobility in the legs. During the 1800s, therefore, the full gaiters were steadily ousted in preference of more practical half gaiters, which became another universal adoption in 1812.

Gaiters also fitted to the soldier's shoes via a strap that passed under the heel. Military footwear was an abiding interest of Napoleon, who regarded it as a much-overlooked key to the operational success of his infantry. The basic shoe was made of black leather, with a heel, a square toe and hobnailed sole and fastened by either a buckle or by laces. The quality and quantity of these shoes often left much to be desired, hence other varieties of shoes and boots were in evidence, particularly among elite regiments and the light infantry, who might borrow styles from other allied nations.

HEADGEAR

Turning to headgear, the five main options available appear wildly impractical to modern eyes, and, indeed, they largely were. One of the worst offenders was the *casque* (helmet), a boiled leather dome with a longitudinal bearskin or horsehair crest and a visor. Resembling the British Tarleton helmet, the *casque* was plagued by issues of poor-quality manufacture – in some cases, the crest was nothing more than a tube of fabric stuffed with straw, which became rotten and stinking. It persisted in service until around 1794, when both the volunteer and regular infantry regiments moved across to the famous *chapeau*, or cocked hat. This quintessential piece of Revolutionary identity was still far from satisfactory in terms of military headgear. The half-crescent of felt that framed the soldier's face was not generally stable, and adornments such

◄ *A shako plaque of the French 100th Infantry Regiment, bearing the Napoleonic imperial eagle. The design of the plate appears to place it after 1810. (PD/CC)*

▶ *A belt buckle of an infantry officer of the Imperial Guard. The eagle motif ran through Napoleonic iconography from 1804, with their suggestions of Roman ancestry. (PD/CC)*

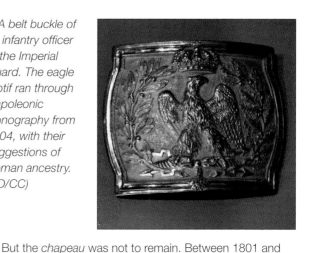

as the cockade and particularly the pompom unbalanced the hat so that it often slumped down to one side. It was not suited to musketry, furthermore, as the right side of the hat would sometimes clash with the stock of the musket when the firearm was in the aimed position, with the soldier's cheek on the upper stock. Soldiers adapted to this reality on the battlefield, literally by turning the hat to face to align front to back, a position that also had the virtue of providing some shade for the eyes. In all other ways the *chapeau* gave no protection for the wearer, but it remained a popular adornment, largely because of the sense of Revolutionary dash it evoked amongst the troops.

But the *chapeau* was not to remain. Between 1801 and 1806 the Napoleonic army shifted to the shako, with the light infantry first making the move and the line infantry following later. Shakos were tall and cylindrical by design. The first model measured some 7in (18cm) high by 9in (23cm) in diameter at its widest point, with some subsequent variations being taller and wider. The shako was made from boiled felt, with some types crowned with a leather top piece. The shako would remain the most prevalent campaign headgear throughout the rest of the wars, offering a measure of head protection from sword cuts and from the weather. It was certainly more practical than the traditional bearskins worn

▼ *M. Lefebre, a sergeant who served in the 2nd Regiment of Engineers in 1815. (PD/CC)*

▼ *Sergeant Taria served as a grenadier in the Imperial Guard from 1809 to 1815. (PD/CC)*

primarily by grenadiers and some elite types of light infantry, but was disastrously impractical on almost every level. This, too, was ousted by the shako in 1812.

The final type of headgear we should acknowledge is the *bonnet de police*, or forage cap. The term here really applies to a whole swathe of different soft headgear, worn during fatigue duties and off-duty hours.

STANDARDISATION OF UNIFORM

It was around these key pieces of uniform that the Revolutionary then Napoleonic armies strove towards measures of standardisation and practicality. The first major key date was the standardisation of the Revolutionary blue *habit* among most line and light formations in 1793, with some points of exception. After this there follows a period of evolution, the main trends of which were the shift from the bicorne hat to the shako plus the gradual spread of loose trousers in preference to breeches. Interestingly, in 1806, Napoleon attempted to turn back the clock by decreeing that the pre-Revolutionary uniform of *les blancs* would be restored, but this quickly proved to be impossible across the entire army, and although a handful of regiments went back to the white uniform, this decree was abandoned in 1807. The final major uniform event of Napoleon's reign were the reforms of 1812, which officially standardised to the short-tailed *habit-veste*, a new-pattern shako, short gaiters and a new style of forage cap.

▼ *A soldier of the Dutch grenadier regiment, a unit of the Imperial Guard, in a traditional white uniform. (PD/CC)*

SPARE CLOTHING ITEMS

In addition to the core items of uniform, however, the infantryman carried a range of spare/utility clothing items. Looking at around 1812/13, the clothing *petite équipement* clothing allocation for an individual soldier would include:

- 3 × linen shirts
- 4 × spare collars
- 2 × pairs of shoes
- 2 × handkerchiefs
- 2 × nightcaps
- 2 × cockades
- 1 × smock frock (worn for fatigue duties)
- 1 × pompom or plume for the headgear
- 2 × pairs of gaiters (one black, one grey)
- 1 × oiled linen shako cover

Much of this clothing, if not worn, was stored in the haversack. Packing such a significant volume of items into a relatively small space required experience and system; individual items were tightly rolled and stored in a proscribed fashion in the interior space.

▼ *Camp life often included collecting copious amounts of firewood to fuel cooking and heating. (Shutterstock)*

THE INFANTRY EXPERIENCE

Much about the infantry experience is explained in later chapters on logistics and tactics, but this chapter should conclude with a summary of the soldier's lot. Life was invariably hard. The uniforms described earlier in the chapter were generally ill-fitting, in poor repair, and gave little protection against the wet weather under which the humble infantryman so often marched and slept.

Chest infections and various other respiratory diseases, not helped by the prolific use of strong tobacco and the occasional inhalation of clouds of gunpowder smoke, were common. But these were the tip of the iceberg when it came to diseases among the soldiery. The general lack of hygienic living conditions, exacerbated by an often inadequate campaign diet, meant that disease could run like wildfire through units. For every single French soldier who died in combat, four died of sickness on campaign. Cholera and typhus were particularly severe maladies, being diseases that thrived in insanitary conditions. Napoleon himself appeared to be concerned about the serious effects of disease on unit efficiency. For example, while on campaign in Italy, he wrote: 'It is better to fight the most sanguinary battle than to encamp the troops in an unhealthy spot.'

PHYSICAL EXHAUSTION

Although battles formed logical landmarks for the infantry, most of their time on campaign was spent marching, fast and for long hours. The regulation pace for French marching was 76 paces per minute for ordinary step and 100 paces for fast

▼ *Infantry re-enactors display their distinctive haversacks and white-flapped gibernes. (DEA / C. BALOSSINI /Getty)*

step, equating to about 2–2.5mph (3.2–4km/h). The soldier might have to maintain this for hour upon hour, in badly fitted or worn-out shoes, although much of the marching would be done *pas de route* (own pace). There are accounts of soldiers being so tired that officers had to beat them awake with the flats of their swords. One fusilier remembered falling down a steep embankment while marching, rolling over and over again – and being asleep by the time he hit the bottom. When the infantry halted, they would set up a rudimentary camp, eat a basic meal, perhaps play a game, then slump into sleep, either lying on the ground in the open or, rarely, in a tent.

THE EXPERIENCE OF BATTLE

Then there was the experience of battle itself. The few accounts from regular soldiers indicate the age-old truths of battle – an overwhelming sense of fear and anxiety, trauma from witnessing violent death, and the release of action. The close ranks of line and column meant that many regular infantrymen would have witnessed truly horrific sights in immediate proximity. Artillery round shot could cause the most spectacular injuries – decapitations, disembowelment, men being split literally in two, limbs smashed off. The impact of a heavy round shot could be so severe that those around the victim might be severely injured by fast-flying ball and/or bone

▲ *Swiss grenadiers in French service fight in a loose skirmishing order. (PD/CC)*

▼ *Constant exposure to gunsmoke would produce thirst, headaches and painful eyes. (Tim Gainey / Alamy)*

INTO BATTLE

In this excerpt, Jean Michel Chevalier, a *sous-lieutenant* in the Imperial Guard, remembers something of the psychological impact of combat:

> It is difficult to say what I felt seeing my comrades, horses and men knocked head over heels. The number of the wounded emerging from the battle, mutilated, dishevelled, carried on stretchers, their faces pale, their bodies covered with dust and blood, the shouts of the dying, the frenzy of fighting men, the collective image of it all troubled my senses in a way that is difficult to define. When I found myself exposed to the enemy artillery batteries, vomiting terror and death into our ranks, I was struck by trembling, but was it fright or dread?...I felt ready to faint ... But we hurled ourselves at the enemy, and then I no longer felt fear. The blood of a Frenchman was coursing through my veins.[6]

6   Forrest 2002: 113

fragments. And throughout this experience, the infantryman would have to operate his musket and follow orders for manoeuvre. The mouth-drying effects of gunpowder and its related smoke would quickly lead to a maddening thirst, and on hot days the physical heat in the buttoned-up uniforms must have been overwhelming. On freezing days, conversely, infantrymen would shiver nearly round the clock.

The humble French infantryman, therefore, was a creature both pitiable and inspiring. With legendary endurance and genuine courage in battle, it was such ragged men who propelled Napoleon to his imperial heights.

3

NAPOLEON'S CAVALRY

The cavalry was the most dashing branch of the
French Army, lauded in fiction and propaganda alike
for their bravura character and audacious actions.
In reality, the cavalry faced the same appalling
dangers as their infantry comrades at ground level,
plus contended with the additional requirement
of managing an often panicked horse through the
maelstrom of combat.

RESTORING THE CAVALRY

Cavalry have always been recruited from the upper-class branches of armed forces, and this was certainly true of the French cavalry under the Bourbons. It therefore suffered proportionately worse under the effects of the Revolution, with huge numbers of trained and talented officers emigrating.

The haemorrhage of personnel was compound by other effects, such as financial and political mismanagement, a lack of training investment by the new regime, and an epizootic epidemic that killed a large number of suitable mounts. By early 1793, it had become evident to even the most republican of politicians and commanders that the deficiencies in cavalry were causing serious setbacks on the battlefield. To counteract this situation, the Convention decreed a levy of 30,000 cavalrymen on 16 April 1793, and began intensive national efforts to requisition suitable horses. The strength and the quality of the cavalry began to improve, but it was under Napoleon that it surged to prominence.

TACTICAL ROLES

Napoleon's original branch of service – the artillery – couldn't have been further away from the style, tactics and equipment of the cavalry, but as an ardent student of military history he fully appreciated the importance of a powerful cavalry force, of a mixed type. He once famously commented that, 'Cavalry is useful before, during and after the battle.'

In the passage below Napoleon summarises or implies some of the key tactical roles of the cavalry: pursuit of an enemy in rout; defence against enemy cavalry; offensive support of infantry and artillery; screening friendly deployment; conducting reconnaissance. Other aspects he could have added (and of which he would have been fully aware) would be breaking enemy infantry lines; making mobile attacks against artillery batteries; cutting the enemy lines of communication; making advance skirmishing assaults on the enemy as he formed up for battle; and mobile and armed foraging expeditions – additions which are far from

▲ *The French cavalry commander Louis Lepic leads his men at the battle of Eylau, 7–8 February 1807. (PD/CC)*

exhaustive. Cavalry was a flexible arm, and Napoleon rightly invested heavily in its expansion and training, especially prior to the campaigns of 1805 and 1812.

NAPOLEON'S REFLECTIONS ON THE CAVALRY

At Jena, the French infantry had won victory with only light cavalry; this victory was inconclusive. But the cavalry reserves arrived and then the Prussians could not rally. Demoralised, they were crushed on all sides and pursued with a sword in their backs. Of 200,000 men, not one crossed back over the Oder. Without cavalry, battles are inconclusive.

[…] General Lloyd asks what use a great deal of cavalry is. For my part, I ask how it is possible to wage anything other than a defensive war, protecting oneself with entrenchments and natural obstacles, when one is not virtually on an equal footing with the enemy cavalry.

Lose a battle, and your army is doomed. Cavalry requires daring, skill, and, above all, not being dominated by the spirit of preservation and avarice. What can be done with great superiority in cavalry, well armed with dragoons' rifles, and with plentiful well-harnessed light artillery, is incalculable. Of the three arms – cavalry, infantry and artillery – none is to be disdained. All are equally important. An army that is superior in cavalry will always have the advantage of covering its moves well, of being informed of its enemy's movements, and of only committing itself to the extent it wishes. Its defeats will be of little moment and its efforts will be decisive.[1]

1 Colson 2015: 215

HEAVY CAVALRY

Napoleon's cavalry were separated into heavy and light categories. Dragoons' unique tactical nature and equipment meant that they sat somewhere in between the two. Here, however, the dragoons are included under the 'heavy' banner, as they were classed at the time.

CUIRASSIERS

At the top of the cavalry tree were the cuirassiers. These were the ultimate heavy cavalry – armour-clad men atop the most herculean of horses. The cuirassier name derived from the cuirass iron breast- and back-plates that encased the cavalryman's torso. This armour, which was highly polished and shone spectacularly en masse, was complemented by an ornate iron helmet, resplendent with a brass comb and horsehair mane. In hand-to-hand combat with swords, the cuirass did have definite value – most sword blows were incapable of penetrating the metal. It provided almost no protection, however, from cannon fire, the great leveller of battlefield class distinctions, but musket balls, particularly at the limits of their range, might be deflected. It should also be remembered that the horses remained critically vulnerable and should the cuirassier be dismounted in muddy terrain, he would struggle to find his feet under the weight of around 9lb (4kg) of body armour. He would find also himself at a distinct combat disadvantage when surrounded by nimble and vengeful infantrymen. The cuirass could also be suffocatingly hot, hence, on some occasions, the cuirassier might abandon his armour in favour of mobility and breathability.

But there is no doubt that the cuirassiers had the power and violence to alter the course of a battle. Napoleon himself said that 'Cuirassiers are more useful than any other cavalry.' They were applied in huge massed charges, driving forward in strength to smash into infantry lines or do battle with enemy cavalry. They were armed with straight-bladed swords – their main weapon – plus carbines and pistols.

The cuirassier label actually came later on in the Revolutionary Wars, as in 1791 the 25 regiments of heavy cavalry in service were simply known as *cavalerie*. The individual regiment was comprised of three squadrons, each of two companies; the total regimental strength being 28 officers, 411 men and 420 horses. The cuirassier name was applied directly to regiments formed from c. 1800, after which the cuirassier arm grew in strength and prestige. At their height of strength, there were 15 regular cuirassier regiments plus a number of provisional regiments, although regiments 13–15 were relatively short-lived, and were removed under the Bourbon Restoration in 1814. As well as the growth in regimental numbers, the interior size of the cuirassier regiments also swelled, so that by the spring of 1807 a regiment had five squadrons totalling more than 1,000 men. Like all the cavalry units of the Napoleonic age, however, the tables of organisation and equipment were volatile, and changed often through decree and through circumstances.

DRAGOONS

The dragoons are an interesting category within the body of Napoleonic cavalry, as they might fight both mounted as medium/heavy cavalry or dismounted as heavy infantry. This reflected the dragoons' origins in the 17th and 18th centuries (Germany is arguably the founder of dragoons),

▼ *The adjustable brass straps on a cavalry cuirass, set on a leather backing. (Shutterstock)*

▼ *Details of a cuirassier helmet, decorated with horsehair. (Shutterstock)*

CAVALRY OF THE GUARD

The Imperial Guard had its own internal body of cavalry regiments, which took the double prestige of both Guard and cavalry status. What is notable about the Guard cavalry is the ethnic diversity of the regiments, and the tactical spectrum formed by the units, from heavy cavalry used for mass battlefield charge to light horse for reconnaissance and mounted skirmishing. The Guard cavalry were as follows:

▼ *An officer of the* Chasseurs à Cheval de la Garde Impériale, *one of the most prestigious of Napoleon's cavalry formations. (PD/CC)*

Grenadiers à Cheval (Horse Grenadiers): The most prestigious formation of the Guard cavalry, this regiment took the nicknames 'The Big Heels' and 'The Gods'. By 1812 it had reached a strength of six squadrons.

Chasseurs à Cheval (Horse Chasseurs): Nicknamed 'The Invincibles' or, by contrast, 'The Emperor's Spoiled Children', the *Chasseurs à Cheval* were raised in 1799 as a four-squadron formation, rising to six squadrons in 1812. In a reorganisation in 1813, the regiment was raised to eight squadrons, with three of the eight becoming the 'Young Guard Regiment'.

Mamelukes: Raised in 1799 from Syrian Janissaries, the Mamelukes were an exotic and ferocious unit, at squadron strength only.

Légion de Gendarmerie d'Elite (Legion of Elite Gendarmes): This four-squadron regiment was raised in 1801, but officially became part of the Imperial Guard in 1803. The police reference in their name alludes to their initial role of palace and headquarters security.

Compagnie de Gendarmes d'Ordonnance (Company of Gendarmes of the Ordinance): This six-company (five mounted, one foot) corps was formed in 1806, with the intention of acting as an elite bodyguard formation, but was disbanded in 1807.

Dragoons: Four squadrons of dragoons were raised in 1806, augmented to six squadrons by 1812. As with the *Chasseurs à Cheval*, two regiments were designated as part of the 'Young Guard Regiment' in 1813.

Lancers: Three ethnic lancer regiments were formed within the Imperial Guard between March 1807 and July 1812. Specifically these were: *1er Chevau-Léger-Lanciers* (Polish), *2e Chevau-Léger-Lanciers* (Dutch) and *3e Chevau-Léger-Lanciers* (Lithuanian).

Gardes d'Honneur (Guard of Honour): Four regiments of the Guard of Honour were raised in April 1813, although incorporation into the Imperial Guard came three months later. Recruited from wealthy volunteers, the regiments failed to cover themselves in glory, being known for poor horsemanship and little in the way of combat awareness.

Eclaireurs (Scouts): Three regiments of scouts were raised in 1813, each regiment having four companies and totalling 250 men. They were disbanded the following year.

when they were intended to deploy rapidly to the battle front on horseback, but would dismount to fight. In the Napoleonic age, the dragoons came to be the most numerous element of the French cavalry, totalling 30 regiments by 1804.

The number of mounted to dismounted companies in a dragoon regiment varied significantly during this period. In 1803, for example, the dragoon regiment consisted of four squadrons of four companies each, with two companies mounted and two dismounted. This establishment went through several shifts until, in 1807, the four companies of each squadron were all mounted, at least theoretically.

The dragoons occupy a curious tactical positioning within the cavalry. Armed with carbines and swords, the dragoons could slip between both light and heavy roles, one moment conducting reconnaissance or escort duties, the next riding in the line of battle alongside cuirassiers. This flexibility was particularly valued in the Peninsular War, where they formed the mainstay of the French cavalry in the theatre.

◄ *A French cuirassier at a re-enactment of the battle of Waterloo, 2011. (PD/CC)*

◣ *Dragoons of the 17th Regiment, the formation's ancestry stretching back to 1743. (PD/CC)*

▼ *An empress dragoon of the Imperial Guard, distinguished by the green uniform and the red helmet plume. (PD/CC)*

LIGHT CAVALRY

Light cavalry was the most dynamic element of Napoleon's field armour. Unencumbered by armour, and on steeds built for speed and manoeuvrability (if they could be sourced, of course), the light cavalry could be directed to make rapid tactical incursions at the most opportune of moments.

HUSSARS

The hussars were a unique brand of cavalry. Egotistical, flamboyant in appearance, absurdly brave in battle, violently independent – the hussars cut a dash on the battlefield and on civilian streets. In a drinking house, the hussars would be quickly identified by their heavy drinking, rowdiness and propensity to start fights. They also had a romantically caddish reputation: 'The hussars were loved by every wife and hated by every husband' was a common saying. It was also easy to spot a hussar, as the French hussars (like most others) retained the classic Hungarian-style dress of fur cap, fur-trimmed jacket and short pelisse, with ornate braidwork crossing the chest. Historian Philip Haythornthwaite adds a notable observation: 'It even spread to their style of hair-dress, fierce moustaches, "queues" (pigtails) and *cadenettes* (braids at the temples) being jealously-guarded regimental distinctions; recruits too young to grow moustaches painted them on in burnt cork until able to produce the real thing.'[1]

Their brash externals, however, should not mask the fact that hussars were superb soldiers. They were masters of sword-fighting, wielding their curved cutting sabres, and, unlike the dragoons – whose horse-handling was often somewhat clumsy – the hussars were excellent riders. Hussars were firmly in the light cavalry category, but their quality and aggression meant that they were used fluidly across tactical roles. They were just as comfortable delivering reconnaissance or skirmishing duties as they were charging en masse on a major battlefield to attack a vulnerable enemy flank.

At their height in 1813, the hussars numbered 13 regiments. The regiment usually consisted of four squadrons (six between 1793 and 1796), with the peak (1807) on-paper regimental strength being 43 officers, 1,000 men and 1,055 horses.

CHASSEURS À CHEVAL

The *chasseurs* were another cavalry body that saw a great expansion under the demands of war. At the beginning of the Revolutionary Wars in 1791, there were 12 regiments of *chasseurs à cheval*, rising to 22 by 1798 and 31 by 1811, making them the biggest portion of Napoleon's light cavalry. A full six regiments of *chasseurs* were actually of foreign origin, specifically the 16th (Belgian), 19th (Swiss, Italian), 26th (Italian), 27th (Belgian, German), 28th (Italian) and

▼ *The Bavarian Chevaulegers-Regiment in battle with the cavalry of the Imperial Guard, Battle of Hanau, 30th-31st October 1813. (FALKENSTEINFOTO / Alamy)*

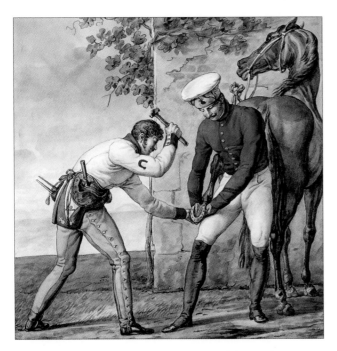

▲ *A caporal-fourrier of the 1st Regiment of Carabiniers re-shoes a horse in this painting by Carle Vernet, one of a series entitled* La Grande Armée de 1812. *(PD/CC)*

30th (German). Many of the *chasseur* regiments were also converted dragoon regiments.

The *chasseurs* largely performed the same roles as the hussars – skirmishing, reconnaissance, pursuit, breakthrough

▼ *A M. Maire, who served as a member of the 7th Hussars from 1809 to 1815. (PD/CC)*

attacks, mobile foraging – but did so on a smaller budget than the ostentatious hussars. (This was actually one of the reasons why the *chasseurs* were more numerous than the hussars.) They should not be regarded as second-class cavalry, however, although doubtless many hussars looked down upon them. Indeed, the battle honours that accrued to many *chasseur* regiments were truly distinguished. The *1er Regiment de Chasseurs à Cheval*, for example, had been raised back in 1651 and was rarely out of action between 1792 and 1815. Battles and campaigns in which the regiment fought include the Rhine (1799–1800), Hohenlinden (1800), Austerlitz (1805), Auerstädt (1806), Eckmuhl (1809), Wagram (1809), Borodino (1812), Bautzen (1813) and Waterloo (1815), to name just the most famous events.

Although the list here illustrates how the *chasseurs* were able to contribute to the big battles, their light roles meant that they were ideally suited to the skirmishing and anti-guerrilla warfare of the Peninsular theatre, where many of the *chasseur* forces served. The *chasseurs* were also quite capable of dismounted fighting, which was another reason why they could make their presence felt in the complicated terrain of the Spanish and Portuguese interior. In terms of weaponry, the *chasseurs* went into battle with curved cutting sabres and carbines.

LANCERS AND CARABINIERS

The *chevau-légers lanciers* (light horse lancers) were a relative late-comer to Napoleon's body of cavalry. The tactical rationale of the lancer had rather fallen from military thinking

▼ *M. Loria, a member of the 24th Mounted Chasseur Regiment and a Chevalier of the Legion of Honour. (PD/CC)*

▲ *French lancers ride into action through chaos at the battle of Waterloo. (Historical Images Archive / Alamy*

in France by the beginning of the Revolutionary era, but it was restored to focus after Napoleon witnessed the solid results of allied Polish lancers during the first ten years of his rule. In 1807, Napoleon actually raised a guard regiment of Polish light horse, called the *Chevaulegere-lanciers de la Garde Imperiale* (Light Horse Lancers of the Imperial Guard).

▼ *Polish light horse lancers of the Imperial Guard during a re-enactment event. These Polish cavalry units were in regular action from 1808 until 1815. (Duncan Miles)*

Initially indisciplined and raucous in behaviour, the Polish guard lancers nevertheless proved to be the most impressive soldiers in battle, and subsequently served with distinction in Spain, Austria, the Netherlands, Russia, German, France and Belgium between 1808 and 1815.

In 1811, Napoleon formed nine regiments of French lancers, again drawing heavily on dragoon regiment personnel to form the bones of the new formations. Part of the reason behind the creation of the lancers was to establish a body of men that could take on the much-feared Cossacks in the impending Russian campaign of 1812, although many of the regiments went on to acquire battle honours for their contribution to the final struggles of 1815.

The defining weapon of the lancers was, naturally, the lance (see pages 78–9 for a more detailed description), but the salutary experience of fighting in Russia in 1812 led to something of the redistribution of weaponry, with the lance taking a reduced role. For example, in 1813 a full company of lancers – 125 men – would each be armed with a sabre, but only 57 of them would carry lances. Other weapons carried by the company included 109 pistols and 61 musketoons or carbines. Obviously these are the theoretical distributions; in reality the actual numbers might vary.

A study of Napoleon's cavalry must not omit mention of the two regiments of horse *carabiniers*, the *carabiniers à cheval*. These two regiments – 1st and 2nd – had actually been formed before the French Revolution, the former in 1693 and the latter in 1776, with the 1st providing the manpower to create the 2nd. During the Revolutionary and Napoleonic Wars, they served with frequency in major battles and campaigns, in the role of heavy cavalry. After a mauling at the hands of Austrian *uhlan* cavalry in 1809, it was decided

▲ *Lancers were dressed in a green coat with turnbacks and lapels of the regimental facing colour. (PD/CC)*

that the *carabiniers* should be given body armour in the same manner as the cuirassiers. In the 1813–14 campaigns, the *carabiniers* seem to have suffered from a depletion in numbers and a reduction in morale and fighting ability – most likely because of the crippling losses they took in Russia in 1812 – and were subject to several routs in the field.

▼ *Some of the equipment items of a French cuirassier, including the steel cuirass and the steel helmet with red plume and black mane. (Shutterstock)*

CAVALRY HORSES

▲ *A French army re-enactor takes his horse to a canter. Galloping would be reserved for the very final stages of an attack. (Alan Balding)*

The lot of a horse during the Napoleonic era was generally not a happy one. The losses of horses – both cavalry mounts and those used in logistics – in almost any campaign was dizzying. During the Russian campaign, an estimated (probably conservative) 175,000 horses died during the epic advance and dire retreat, but even the victorious campaigns depleted the ranks massively. Thus the acquisition of horses proved a perennial problem for Napoleon's cavalry. Strictly speaking, each type of cavalry required a horse of specific stature. The heavy cavalry naturally needed the most sizeable creatures to carry them, if not at a gallop, then at least at a brisk trot. The light cavalry required smaller horses, but ones capable of speed, manoeuvrability and dash. By 1812, the exact height specifications for cavalry horses were as follows:

Cuirassiers and *carabiniers*: 61–63in (155–160cm)
Dragoons and artillery: 60–63in (153–160cm)
Chasseurs and hussars: 59–60in (149–153cm)
Lancers: 57–59in (146–150cm)
Polish *uhlans*: 56–60in (142–153cm)

In reality, the chronic shortage of horses meant that these standards were not often met, and many horses ill-suited for cavalry life went into the field. France had some areas famed for their horsebreeding, particularly Normandy and Burgundy, but vast numbers of horses were also acquired from allied or conquered states. Germany, above all, was revered for its heavy horses suitable for cuirassiers, but horses also came from Poland, Hungary, southern Russia and even Turkey and Syria.

CAVALRY WEAPONS AND FIGHTING TECHNIQUES

Cavalry warfare was a uniquely demanding form of combat. Not only did the cavalryman have to manipulate and control his mount – no easy matter on a battlefield – but he also had to fight from horseback, performing complex physical moves. The way he fought was, to a large extent, dictated by the weapons he carried, each of which imposed a varied set of opportunities and limitations.

◀ *A sword issued to cuirassiers or dragoons, c. 1810. (INTERFOTO / Alamy)*

THRUSTING SWORDS

Throughout history, the development of swords and swordsmanship has been largely governed by a single question – which is superior in battle, a thrusting sword or a cutting sword? Thrusting swords are typically long, straight sided, sharpened on both sides, fairly rigid and feature a particularly sharp penetrating point, designed to pierce the enemy's body and run deep inside; their ideal target point is the torso, which offers the highest probability of piercing a major organ. Cutting, or slashing, swords, by contrast, are usually curved in profile, with only a single sharpened edge (or the outer side of the curve), tend to have more flexibility (to cope with the impact of the blade edge on the target) and are used to deliver an open, slicing cut on the opponent; here the ideal target points are the head, neck, shoulders, arms and upper thighs.

The debate within the French cavalry service was a heated and entrenched one. The advocates of the thrust argued that a deep penetrating wound carried with it a much higher incidence of mortality than cutting injuries, plus had some tactical advantages. One of the famous proponents of the thrust, French officer Antoine de Brack, who served with both the hussars and the lancers, stated: 'It is the points alone that kill; the others serve only to wound. Thrust! Thrust! as often as you can: you will overthrow all whom you touch, and demoralise those who escape your attack, and you will add to those advantages that of always being able to parry and never uncovered.'[2]

What evidence we can gather seems to support the proposition that thrusts were inherently more lethal, as a blade penetration to the torso would produce internal bleeding (almost impossible to control at the time, compared to external injuries) and direct damage to vital organs, resulting in death by blood volume shock or organ failure. The slashes from sabres and other cutting weapons were generally hideous, and they could certainly be fatal if they opened up a major blood vessel, or if the unfortunate enemy was beheaded at a stroke (the Mamelukes in French service proved especially adept at this grim feat). But testimony from the informative French surgeon Dominique Larrey indicates that despite initially appalling appearances, many cutting injuries could be successfully repaired, with the victim going on to make a functional recovery, albeit often with some socially shocking scarring or disfigurements. If the analysis extends to non-French sources, then the evidence further stacks up in favour of the thrust. Captain William Bragge, a British cavalry officer who served with the 3rd (King's Own) Dragoons during the Peninsular War, noted that following a clash at Bienvenida in April 1812: 'Scarcely one Frenchman died of his wounds although dreadfully chopped, whereas 12 English Dragoons were killed on the spot and others dangerously wounded by thrusts. If our men had used their swords so, three times the number of French would have been killed.'[3]

As a broad rule, the French heavy cavalry (much like heavy cavalry everywhere), tended to prefer the straight-sided thrusting sword. Their choice was related specifically to the manner of their attack; deployed in a direct charge against an enemy mass, the heavy cuirassier or dragoon would add the momentum of the horse behind the thrust of the sword. During the charge, the sword would generally be extended out, down the side of the horse, the point angled forward and down towards the enemy, the blade often held parallel to the ground

2   Quoted in Nosworthy 1995: 287
3   Quoted in Nosworthy 1995: 288

so that it would slip between the victim's ribs rather than stick between them. The key technique for the cavalryman to master was the withdrawal, pulling the sword quickly out and clear the second it had penetrated the enemy's body. Failure to do this cleanly would often result in either a lost sword or a sprained/broken wrist, or even a dismount. Although the straight sword was a thrusting weapon, the cavalryman might also follow up a successful thrust with a backhand slash to the enemy's head or neck, just to make sure.

CUTTING SWORDS

'Cutting swords' generally refer to the sabres used primarily by the light cavalry. Having laid out the terminal advantages of the thrusting sword above, it might seem open to question why anyone would use the curved sabre at all, apart from tradition. Yet the sabre offered advantages not possessed by the straighter blade. On the question of lethality, for example, while strike-for-strike sabre blows might not have produced as high a death toll, they inflicted an extremely high rate of terrible injuries, awful gaping wounds that, if they did not kill the victim, would certainly result in his withdrawal from battle and possible permanent retirement from the armed services.

A further advantage of the sabre was that it did not quite require the same keen eye to be effective in action. A decisive thrust strike required some focused accuracy, which was not always easy to attain in the swirl of mounted combat. The swordsman also had to 'recock' his arm to repeat the thrust, and it would be easier for an opponent to perceive the intended line of attack. The sabre, by contrast, could be wielded in all manner of ways – backhand, forehand, downward, diagonally, as well as across the body and even behind – and a well-trained swordsman could transition between these lines fluidly, without stopping, confusing the opponent and maximising the

THE *AN IX* CAVALRY SWORD

A classic example of a straight-sided sword for French heavy cavalry is the *An IX* sword, which was introduced in 1800–01 as an attempt to standardise the many patterns of heavy cavalry swords then in service. The basket-type hilt featured a large 'cage' of four brass bars that wrapped around the user's hand, to protect it from hostile sword blows and to aid retention of the weapon. The wooden handgrip featured a leather covering plus wire grips, giving the cavalryman a high degree of purchase on the weapon even if his hands were sweaty or covered in blood. The key feature was the long, straight blade. This measured 38½ in (98cm), with the length meaning that the cavalryman could engage all targets on the ground from the mounted position. To ensure that the long blade was not too heavy to wield, fullers ran down each side, which also served to make the blade more resilient to impacts.

opportunities for hits. It could also inflict damage across the full range of its sharpened edge, which reached up to a yard/ metre in length, hence even a glancing blow could open up an injury. For this reason, the sabre was often a more useful tool in a melee battle, when enemy cavalry or infantry were on all sides. In addition, although the straight sword and curved sabre obviously had preferred styles of fighting built into their design, the former was still capable of slashing as was the latter of thrusting – it was never exclusively a matter of either/or. When

▼ *A re-enactment of cavalry vs cavalry combat. Note how exposed the horses' heads are to blows. (Alan Balding)*

▲ *French cavalry and infantry receive a charge from
Brandenburg hussars at Leipzig. (Chronicle / Alamy)*

making a cutting stroke, the ideal was to strike the opponent on
a lower part of the blade and then draw the blade across in a
slicing motion; a straight-on impact blow would cause far less
damage.

Up to 1800, there was no universal light cavalry sword.
The hussars and the *chasseurs à cheval* each had their
own traditional patterns. The hussars opted for a classic
Hungarian-type curved sabre, with a wide, flat blade and a
basket hilt, while the *chasseurs à cheval* took a straighter and
narrower blade, leaning more towards the thrust, married to
a half-basket hilt. An attempt at standardisation between the
two types came in 1800, with the *An IX* light cavalry sabre.
The broad curved blade was retained, measuring 36in (92cm)
in length in an overall sword length of 42in (107.5cm). It
featured a three-bar basket hilt design that was to be highly
influential across all 19th-century sword design. Overall
weight was 2lb 10oz (1.2kg), enough weight to give the
sword a natural momentum behind the swing.

An improved version of the *An IX* – the *An XI* – was
produced from 1802. The main enhancements were a
sturdier scabbard (the former version proved vulnerable to
damage, causing the sword to stick) and a hand guard that
stretched all the way back to the pommel, to provide better
protection. It was a fine and respected sword, but although
it was taken up by the *chasseurs à cheval* and later the
lancers, the hussars tended to stick with their traditional
sabres, maintaining their reputation for anything that defied
convention.

FIREARMS

We have already analysed Napoleonic muskets and carbines
in some detail in the preceding chapter, but there are some
points of note regarding the relationship between the cavalry
and gunpowder weaponry. Flintlock weapons obviously
presented the cavalry with some practical handling issues,
particularly relating to carrying, aiming and reloading. Aiming
was probably
the least of the
concerns, as the
cavalry would
typically ride
up close to the
enemy ranks
and open fire at
close ranges into
a massed target
with musket,
carbine or
pistol. Generally

▶ *A French
hussar re-
enactor, wearing
the bearskin
colpack instead
of the regulation
shako. (Alan
Balding)*

▲ *French cavalry organise themselves into line of battle at Austerlitz, with artillery support behind. (PD/CC)*

speaking, the only accuracy required was to point the firearm in the general direction of the enemy, although mounted/dismounted troops such as dragoons would still pride themselves on the ability to handle muskets properly.

There were several patterns of cavalry carbine available to the cavalry, including the Pattern 1777 Cavalry carbine (1779), Pattern 1777 Carabinier carbine (1781), the Pattern 1786 Hussar carbine (1786) and the Model 1777/*An IX* Dragoon musket (1800). All had their individual traits, but the common denominator was shortened dimensions, principally a reduced barrel length. Despite this, cavalry firearms were still sizeably awkward pieces to handle on horseback. The Model 1777/*An IX* Dragoon musket, for example, had an overall length of 55in (1.4m) and weighed 8lb 11½oz (4kg). It was thus carried in a special holster by the side of the saddle, pre-loaded and ready to be drawn and fired at the right moment. Other shorter weapons would generally be carried on the back using the weapon's integral sling. Pistols, if possessed, would be placed in a holster either worn by the cavalryman or fitted to the saddle.

Although firearms were standard issue for cavalry, there is some evidence that the awkwardness of using them meant many men disregarded them. Contemporary illustrations of cavalry often show the men without firearms of any sort. Some inspections of cuirassier regiments found that only 20 per cent of the men had pistols with them, and many did not seem to possess basic musketry items, such as cartridge boxes (although cavalrymen often stored cartridges in their pockets).[4]

---

4   http://www.napolun.com/mirror/napoleonistyka.atspace.com/French_Cavalry.html

A CAVALRY SWORD ENGAGEMENT

Flemish *carabinier* Joseph Abbeel describes a sword action at the battle of Borodino (7 September 1812):

> After we had executed several charges on the cavalry of the enemy, I finally got wounded – at half past two in the afternoon – for the first time. In a charge on the dragoons of the Tsar, I moved myself a little bit to the side to make it easier for me to follow them. But one of them came to me and cut off the reins that I held in my hand. Without the leather of those bridles I would certainly have lost a thumb and a finger of my left hand. Immediately I took the watering rein [bridle strap used to bring the horse to a river and let it drink] in my bloody hand and I used my spurs. My attacker thought he could escape me, but he didn't get far because he didn't have a copper or iron jacket as we have, which could protect him against the thrust of my sword. After this was done, I returned to my regiment with my sword full of blood. When my lieutenant saw that I was wounded and that I could not use my reins anymore, he wanted to send me to the infirmary, but I told him that I was not seriously wounded and that I would soon be able to put my hands on another pair of reins.[5]

---

5   Gavaert 2016: 116–17

◄ *These French hussars of the 4th Regiment, moving forward in open order, are armed with short cavalry carbines, which were approximately 45in (114cm) long. (PD/CC)*

▶ *A French cavalryman's cloak, from c. 1812. (Nick-D, PD/CC)*

▼ *Lithuanian Tatars – Lithuania provided some 4,000 cavalry for French service in 1812. (PD/CC)*

LANCES

The lance became a key weapon of, naturally, regiments of lancers, but also of various other *chevau-léger* (light horse). Physically, the French lances moved away from the prodigious weapons of the Polish past, which could measure up to 14ft 9in (4.5m). Instead, the typical lance measured about 9ft (2.75m) long, with a shaft of hardwood terminating in a flattened, diamond-shaped blade head, which could deliver a deep penetrating wound. Extending out from the blade down the shaft were steel straps called langlets; these not only strengthened the shaft around the point most susceptible to impact, but also helped to prevent enemy soldiers chopping off the head with a sword strike. About halfway down the shaft, at the lance's centre of gravity, was a leather grip section, plus a leather loop that twisted around the hand and wrist to prevent the lance from being lost in action. There was also a steel cap at the other end of the lance, to protect the wood when the weapon was rested on the ground.

As with most other weapons of the era, the lance prompted lively debate over its merits and demerits. One of the clearest statements of the application of the lance came from Marshal Auguste de Marmont, who saw broad service in both the Revolutionary and Napoleonic Wars. After the conflict he presented his reflections in *The Spirit of Military Institutions or Essential Principles of War* (see box on the facing page).

Marmont's claim that the lance was an inferior weapon when faced by sabre-armed cavalry is initially surprising, as the greater stand-off distance of the lance – about 5ft (1.5m) greater than that of the sword – would appear to suggest

THE LANCE IN COMBAT

In the following passage, Marshal Auguste de Marmont considers the application of the lance in the context of both infantry and cavalry combat.

The lance is the weapon of the cavalry of the line, and principally destined to combat infantry. The sabre cannot take its place; what use will cavalry make of sabres if the infantry remains firm, and is not afraid? The horsemen cannot sabre the foot-soldier, because the bayonets keep the horse at too great a distance. On the other hand, if the horse, which remains the only offensive arm of the horseman, be killed, it falls and makes a breach, and this breach gives to those who are near it the means to penetrate. On the whole, the advantage of the struggle then is with the infantry. On the contrary, suppose the same line of cavalry, furnished with a range of pikes preceding the horses by four feet, and the chances of success will be entirely different.

But for light troops the sabre is better suited than the lance; in hand-to-hand conflicts a short weapon is managed with more facility, and is more advantageous, than a long one. All things being equal, it is certain that a hussar or a chasseur will beat a lancer; they have the time to parry and thrust again before the lancer, who, beset by them, will be obliged anew to resume the defensive. [...]

To resume. I am, then, authorized in saying that the lance should be the principal weapon of the cavalry of the line, and the sabre only an auxiliary one; and that the armament of light troops should consist in sabres and fire-arms. Undoubtedly, routine and contrary prejudices will yet, for a long time, combat these principles, whose truth seems to me, however, to be perfectly demonstrated.[6]

6 Marmont 1862: 78

that the lancers could inflict attrition on enemy cavalry before they even came into range. This was indeed true, but not decisively so. Experience, particularly when fighting against Cossack troops in the East, showed that if a formation of lancers could be broken up, and the sabre-armed light cavalry moved in to a close-quarters fight, then the lancers struggled to bring the points of their lengthy weapons to bear on the proximate enemy. Partly for this reason, a good number of men in a lancer regiment would go into action purely with sword and carbine.

Yet as Marmont explains, the lance really came into its own in the context of cavalry vs. infantry combat. The lance outreached the bayonets of the infantry by some considerable margin, meaning that even infantry who had adopted the classic square defence were still vulnerable to the lancers. Marmont proves his point by referring to an incident in the battle of Dresden on 17 August 1813. Despite the fact that heavy rain had rendered most muskets inoperable, Austrian infantry still managed to repulse multiple attacks delivered by French cuirassiers, with the infantry fending off the mounted assaults purely through a bayonet defence in squares. Marmont notes that the block was eventually overcome by preceding another cuirassier assault with an attack by some 50 lancers, who managed to hack open the Austrian squares, leading to their total destruction.

The lance was a powerful addition to the French cavalry, but, like all weapon systems, it had its tactical place and time. The diversity of the heavy and light cavalry types meant that a judicious corps or division commander had a range of mounted options at his disposal.

▶ A M. Verlinde, a surviving member of Napoleon's 2nd Lancers in 1815. He is wearing the Saint Helene medal, issued on 12 August 1857 to all veterans of the wars of the French Revolution and the Napoleonic era. (PD/CC)

BATTLEFIELD EFFECT

The cavalry was an 'arm of decision', a body of men who by virtue of their horses could surge around the battlefield at ten times the speed of a running man. When drawn up on the battlefield, they were often positioned just behind or in between the infantry formations, ready to conduct a fast exploitation when the moment presented itself.

RIDING INTO BATTLE

More about the detailed tactics of the cavalry is considered in Chapter 6. Here, however, we will reflect upon the general experience of cavalry in combat. To do so, we must never overlook the behavioural and physical characteristics of the horses upon which they rode. The collection of mounts on which the men went into battle were not a uniform mass of animals, but rather an assortment of beasts exhibiting highly variable levels of experience and temperament.

A big issue during campaigns, with their typically high losses amongst cavalry horses, was that new mounts might not have benefited from the appropriate length of training – it could take up to two years to train a military horse that was somewhat conditioned to the thunder and chaos of battle.

But even if a horse were fully trained, the contact with battle itself could undo the discipline and obedience of even a seasoned and veteran mount. Having once experienced the agonising sting of a non-fatal musket ball or bayonet thrust, or been startled by the sheer horror and noise of battle, many horses could develop the equestrian equivalent of PTSD. Such traumatised animals, plus horses unaccustomed to battle in the first place, could result in unpredictable formations on the move, and a scattering effect once the cavalry came to blows with the enemy. In melee actions, the cavalryman might actually expend more of his energy

▼ *French cavalry surge past Napoleon at the battle of Friedland on 14 June 1807. (PD/CC)*

controlling and directing his horse than actually wielding his weapons in anger.

Many factors dictated whether a cavalry force might take the field in action. Much depended upon the moral courage on both sides. Although cavalry were certainly a genuine battlefield influencer, a substantial part of their effect was derived from psychological impact, particularly when unleashed against infantry. One British officer remembered an encounter with French heavy cavalry: 'A considerable number of French cuirassiers made their appearance, on the rising ground just in our front, took the artillery we had placed there, and came at a gallop down upon us. Their appearance, as an enemy, was certainly enough to inspire a feeling of dread – none of them under six feet; defended by steel helmets and breastplates, made pigeon-breasted to throw off the balls. Their appearance was of such a formidable nature that I thought we could not have the slightest change with them.' Although the British officer's reaction to the cavalry charge was both understandable and common, if the infantry held their nerve and took up a strong defensive position – ideally a square – then they had a decent chance of surviving the enemy charge. Neither horses nor riders had any incentive literally to smash into a bristling wall of bayonets, so the tempo of the charge would be replaced by a jostling action around the edges of the infantry formation. In fact, one British officer who fought at Waterloo actually found that his men grew to almost welcome the rush of enemy cavalry, as he discovered that after the initial thunderous charge 'no actual dash was made upon us'. Furthermore, the British troops also learned that once the French cavalry took to the field, the French artillery was compelled to stop firing, giving the infantry a break from the endless hails of shot and canister.

Yet while stoic and well-trained infantry might indeed cope with the enemy charge, there is no doubt that the appearance of the mounted troops was a uniquely dangerous moment for the opposing ranks. Proof of just how devastating well-executed cavalry attacks could be can be illustrated by looking at one element of the battle of Albuera during the Peninsular War.

CASE STUDY: THE BATTLE OF ALBUERA

By 16 May 1811, the French-held Spanish town of Badajoz had been under siege, for just over three weeks, by a combined Anglo-Portuguese force, commanded by Sir William Beresford. Napoleon, wishing to break the British grip in the Peninsula, sent a French army of about 24,000 troops, led by Marshal Soult, to relieve Badajoz, buoyed by what would be inaccurate reports of the British strength and condition. In fact, the British forces had been bolstered by the arrival of a Spanish army under General Joaquín Blake, taking the complete Allied disposition up some 35,000 troops. Forewarned of the French advance, the Allied forces moved out and took up positions along a ridge around the village of Albuera, through which the French were expected to move.

Battle was joined around Albuera on 16 May, with the French taking the early initiative. Soult threw a feint against

▲ *A M. Dreuse of the 2nd Light Horse Lancers of the Guard, in full dress uniform. (PD/CC)*

the Allied centre, but then launched his main attack against the Allied right flank, hitting the Spanish forces hard. Beresford now spotted the threat, and pushed forward the 2nd Division, headed by Lieutenant-Colonel John Colborne's 1st Brigade, which was engaged in a blistering musketry and artillery duel with the French. Steadily, the 1st Brigade began to push the French forces back. Unwittingly, they were opening up their right flank to counterattack, and the commander of the French cavalry – General Marie Victor Latour-Maubourg – timed the moment perfectly to launch a strike by the 1st Vistulan Lancers and the 2nd Hussars. Utilising the advantage of a drenching rain and hail storm, the French cavalry smashed into the British lines before most of Colborne's troops had the opportunity to form themselves into a square, the standard defence against cavalry attack. The result was an astonishing massacre. The Polish troops in particular, known for their ferocity and mercilessness, ran their lances through dozens upon dozens of panicked British troops, the length of the lances far exceeding the reach of the infantry muskets and bayonets. Three of the British battalions – the 1/3 Foot, 2/48th and 2/66th – were virtually destroyed, with losses varying between 60 and 85 per cent. Only the fourth battalion, the 2/31st, was able to form itself into a square and survive the clash, albeit with heavy losses.

The battle of Albuera ultimately worked out indecisively for both sides, but the destruction of Colborne's brigade is a horrifically perfect illustration of how cavalry could be used on the battlefield, and how the French cavalry could channel lethality to a decisive point.

4

FRENCH ARTILLERY

Napoleon was an artilleryman through and through.
He one famously remarked that 'Great battles are
won with artillery.' As this chapter will demonstrate,
such a statement is rather stretching the point.
But there is little doubt that artillery could alter the
outcome of an engagement, if integrated properly into
wider offensive and defensive tactics.

ARTILLERY REFORMS

The importance of artillery in the French Army had been recognised well before the Revolution of 1789. A landmark year was 1776, in which the French officer and engineer Jean-Baptiste Vaquette de Gribeauval became France's Inspector-General of Artillery, and promptly set about reforming every aspect of artillery production, tactical distribution and organisation.

Moving beyond the previous 1732 artillery system, developed by Lieutenant-General Jean Florent de Vallière, Gribeauval's biggest change was to rationalise the wide variety of field artillery pieces in use down to three principal types: 4pdr, 8pdr and 12pdr guns, plus a 6in (152mm) howitzer. (The 'pounder' measurement refers to the weight of round shot.) To make these pieces more mobile on the battlefield, he reduced their weight by shortening the barrels and making improvements to the carriages. To keep the performance of the guns with shorter barrels, however, Gribeauval switched from casting barrels around a clay cylinder core – which tended to produce subtle calibre variations between each gun – to casting solid barrels, then drilling out the bore with an extremely precise cutting machine. This way, not only was each bore of each gun exactly the same diameter, but round shot manufactured with equal precision fitted more precisely into all guns, resulting in less gas leakage around the shot and therefore greater velocity and accuracy.

▼ *This French cannon at a re-enactment camp is fitted with a muzzle tampion to protect the bore from rust when not in action. (DEA / C. BALOSSINI / Getty)*

THE GRIBEAUVAL SYSTEM

What Gribeauval was striving for was an early example of uniform mass production, which he applied to all parts of the gun, carriage and limber. For example, wheels and many other parts of the gun carriage were standardised and made interchangeable, which meant that it became relatively easy for a gun crew to obtain and change parts that were broken under field use. At the same time, the iron – rather than wooden – axletrees on gun carriages made them physically more durable and less likely to break anyway. Another innovation was the introduction of screw-type mechanisms for adjusting gun elevation, meaning fire control became more precise. When a field gun was on the move, it was now pulled by draught horses arranged in double files rather than single files, which meant that the pulling capacity of the horse team was increased, while the length of artillery columns decreased.

Yet beyond the material changes, Gribeauval also took a look at the distribution of weaponry among the French Army. Most significantly, he raised the gross number of barrels available to the frontline battalions. The following table illustrates the differences of artillery guns, horses and caissons (wagons carrying ammunition and supplies)

▲ *The 12pdr was the heaviest practical field gun on the Napoleonic battlefield. (PD/CC)*

▲ *The rear end of a Gribeauval 8pdr cannon, manufactured in the year of the Revolution. (PD/CC)*

▼ *A maréchal des logis of the Imperial Guard horse artillery. (Photo 12 / Alamy)*

available to 100 battalions of army troops in the field, comparing the Vallière and Gribeauval systems:[1]

	Vallière system	Gribeauval
Artillery pieces	150	200
Horses	1,720	2,840
Caissons	230	440

Buried within the top line of these figures is also the fact that the bulk of the increase in gun types was focused on the longer-range and harder-hitting 8pdr and 12pdr guns – from 60 to 160.

The Gribeauval system was enormously influential, not only in France but further afield – Austria, Great Britain, Prussia and Russia all took notice and were influenced to some degree by the innovations. The next major innovation in the French artillery system would come in 1803, when Napoleon modified it in favour of the new *An XI* (Year XI) system, with further major changes in 1809. But there was no doubt that Napoleon and the French forces saw the practical fruits of Gribeauval's system on campaign.

EGALITARIAN SERVICE

Allied to a sound system of artillery, Napoleon also leant upon the fact that of all the services in the French armed forces, the artillery was the one least affected by the Revolution. The Revolution and emergent republicanism turned an unfriendly radical gaze upon many French officers who were of noble or landed birth, or who remained loyal to a monarchical model of government. Feeling unwelcome in their own land, huge numbers emigrated, especially from the cavalry and navy, but the infantry was also badly affected. The artillery, by contrast, was a more technical and therefore egalitarian service, more attractive to the reflective engineer than the dashing young noble. Thus its manpower and expertise stayed relatively constant during the Revolutionary Wars.

1 McNab 2009: 66

ARTILLERY ORGANISATION

Army artillery was subdivided into three fundamental categories during the Napoleonic era – field artillery, horse artillery and siege artillery. In the open battlefield engagements that characterised most Napoleonic actions, it was field and horse artillery that provided the heavy firepower, and achieving the right dispositions and deployments of both were critical in the attempt to achieve fire superiority.

FIELD/FOOT ARTILLERY

Field artillery refers to artillery intended for battlefield use on campaign, hence it had to be practically mobile, i.e. it could be drawn into action by a reasonable number of horses and, once deployed, it could be adjusted for aiming by the physical efforts of the gun crew. More properly, this type of artillery was known as *artillerie à pied* (foot artillery); although the guns themselves were pulled by horses, the men of the *artillerie à pied* marched alongside them, in contrast to the fully mounted troops of the horse artillery.

The organisational story of French artillery during the Revolutionary and Napoleonic wars is one of progressive expansion. In 1791, there were a total of seven *régiments d'artillerie à pied*, each consisting of two battalions plus a headquarters. Each battalion was in turn divided into ten companies or batteries, with each battery having eight guns at its disposal, typically six cannon and two howitzers. Each battery was subdivided into four two-gun sections, with the paired guns positioned together on the battlefield and working in cooperation. Total manpower for these elements was 1,297, plus an extra 400 men during wartime campaigns. Each regiment also had its own depot and artillery school

and its own support units, specifically pontooners, who built bridges and laid road surfaces to keep guns moving, and *ouvriers* (artisans), who were responsible for the construction and repair of gun carriages, limbers, wagons and other vehicles. There were also *armuriers* (armourers) who maintained and repaired the guns themselves.

The expansion of the artillery gathered apace during the Revolutionary Wars. In 1795, the artillery complement was raised to eight regiments of foot artillery and eight of horse. By 1801, the number of companies per battalion had also risen to 20, meaning that each regiment now had a basic manpower of 1,888. The size of the artillery general staff had also grown to more than 230 people, presiding over a force that now numbered 28,000 men in total. During Napoleon's years as first consul and then emperor, the number of companies per regiment rose to a peak of 28 (by 1813), and a ninth foot artillery regiment was added in 1810. Overall strength of the artillery arm (including horse and siege artillery) was a mighty 80,273 by the end of March 1814.

A single artillery company was a significant logistical entity in its own right. Each 12pdr gun, for example, had its own limber plus two ammunition caissons (wagons). The battery would be further supported by between six and eight other vehicles. All the vehicles required the horses to draw them – a single 12pdr gun needed a team of six horses – plus all the associated forage and equestrian equipment. Supplies were also required for the manpower of the company.

▼ *(Left to right) Foot artillery troopers ram home shot and powder; a soldier of the artillery train (left) talks with a gunner; a mounted officer of the Guard Artillery train and a field artillerist. All artworks by Bellange. (PD/CC)*

HORSE ARTILLERY

The *artillerie à cheval* (horse artillery) was the most mobile element of the Napoleonic artillery. The combination of specially lightened guns and ammunition, plus the fact that all horse artillerymen were mounted, gave horse artillery the ability to manoeuvre around the battlefield with speed and a sense of opportunity, hence they were also known as *artillerie légère* (light artillery). Horse artillery was still in its infancy by the onset of the Revolutionary Wars, having been pioneered by the Russians then, in response, by the Prussians during the Seven Years' War (1756–63). The idea of horse artillery in the French forces was presented to the National Assembly in September 1791, by a group of young officers, and the first units – nine companies – were raised the following May.

Having quickly proved their utility in the early actions of the War of the First Coalition, the horse artillery units rose quickly in numbers, going from nine companies to 40 in the period 1792–93. Across the whole period of the Revolutionary and Napoleonic Wars, the number of regiments of horse artillery wavered, through various cost and tactical reasons. In 1794 there were nine regiments, each of six companies, with two companies composing a squadron. The number of horse artillery regiments was reduced to six in 1801. A seventh regiment was temporarily created in 1810, prior to its absorption into the 1st and 4th regiments,[2] and from 1799 the Imperial Guard also contributed a horse artillery element, rising to three squadrons of two companies each in 1806, and falling to two squadrons in 1808 to reflect the creation of the Guard foot artillery. A full complement of three squadrons was restored in March 1813, and in 1815 four companies of Guard horse artillery were in action.[3]

At company/battery level, horse artillery units usually had six or eight guns in total, generally 8pdrs plus a light field howitzer; the most typical combination was four 8pdrs and two howitzers. All the men within the horse artillery were

2   Haythornwaite 2017: 50
3   Haythornwaite 2017: 50

▲ *Re-enactors fire a reproduction 4lb field cannon. The gunner has just touched the vent hole with the slowmatch on the linstock. (Duncan Miles)*

trained cavalrymen, a fact visually reflected in the dash of their hussar-style uniforms and tactically reflected in their rapid and sometimes foolhardy deployments to the most intense sectors of the battlefront. In 1807, a full regiment of horse artillery, consisting of a staff plus six companies (two companies formed a single squadron), had a manpower of 15 staff and strength of about 114 men each company, adding up to total regimental strength of around 700 men.

▼ *A French 12pdr fitted to its two-wheel limber. Note also the water bucket suspended underneath of the carriage for transit. (DEA / C. BALOSSINI / Getty)*

In 1815, the textbook complement of a foot artillery battery was as follows:

- 2 captains
- 2 lieutenants
- 1 sergeant-major
- 4 sergeants
- 4 corporals
- 1 furrier
- 2 drummers
- 20 gunners of 1st Class
- 48 gunners of 2nd Class
- 4 metal workers
- 4 *ouvriers* (artisans)
- 13 woodworkers and artificiers

SIEGE ARTILLERY

Siege artillery was a special category within the Napoleonic artillery. Because sieges were actually a relatively infrequent occurrence in the Revolutionary and Napoleonic Wars, and were something of an unwelcome intrusion in Napoleon's adherence to mobile warfare, there were no actual dedicated siege-artillery units, but rather field artillery units were repurposed for sieges with the appropriate ordnance. The chief weapons suited to siege actions, i.e. those with the power to smash down battlefield, fortress or city wall defences, were the 16pdr and 24pdr guns – although 12pdr and 8pdr guns were also used – plus an 8in (20cm) siege howitzer and four different varieties of mortar, the largest of these reaching

15in (381mm) in calibre. In design, the guns were largely those of the Vallière system, albeit on carriages modified under the Gribeauval system. The chief advantage of the big 16pdr and 24pdr guns was their range and force. A 16pdr, set at a 45-degree elevation, could reach out to strike targets at 4,702yds (4,300m), while a 24pdr at the same elevation had an effective range of an impressive 5,249yds (4,800m).[4] Furthermore, each strike of the heavy round shot would take out huge chunks of even the sturdiest fortress *enceinte*.

Yet on the flip side, these guns were impractically heavy for anything other than the most static work. The 16pdr had a barrel weight of 4,400lb (2,000kg), while a 24pdr was 6,028lb (2,740kg). Compare this against a standard 12pdr field gun – 3,410lb (1,550kg) – and it is evident how much of an

▼ *French heavy siege guns bombard the Dutch town of Naarden in April 1814. (Shutterstock)*

4   McNab 2009: 82

additional physical burden the heavy siege guns imposed on an army. Howitzers and mortars were the other side of siege artillery.

Howitzers fired explosive 'common shell' (see 'Ammunition' on pages 96–7), either lobbing shells directly over the fortress walls into the interior, or firing short to create ricochets that clipped the top or skirted just over outer defences. Mortars were stubby and basic weapons; the short and immensely thick barrel was often set at a fixed, high angle on a heavy wooden 'bed' that sat directly on the open ground, with the earth acting as a recoil absorber. The ranges of the mortars varied significantly depending on the calibre of the gun, weight of the shell, and the quantity of powder used – because the mortars generally had fixed barrels, varying the powder charge was the chief way of controlling the overall trajectory and range – but typical combat ranges would be about 500–1,500yds (460–1,370m). Mortars also had the useful function of firing early illumination shells, created by filling an iron frame with a bright-burning incendiary mixture.

Siege warfare was a hefty business logistically and temporally. For example, during the siege of Almeida from 25 July to 27 August 1810, during the Peninsular War, Marshal Michel Ney's siege force included more than 100 guns operated by 3,124 men, 3,222 horses and 1,100 oxen. (Sixteen oxen, arranged in eight pairs, could be required to pull a single 24pdr gun in difficult conditions.) Still, on this occasion the French effort seems to have paid off. A single shell hit the castle's central powder magazine on 26 August, resulting in a wall-splitting explosion that killed or wounded 900 men. The defenders were forced to capitulate the following day.

▲ *A Gribeauval 12in mortar could throw a 150lb (68kg) shot, albeit over short ranges. (PD/CC)*

▼ *The Gribeauval 6pdr cannon, intended (unsuccessfully) to replace the 4pdr and 8pdr. (PD/CC)*

GUNS AND EQUIPMENT

The French field army was principally armed with 4pdr, 8pdr and 12pdr guns, and the 6in (152mm) howitzer, of the Gribeauval system. This system provided a versatile range, with the 4pdr gun providing very mobile but light fire, while the heavier 8pdr and 12pdr weapons were better suited to hitting protected positions. The howitzer was ideal for hitting targets behind terrain features.

▲ *Gribeauval 12pdr cannon displayed outside the Musée de l'armée, Paris. (PD/CC)*

▼ *A French cannon in Les Invalides. Note the studded wheels to improve battlefield traction. (PD/CC)*

AN XI SYSTEM

As indicated above, the Gribeauval system received a significant overhaul in 1803, with the introduction of the *An XI* (Year XI) system. Inspired by suggested changes proposed by the inspector-general of artillery at that time, Auguste Marmont, Napoleon commissioned the re-evaluation of the types of cannon used on the battlefield. The *An XI* system featured a range of changes across the spectrum of gun types, but the most significant was the theoretical replacement of the 4pdr and 8pdr field guns with a 6pdr. Based partly on experience of using captured 6pdr weapons, it was reasoned that the 6pdr offered much of the mobility of the 4pdr, but gave a firepower nearly equivalent to that of the 8pdr. By replacing the two types with a single gun, it was also felt that the artillery commanders in the field would have fewer decisions to make about which type of gun to deploy.

Partly for production reasons, partly for tactical ones, the transition to the 6pdr was never fully implemented in the French artillery forces. Many gunners were not emphatically convinced that the 6pdr covered the tactical or firepower options provided by the 4pdr and 8pdr. The 6pdr carriage also had some structural weaknesses, which rendered it prone to breakage on the battlefield. Furthermore, by 1808, captured Prussian and Austrian stocks of 6pdrs had reached such an extent that production of further French models was cancelled. In no sense did the introduction of the *An XI* system entirely replace the 4pdrs and 8pdrs.

THE ARTILLERY TRAIN

Napoleon made important innovations in the system of artillery transportation and supply. Prior to 1800, the wagons of the *train d'artillerie* (artillery train) – the supply system that accompanied the artillery on campaign – were manned by civilian drivers. Understandably enough, such men were not always the most steadfast when thrust into the heat of battle. On 3 January 1800, under direct command of Napoleon himself, the *train d'artillerie* was fully militarised through 28 articles that covered every aspect of its administration, organisation, manpower and operational functions, even its uniform codes. Crucially, the civilian drivers were replaced with professional soldiers, who were carefully selected for character and competence. The initial structure of the new artillery train was eight battalions of five companies each, although after the fighting of 1800 the number of companies per battalion was increased to six, with each battalion commanded by a captain and each company by a lieutenant. The individual companies of the artillery train were parcelled out to support companies of artillery in the field, with the 1st company – regarded as an elite – often being sent to the horse artillery, rather than the foot artillery.

The relentless pressures of war during the imperial period meant that by 1810 there were no fewer than 14 artillery train battalions. This strength was further increased by the wartime exigency of 'doubling', in which a cadre of men from a battalion was peeled away and used to form a new temporary battalion, designed with the suffix *bis*.[5] This ability of the artillery train to scale up to meet conflict demands, plus its general professionalisation, were crucial steps forward in maximising artillery's capacity to influence a major military campaign.

---

5   See Kiley 2004: 108

TYPICAL COMPOSITION OF AN ARTILLERY COMPANY (1815)

- 1 sergeant-major
- 4 sergeants
- 1 furrier
- 4 corporal
- 2 trumpeters
- 24 drivers of 1st Class
- 60 drivers of 2nd Class
- 2 blacksmiths
- 2 harness makers.

▲ *Napoleon directs cannon against royalists in Paris, 1795.* (Hulton-Deutsch Collection/CORBIS/Corbis via Getty Images)

► *The bulk of the artillery ammunition was transported in large caissons like the one shown here. The large caisson for the 12pdr guns could carry 48 rounds of ball and 20 rounds of canister. (PD/CC)*

THE CANNON IN BATTLE

In the age of Napoleon, the weapons that fell under the category 'artillery' were largely similar in their overall fabrication. In-service artillery pieces were invariably smoothbore – i.e. without any internal rifling – and muzzle-loaded, with each shot requiring a team of men to repeat the loading and firing process in all its steps (see opposite page). A basic understanding of the parts of a cannon is necessary to grasp the innovations and standardisations of artillery in the French Army.

THE BARREL

The main part of a cannon was, of course, its barrel. French guns were typically made of bronze (often, confusingly, called 'brass'). The use of bronze was in sharp contrast to, say, Britain's artillery, which made prolific use of iron-barrelled guns. Bronze cannon were more expensive to make, both in terms of the raw materials and the production process, but the trade-off was that bronze actually handled the stresses of firing better than iron, being less liable to sudden and unpredictable bursting. (If a bronze barrel did burst, it would usually just split, rendering the gun useless but without lethal effect on the gun crew; iron guns, by contrast, could literally blow apart on failure.) However, although bronze would withstand the internal propellant detonations better than iron, it was actually more susceptible to problems from overheating during prolonged and rapid firing. The barrel would soften to the point that it suffered 'barrel droop' towards the muzzle end. In fact, one way of destroying a bronze cannon, to prevent it falling into enemy hands, was to

▲ *Re-enactors emplace a battery of 12pdrs ready for firing. Note the sponge buckets between the wheels, holding water for barrel swabbing. (Shutterstock)*

▼ *An ornate bronze basilisk handle on a late 18th century French cannon.(Alamy)*

FIRING A CANNON

The essential procedure of firing any sort of cannon followed similar lines, with some variations depending on the size of the gun (which affected the size of the gun team), the carriage format and the type of ammunition. Two men typically stood at the muzzle end: a 'loader' and a 'spongeman'. It was the loader's responsibility to place the powder, wad and projectile into the muzzle. The spongeman drove these down to a snug fit in the chamber using a rammer head on a long pole. At the other end of this pole would be a thick sponge. This was used if the cannon had already been fired. The sponge was dipped in a bucket of water, and the bore was swabbed out prior to loading to ensure that any burning embers left over from the previous shot were extinguished; leaving these smouldering in the barrel could result in a premature explosion when the new propellant charge was inserted.

As the loading procedure was enacted, another member of the gun crew – the 'ventsman' – would place his thumb, encased in a leather pouch, over the vent hole at the rear of the cannon. This measure prevented air flowing through the vent hole under pressure as the gun was loaded; such an air flow could fan into life any embers still left smoking after the bore had been swabbed. Once the cannon bore

had been loaded, the ventsman then inserted a long wire 'pricker' down through the vent hole to puncture the propellant sack, exposing the contents to ignition; the action had the added benefit of clearing out the venthole of powder residue. (This measure was omitted if the gun team had loaded the cannon with loose powder.)

In the vent hole, the ventsman then inserted a 'firing tube' – a reed, metal or paper tube filled with gunpowder and incendiary accelerants. The top of the tube was covered with a flannel, but this flannel was soaked in saltpetre and spirits of wine, so that it could be directly ignited by the gunner rather than being removed before firing. To fire the cannon, another member of the gun crew would apply a 'portfire' – a wooden handle holding a length of hot-burning quick-match – to the firing tube, resulting in the tube's gunpowder igniting, sending a flame down the length of the vent into the chamber, where it would ignite the main gunpowder charge and fire the gun.

▼ *The gunners at the front of the cannon swab out the barrel and then ram home powder and shot. The gunner in the centre of the rear group holds a linstock.*
(DE ROCKER / Alamy)

▲ *The initial and emblem of Napoleon, carved into the upper face of a Gribeauval cannon. (PD/CC)*

◄ *A top view of a Gribeauval 12pdr. This perspective shows to good effect the double-bracket type of trail, the cannon framed by two parallel wooden planks, known as cheeks or brackets. (PD/CC)*

dismount it from its carriage, prop it up between two barrels and light a fire under the middle. The heat of the fire would cause the tin in the bronze to melt and strip out, causing the gun to sag in the middle. But bronze counterbalanced this problem with a practical benefit. Although bronze is actually 20 per cent heavier than iron, less bronze was required to make a barrel of the requisite strength, and therefore bronze guns tended to be lighter than iron guns. This weight saving meant that bronze guns were particularly good for mobile field artillery pieces.

The bore of the French bronze cannon was drilled out after casting, and polished smooth. The actual length of the barrel was a matter of much consideration. In strict ballistic terms, the longer the barrel the greater the muzzle velocity, range and penetration achieved, as the lengthier barrel provides a greater distance over which the propellant gases are imparting acceleration to the projectile. For practical reasons, however, cannon barrels were never at theoretically optimal length because making them so was impractical for weight, cost, engineering and mobility considerations. Thus it was that cannon barrels were in length usually 12–24 times

the diameter of the bore, with the particularly short lengths being reserved for howitzers, which relied upon a slow, high trajectory rather than the fast, flat trajectory of field guns.

THE BODY

Externally, the outer profile of the cannon swelled out into a 'lip' at the muzzle end; the flared metal helped to prevent the muzzle splitting during fire. The body of the cannon then became progressively thicker from front to back, with sequences of reinforcing rings and a very thick breech end to withstand the detonation of the primary charge in the chamber. On the sides of the cannon were the trunnion projections, which formed the mounting interface with the carriage. At the very rear of the cannon was the *cascabel*, a knob-like projection used to adjust the gun's elevation; the cannon's screw-type elevating mechanism might run up inside the *cascabel* projection. Atop the breech was the vent hole, which ran down into the chamber at an oblique angle of about 45 degrees; the angle meant that when the gun fired, the spent firing tube was blown out safely to the rear, away from the gun crew.

CARRIAGES, LIMBERS AND TRANSPORTATION

The functionality of an individual piece of French field artillery rested on four main physical elements, apart from the gun itself: the carriage, the limber, the caissons and the horses. Carriage design had some variations between each individual piece, but the standardisation of Gribeauval brought a measure of harmony. French field gun carriages were mostly two-wheeled double-bracket systems, with the barrel mounted on supports that connected two parallel wooden planks, or brackets, either side of the gun. The French used a split-trail design. The support trail opened out into a broad V-shape to give the gun its requisite stability, although all artillery pieces would shift substantially under recoil with every shot. The split trail was closed up for movement, and hooked up to a two-wheeled limber, which provided the interface between the carriage and the horses pulling the whole configuration.

Prior to Gribeauval, the limber also carried a substantial amount of ammunition, but this system was reformed in preference of a limber mounting just a small box of 'ready supply' ammunition, which could be brought into action immediately; the main supply of ammunition came from the caissons behind. Dotted around the carriage and limber were most of the pieces of kit and equipment necessary for operating the cannon. Hooked up to the limber would be the horses, arranged in pairs. Typically it took four horses to pull a 4pdr gun and six to pull an 8pdr or 12pdr. Trailing behind the moving gun and limber came the caissons, basically four-wheeled wagons about 11ft (3.4m) long. The caisson's wooden body was divided into sections for prepared ammunition and for various pieces of gun kit, such as tool boxes and digging tools. The number of caissons allocated to each gun varied according to calibre, from two for a 4pdr up to five for a 12pdr.

▼ *The 4pdr Gribeauval cannon (seen here on a US battle site) was the lightest French field artillery piece. It had a maximum range of 1,200 yards (1,100m), but an effective range more in the region of 700 yards (640m). (PD/CC)*

AMMUNITION

As we shall see, exploding shells (or 'common shell') were available on the Napoleonic battlefields. Yet, ultimately, most of the damage delivered by artillery of this era was done via the brute kinetic energy of inert iron, delivered in various sizes and configurations.

ROUND SHOT

The most common ammunition type used on cannon was round shot – the cannonball. These solid balls of iron relied purely on kinetic energy to deliver their effects, offering the highest muzzle velocities of the ammunition types, in the region of 500–2,000ft/sec (152–610m/sec), depending on the calibre, length of barrel, powder charge etc. The title of the gun – e.g. 4pdr or 12pdr – indicated the weight of the round shot fired. Note that the horse artillery, given the priority they placed on light logistics and mobility, often used round shot that had been hollowed out as a weight-reducing technique.

The propellant charge for round shot was usually calculated in the region of a third of the weight of the shot. Up to around 1800, loose powder was still seen in battlefield use. A gunner used a wooden *laterne* literally to spoon the propellant into the barrel before it was rammed down. But

▼ *Round shot and grapeshot balls found on the Waterloo battlefield. (Arterra Picture Library / Alamy)*

this method was becoming archaic, and instead artillerymen used what was in effect a unitary cartridge to speed up the process. In this system the propellant came pre-measured in a flannel or serge bag, with the bag boiled in glue to add a degree of waterproofing. A wooden sabot, cut precisely to the diameter of the bore, was fitted into the neck of the bag and tied in place tightly; the sabot in effect acted as a replacement for the wadding traditionally used to provide a buffer and means of gas obturation between the powder and ball. The front end of the sabot cupped the round shot, and these two components were also secured in place by iron straps, which crossed over the top of the shot and were nailed to the body of the sabot. Thus propellant, wadding and shot were combined in a single unit, which dramatically improved rates of fire over separately loaded components. For a well-trained and combat-experienced field-gun crew, a rate of fire of 4rpm was possible, although with heavier calibres and the natural friction of combat the practical rate of fire might be more in the region of a single round per minute.

▲ *Canister shot had a fearsome anti-personnel effect on exposed infantry ranks. The thin tin canister ripped apart on leaving the muzzle. (PD/CC)*

▶ *From left to right: canister shot, round shot and fused exploding shot, each type of projectile attached to its powder charge bag. (PD/CC)*

CANISTER

Round shot essentially was a point-target munition, designed to throw all its kinetic energy at a single point or along a single track in space. Canister, by contrast, was an area weapon, rather like a huge artillery shotgun. The intention behind canister was as a short-range anti-personnel/anti-horse weapon, with the numerous balls inflicting multiple casualties over a wide area. A canister round consisted of a thin, fully enclosed cylinder of tin, which fitted – albeit not too tightly – into the bore of the cannon. A wooden sabot sat at the bottom of the cylinder, and inside the cylinder were multiple small iron balls, packed in sawdust to achieve consistent spacing and to cushion the shot against the impact of firing. Canister shell was loaded in the same way as round shot, but on firing, the canister ruptured as it left the muzzle, leaving a hail of shot flying onwards in a widening conical pattern. The size of the shot varied, from 'light canister' which weighed around 1oz (28g), to 'heavy canister' (sometimes referred to as 'grapeshot') which was about 3oz (85g); heavy canister was usually placed in a canvas bag rather than a tin cylinder, but worked in the same way.

A French 4pdr canister round would usually contain 63 individual pieces of light canister or 28 pieces of heavy canister; the figures for a 12pdr, by contrast, were 112 or 46 pieces.[6] *In extremis* a gun crew might improvise a form of canister by loading the barrel with musket balls, nails, horseshoes – anything that could be blasted out for anti-personnel effects. Although this sounds ferocious, it was almost always avoided unless the cannon was abandoned or the crew was threatened with death, as after a few such shots the bore of the gun could be irreparably damaged.

COMMON SHELL

Common shell was the third main type of battlefield ammunition, and was generally fired from howitzers and mortars. The shell had an explosive fill, with the walls of the shell about one-sixth of the shell's overall diameter.[7]

Terence Wise, in his recommended work *Artillery Equipments of the Napoleonic Wars*, here explains the fuze system:

> The fuze was either reed or drilled beech-wood containing strands of quick-match and a composition of saltpetre, sulphur and mealed powder. The top was capped with parchment and the outside marked with cuts spaced at half seconds of burning time apart. The gunner had to cut the fuze to the required setting and insert it into the shell before firing, and to speed up this process it was not uncommon for some fuzes to be cut lengths probably required in the forthcoming battle and inserted into shells which were then stacked in their respective batches.[8]

The goal for the fuse-setter in all this activity was ideally to have the shell explode as air burst or just as it struck the ground, as the dispersal of the shell-case fragments was its main wounding mechanism. The fuse would be lit automatically by the firing of the main propellant charge, and then would burn down as it flew through the air. The shell itself was weighted on the opposite face to the fuse, so that if the shell struck earth it would do so without crushing and extinguishing the fuse.

6   Wise 1979: 17

7   Ibid.
8   Ibid.

ACCURACY AND EFFECTS ON TARGET

The lack of rifling, stabilised shells and precision sighting mechanisms meant that all cannon suffered from an inherent inaccuracy that became more pronounced over range. By way of example, the great German military reformer Gerhard von Scharnhorst (1755–1813) conducted artillery accuracy trials during the Napoleonic Wars, producing results that reflect the sobering limits of contemporary artillery pieces.

SCHARNHORST'S ARTILLERY TRIALS

A 6pdr and a 12pdr cannon were fired repeatedly over a 30-minute duration at a target of boards some 200ft (61m) wide by 6ft (1.8m) high. The type of fire, either 'direct' at the target or 'ricochet' – skipping the round shot off the ground into the target – was tested at three different ranges to judge which was most effective. Putting aside, for now, the results for the ricochet shots, at 1,800yds (1,646m) the 12pdr fired 180 direct shots at the target, and achieved precisely no hits. At 1,350yds (1,234m), the 6pdr rattled off 240 shots and once again made no hits of the target, while the 12pdr fired 180 and opened the scores with 16 strikes. At 900–1,000yds (823–914m), the 6pdr and the 12pdr repeated the same rates of fire as previously, but this time both scored 20–30 hits on the target.[9]

These figures bring out a couple of points. First, regardless of the type of cannon, it was largely the case that the maximum *effective* range of field guns at this time was about 1,000yds (900m). Yet at this range, the hit rates were still profoundly low. Now consider that this was the gun crew firing against a *static* target, not a moving and offensively dynamic enemy in potentially convoluted terrain, and we can straight away see that cannons firing round shot were not quite the absolute killer that we hold popularly.

9 Nosworthy 1995: 390

An important consideration here, however, is that these figures represent direct fire at the target. Gun laying in the late 18th and early 19th century was a rudimentary affair. Elevation would be altered via a screw adjustment device that connected with the base of the breech. Elevation corrections would typically be quite minor, in the region of 1–3 degrees. There was no traverse mechanism; this was performed by the gun crew literally dragging the gun around using handspikes hooked into the trail. This was a slow business, made more challenging on the battlefield on account of the huge plumes of obscuring white-grey smoke that filled the air after every shot.

RICOCHET FIRE

A more effective alternative to direct fire was 'ricochet' fire. Here the gun crew fired the round shot so that it struck the ground in front of the target, and then skipped on at low level, scything through multiple ranks of enemy soldiers or horses between every bounce. Ricochet firing offered the potential to maximise casualties, as a heavy ball was quite capable of maintaining its dire momentum through multiple individuals without much trouble. Even at the end of its run, as it trundled along the ground, it could still carry enough kinetic force to smash a foot off.

Ricochet fire also had a significant psychological effect, in that the enemy would literally see the impacts on the

◀ *Using a linstock, a British gunner touches his slow match against the vent hole of the cannon, causing the cannon the fire. Note the sheer volume of smoke produced by just a single shot. (Christine Pet-Sepers)*

▶ *Napoleon, being an artillerist himself, was a great supporter of the artillery arm. This artwork shows Napoleon (right) personally handling cannon at the siege of Toulon. (Granger Historical Picture Archive / Alamy)*

ground in front of them, and then attempt to predict and dodge the bounce trajectory. This natural reflex often caused ranks of infantry to break up, hesitate or halt, as each soldier focused on the act of survival rather than maintenance of order. Furthermore, ricochet could deliver a considerably higher ratio of hits on an area target. In the artillery trials by Scharnhorst outlined opposite, exactly the same tests were performed using ricochet. Whereas at 1,800yds (1,646m) the 12pdr scored no direct-fire hits, with ricochet it managed 36, and at 1,350yds (1,234m) ricochet fire struck the target 45 times, as opposed to 16 times for direct fire. For the 6pdr at 1,350yds, zero hits with direct fire contrasted with 60 hits with ricochet. At the 900–1,000yds (820–900m) range, for both 6pdr and 12pdr guns the ricochet fire delivered about three times the hits of direct fire. These trials were, of course, conducted under ideal conditions. In reality, and on a churned battlefield with irregularities, slopes and objects in the landscape, it was much harder to deliver. Just one or two degrees of elevation misjudgement could result in the round shot either burying itself in the ground at first strike or flying over the heads of the enemy. Ricochet fire also relied on hard, dry ground – soft and muddy terrain could simply soak up or drag on the ball, quickly depleting its velocity.

CANISTER EFFECTS

Canister, of course, optimised its effect by spreading its impact over a wide cone. Used optimally, canister could certainly have a truly harrowing effect on the enemy, dropping entire ranks of infantry in a gale of iron balls. Yet the potency of canister can be overestimated. The issue with canister was that, much like a shotgun, the area effects decreased significantly with range, as the projectile spread kept widening at the same time as the kinetic energy of each ball decreased. So, for example, at 100yds (90m) from the muzzle, the shot cone was around 32ft (9.7m) in diameter; at 200yds (183m) it was roughly 65ft (19.5m); and at 300yds (275m) it was 96ft

(29m).[10] Remember that this spread was on the vertical as well as the horizontal axis, meaning a large percentage of the balls simply buried themselves into the ground or flew into the sky.

Although investigations conducted by French artillerist Louis de Tousard concluded that canister shot produced twice as many casualties as round shot at ranges under 800yds (730m), the figures are still not quite as terrible as one might expect. For example, in test firings against a target the same size and shape as the front face of an infantry line, a 4pdr at 600yds (550m) with large canister achieved only 8–9 hits, the same as an 8pdr at 700yds (640m) and a 12pdr at 800yds (730m). The best results were naturally achieved with small canister at short range – the 12pdr managed 40 hits with small canister at 400yds (365m), the same as the 8pdr at 500yds (457m); the 4pdr delivered 21 hits at 400yds (365m). These latter figures are starting to sound impressive, and do hint at the power of canister. Yet there is no denying that a high percentage of the balls hit nothing of value at all.

COMMON SHELL EFFECTS

Common shell also delivered a combination of physical and psychological effects. If the gunner judged the moment of detonation correctly, multiple enemy troops might be killed or injured in a single detonation, suffering primarily from fragmentation injuries. It also had a startling effect on horses; if it didn't physically harm them, it would generally cause them to rear and bolt, breaking the integrity of their ranks. Similarly, if a common shell landed on the ground amidst infantry, and sat there with its fuse sputtering down, self-preservation would cause the men around the bomb to break ranks and attempt to give the shell some distance. Yet common shell was rarely fired in the volumes or with the necessary accuracy to have a major influence over the outcome of an engagement.

---

10 Wise 1979: 17

ARTILLERY TACTICS

From a tactical viewpoint, artillery's basic purpose was to inflict attrition upon enemy personnel and/ or destroy protected positions. Long-range guns were especially useful for engaging enemy troops as they were attempting to form up into ranks, or as they were advancing forward to the battlefield, causing demoralising casualties and command indecision even before the main clash of forces.

Cannon might also engage in counter-battery fire with enemy cannon, and there was a lively debate about whether this was a better use of the guns than directing them against the infantry. Because of the difficulties of striking distant point targets, however, it was generally decided that firing on infantry and cavalry was preferable to counter-battery use, although there are good combat examples of effective counter-battery fire, particularly if an attacking artillery battery could manoeuvre unseen to a firing point that provided surprise enfilade along the enemy guns.

RANGE

The best targets were, naturally, close-packed ranks of men and horses across a wide frontage, with the size of the target compensating for the general inaccuracy of the weapons. At longer ranges of 500–1,000yds (450–900m),

▼ *Intelligent artillery officers would use landscape features – such as the tree in the background – to provide protective cover and a degree of visual concealment. (Shutterstock)*

round shot delivered some of the most harrowing fire, as it had the most extended reach. As the enemy advanced forwards, the gunners would usually, ammunition supply depending, work progressively down through heavy and then light canister, concentrating their fire on formations that were most threatening, or attempting to open up weak points for exploitation by friendly cavalry or infantry. (Canister was typically only about 15 per cent of the total ammunition carried, which was another reason why it was reserved for close-range use.) It was important for the artillery officer to have a firm sense of the moment he would begin firing; nervous infantry officers often harassed battery commanders to open fire at excessive range on the enemy, in the hope that the artillery could critically weaken the opponents prior to the clash of infantry ranks. A sage artilleryman might have to resist such pressures, as fire at ranges beyond 1,000yds (900m) could be of limited effect, and could serve only to deplete ammunition unnecessarily. Of course, he might have to comply simply due to the pressures of seniority of command.

▲ *The muzzle of a French cannon captured at Borodino shows sobering evidence of the impact of round shot. (Boris Zamanskiy / Alamy)*

TEMPO

The tempo of fire was also a matter of discipline and judgement. Generally speaking, artillery batteries avoided unified salvo fire, as after each rippling blast there would follow an extended silence of at least 15 seconds from the guns, as they undertook reloading, and the enemy would use such time wisely to advance. Thus the French method,

▼ *At the battle of Ligny (16 June 1815), Napoleon and his staff survey the battlefield from the hill while an artillery team struggles to free a gun from the mud. (PD/CC)*

as advocated by Gassendi and others, was for the guns to fire individually. This naturally produced a staggered battery fire with few opportunistic gaps. A slightly more disciplined approach was for two guns (artillery pieces usually operated in pairs) to alternate their fire in a regular rhythm.

LOCATION

For the artillery to be at their most effective, intelligent siting was important. Although the guns were perfectly capable of firing over the heads of infantry in front, this positioning was not popular – the noise of low-flying shot was disquieting, and accidents would happen. Thus gun batteries acting in infantry support were located on the flanks and at intervals in the infantry formations, with the regimental or battalion commander attempting to ensure that while his guns were placed at multiple points, they were not so widely scattered that their fire was dispersed.

One interesting Napoleonic development in artillery placement was to set the guns actually ahead of the main body of infantry they were intended to support. Historian Brent Nosworthy here explains:

> The traditional practice had been to place artillery on either side of an infantry body to produce a cross fire; however, this ceased to be practicable if the infantry was sufficiently wide. Unlike earlier times where the artillery was placed relatively near the line, by Napoleonic times batteries were often pushed to more advanced positions, between 60 to 150 metres in front of their supporting formations. These more advanced positions minimised or eliminated casualties among the supporting formations should a caisson explode. This trend was also, however, partly in response to the ever-increasing presence of friendly skirmishers. Artillery along an infantry line would have to be silenced as soon as the friendly skirmishers were sent out or risk firing on their own troops. Artillery in an advanced position had a much easier time supporting the skirmishers by continuing to fire on their common enemy. Of course, the artillery could not be placed too far in front. It always had to be close enough that the infantry could come to their timely support if attacked.[11]

Nosworthy illustrates the point that artillery, to be most effective, had to work in a cooperative venture with the infantry, and that the rise of the light infantry affected artillery tactics as much as infantry tactics. His final cautionary sentence, however, reminds us of the fact that artillery in isolation was particularly vulnerable, in much the same way as modern armour requires infantry protection for its survivability. Artillery positions would usually be supported by an infantry screen to guard the guns against cavalry or infantry attacks, particularly from the flanks.

Adding to the calculations outlined here by Nosworthy were the issues of terrain. Artillery commanders had to avoid

11 Nosworthy 1995: 386–87

DESCRIPTION OF AN ARTILLERYMAN, FROM ST HILAIRE'S *HISTORY OF THE IMPERIAL GUARD*, BK IX (1809)

▲ *French Guard foot artillery operate a 12pdr cannon, the man on the left swabbing out the barrel. (PD/CC)*

The foot artillerist was a large and lanky fellow; he had the slightly arched back found in all men who devote themselves to operations of force. His character was as severe as his uniform; he spoke little, and his meditative air, although he was only a private, made one soon guess that he belonged to an erudite arm, to a corps special to Napoleon, more or less justified in his preferences, placed before all the others, without exception even those of his engineers. On seeing the artillerist of the Old Guard, one would have said that the smoke of the cannon had blackened his hair and his face. His step was a little heavy, and on this standpoint he was far from resembling his brother in arms, the horse artillerist. This one, under more than one report, was joined together with the types of the horse chasseurs of whom he wore the uniform, except in colour. He was alert in his movements, and seemed to be able to hold in place. Off duty he was not the same man anymore; as soon as he saw neither his horse, nor his pieces anymore, he seemed sad; he could not enjoy the leisure of the garrison; he needed labours and the noise of the camp life. He had this in common with the foot artillerist.[12]

12 https://www.napoleon-series.org/military/organization/frenchguard/
sthilaire/c_sthilaire9c.html – accessed 9 May 2018

▲ *French artillery on campaign in 1809. The majority of artillerists would move between battlefields on foot, just like regular infantry. (PD/CC)*

placing their guns so that they fired up or down particularly steep slopes, which made sighting far more difficult and affected the options for using ricochet fire. Elevated ground could be a positive placement, but only if it was not too high; very elevated platforms might result in impractical depression of the gun barrels, plus the ascent to the post often meant that subsequent options for manoeuvre might be limited. Placing the guns on a single prominent but restricted feature also raised the threat of being outmanoeuvred by enemy infantry. The commander had to 'read' the terrain in front of him, looking for (and ideally avoiding) shot-trapping or shot-deviating features in his field of fire, such as ditches, muddy patches, very thick vegetation, trees or sharply angled slopes. The ideal position for an artillery battery was on the summit of a gently sloping hill, positioned just on the reverse slope for additional protection and firing down onto enemy formations clearly presented in front.

LIMITS OF ARTILLERY

Although artillery had true battlefield muscle, we must avoid the impression that it was always dominant in the clash between cannon and infantry. In reality, when faced with a determined body of foot soldiers led by an experienced commander, the big guns were in a precarious position. Intelligent infantry commanders would use the terrain to provide cover or concealment on the approach to the guns. The battlefields would have been wreathed in thick gunpowder smoke, which in itself could be used to provide a degree of concealment for an offensive manoeuvre against artillery. Even if the artillery crew could just about see the enemy, the smoke could make judging distance, and therefore accurate sighting, difficult. Moreover, the infantry commander could make frequent adjustments to the regularity or speed of his advance. Resighting a cannon was a slow business, and good infantry officers knew this. By suddenly speeding up, slowing down, shifting to the left or the right, or even stopping momentarily, the infantry could make life hard for the gunners, and could reduce the levels of casualties suffered on the approach. As soon as the troops were in musket range, then the gun crews themselves could be subject to harrowing fire.

Beyond the infantry, cavalry were also a major threat to the guns. A man and mount together presented a very sizeable target, especially vulnerable to canister fire. But the speed of their advance and their ability to manoeuvre fast around flanks made them a respected foe for artillerists. Many cavalry attacks on artillery were indeed repulsed, and often with horrible casualties. The cavalry assaults that tended to do best were those where the cavalry commander had done proper prior reconnaissance, and had developed a strategy to confuse the guns as to their aiming point, generally by attacking from different points of the battlefield, or using skirmishing cavalry to disperse fire away from a sudden rush by the main force.

But artillerists would usually not give up their guns easily. If a gun had to be lost, the gunners would render it useless by some means – possibly by setting a fire under the barrel, but more typically by 'spiking' – driving a long purpose-designed spike down into the vent hole.

Whatever the risks and difficulties it faced, artillery was certainly at the heart of the French Army's battle-winning capability. It was deployed in huge numbers and with equally

▲ *French gunners at Hanau, 1813, resort to muskets and even ramrods to protect themselves against an enemy cavalry attack. (Chronicle / Alamy)*

huge effects. At Leipzig, for example, Napoleon had 600 guns facing 900 enemy cannon, a clash that saw some 150,000 rounds of ammunition fired over the three-day battle. Napoleon once remarked that 'With Artillery, War is made.' Given the scale of its application in his imperial wars, few could argue with that statement.

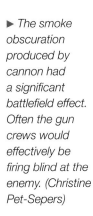

► *The smoke obscuration produced by cannon had a significant battlefield effect. Often the gun crews would effectively be firing blind at the enemy. (Christine Pet-Sepers)*

5

ON CAMPAIGN: LOGISTICS IN ACTION

Napoleon has left history with arguably two of the most famous quotations on the topic of logistics: 'The amateurs discuss tactics: the professionals discuss logistics', and, 'An army marches on its stomach.' Certainly, Napoleon appears acutely aware of the centrality of logistics in effective war-making, reflected in his memory of logistical details. He clearly understood that mundane planning and a well-organised system of logistics could make the critical difference between victory and defeat. Yet on occasions, his disdain of logistics in favour of manoeuvre could have disastrous consequences.

A LOGISTICAL PIONEER

In *Supplying War: Logistics from Wallenstein to Patton*, military historian Martin Van Creveld makes a striking claim: 'It was, in fact, his [Napoleon's] inversion of the relationship between sieges and battles – between the relative importance of the enemy's fortresses and his field army as objectives of strategy – that constituted Napoleon's most revolutionary contribution to the art of war.'[1]

The theory behind Van Creveld's statement is that prior to Napoleon, the focus of military campaigns was heavily skewed towards taking fortresses and cities through siege. The problem with this approach, from a logistical point of view, was that an effective siege required a troop ratio of 7:1 in favour of the besiegers, and thus a very large body of men needed supply in a static location. All supplies necessary to keep the siege alive had to be brought to a single location by long chains of transport, or extracted from the local area, which would quickly be depleted. Napoleon unchained his strategy from fortresses and allowed his armies the ability to access fresh supplies repeatedly while moving across a territory, through a process of living off the land. As we shall see, Napoleon's logistical understanding was far from infallible, yet Van Creveld is correct in implying that Napoleon pioneered a more flexible approach to logistics, keeping his men on the move and preventing them being dragged down

by limited supplies. On many occasions the improvisational nature of the field logistics was a matter of circumstances, not choice. As we shall see, furthermore, when it came to logistics the gap between intention and reality could be especially broad.

ATTENTION TO LOGISTICS

Historical appraisals of Napoleon's relationship to logistics are highly variable. A classic view is that Napoleon's strategic and tactical energy, his focus on securing speed and tempo in operations, made him disregard important logistical matters. There is certainly substance for such an argument, because at times Napoleon seemed wildly optimistic about what could be achieved with improvisational logistics. During his Egyptian campaign, for example, Napoleon was enthusiastic about continuing the advance of his parched, tired and hungry army beyond Egypt and Syria all the way to northern India, emulating the conquests of Alexander the Great through daily advances of 15 miles (24km), maintained for months on end. Such visions were, to a large degree, bullish and speculative grandstanding, but in Russia in 1812 the catastrophic consequences of ineffective long-duration logistics became shockingly clear.

---

1   Van Creveld 2004: 41

▼ *Napoleon retreats towards Soissons after the defeat at the battle of Laon (9–10 March 1814). (PD/CC)*

▲ *A supply wagon of the Imperial Guard. The burden of weight on the horses is evident here; many horses died under the unequal struggle to pull loads. (PD/CC)*

▼ *The French soldier was famed for his ability to cross great distances on foot at speeds often not expected by their opponents. (Lanmas / Alamy)*

Conversely, we cannot say to any degree that Napoleon was disdainful of logistics – far from it. His field orders prior to battles and campaigns often demonstrate an acute understanding of the minutiae of logistical matters, and his published statements clearly show a man who knew that poor logistics could evolve into military disaster. In Napoleon's first major command in Italy, he demonstrated a real level of care in supply matters, transforming a bedraggled and under-resourced army into a war-winning force. And even in the ill-fated Russian campaign, Napoleon's intense attention to logistics still ensured that his army had the means to advance all the way to Moscow, fighting a major action at Borodino along the way – such an advance would be difficult for any army, even today. Indeed, Van Creveld's analysis convincingly argues that Napoleon was in many ways a master of logistics, albeit one coping with the scale of his ambition in relation to the means of supply.

Regarding the Ulm campaign, Van Creveld notes that:

If some supplies nevertheless got through, if the army did not starve, nor the majority of its units disintegrate, this was due, not to any supposed neglect of logistical considerations but to a triumph of foresight, organisation and leadership. […] it is therefore no accident that, precisely during this period, we find him [Napoleon] dozens of miles behind his advanced spearheads and allowing his care for logistic organisation to seriously interfere with his conduct of operations.[3]

Van Creveld also explains that the Russian campaign had, in many ways, decent logistical foundations, albeit ones progressively undone by external factors, including French logistical indiscipline amongst some units and the actions of the enemy. So while Napoleon's logistics did occasionally fail, through myriad reasons, and the possibilities of 'living off the land' were at times overestimated, it cannot be said that Napoleon showed contempt for logistics – quite the opposite.

3   Van Creveld 2004: 72

ADMINISTRATIVE ORGANISATION

At the beginning of the Revolutionary Wars, the French military logistical system left much to be desired. One immediate point of clarification is that Napoleon did not introduce the system of organised foraging into French military thinking; the natural evolution of campaigns had made it a necessity for any army that was on the move, for centuries before.

▲ *Five senior French army staff, including a chief surgeon, pharmacist and doctor, c.1804. (PD/CC)*

▼ *Two French re-enactors at rest, one performing a clothing repair – on Sundays there would be a general regimental inspection. (M. Mathews)*

Under the monarchy, prior to the Revolution, responsibility for supply matters was allocated to a senior *Intendant d'Armée*, of which there were two in 1788 – plus about 150 supporting staff, made up mainly of chief commissaries and commissaries. A distinctive figure under the old regime was also the *Intendant Civil*, a provincial official who, in times of war, would serve to organise logistics in his province or region, if it were actually involved in the campaign fighting.

ADMINISTRATIVE WEAKNESSES

In September 1791, this system was replaced by the Assembly with an administration consisting of 23 commissaries and 134 war commissaries.[4] Yet the campaigns of 1792 and 1793 immediately showed up the limitations of this system, as troops fighting for France often did so with inadequate or incomplete uniforms, poor or, commonly, no footwear, and often empty stomachs. Root causes were poor financial management, the unexpected size of the armies and campaigns, and the struggle for a wholly civilian supply administration to get its head around military requirements.

Reforms of the system therefore followed. In July 1793, senior officials in Paris (specifically Lazare Carnot, Pierre Louis Prieur and Robert Lindet) enforced central responsibility for matters relating to supply and transport. The delivery administration was also amplified, with the appointment of some 300 commissaries of varying seniority, plus a commissary-in-chief taking his place amongst the headquarters of every army.

NAPOLEON'S REFORMS

Despite the reforms, logistics remained challenging throughout the era of the Revolutionary Wars, and Napoleon set about rationalising the system as he rose to power through the late 1790s and first years of the 1800s. A major first step came on 8 March 1802 with the establishment of the Ministry of War Administration, headed at first by Jean François Aimé Dejean, a former commander-in-chief of the Army of the North. From now on all Ministers of War Administration would be general-rank officers, although the supply network beneath them would remain in the hands of civilian contractors. Over the next two years, the system was refined in terms of increased numbers of inspectors and commissaries,

4 Rogers 1974: 92

▶ *A portrait of Jean François Aimé Dejean, a talented officer who had a formative effect on French military adminstration from 1802. (PD/CC)*

with more targeted responsibilities for overseeing various aspects of army supply and administration, both while on garrison duties and in the field.

A key role to emerge from this time was that of *Intendant-général* (Inspector-General) of the army, at first occupied by Claude Petiet but performed most memorably by Pierre-Antoine-Noël-Bruno Daru from 1809 until 1812. The Inspector-General was in charge of all matters pertaining to military transport and supply for armies in the field, but his responsibilities stretched even into matters concerning soldier health and pay. Daru in particular had enormous authority over the minutiae of campaign logistics, but he and Napoleon were also reliant upon the unilateral efforts of corps logistical staff. Each corps and division headquarters staff had its own head of logistics, who would attempt to enact the supply orders coming down from the Inspector-General or his immediate superior.

S. E. M.^le Comte de Jean premier Inspecteur Gal du Génie, Grand - Trésorier et Grand - Aigle de la Légion d'honneur.

▼ *Pierre-Antoine-Noël-Bruno Daru. Like Napoleon, Daru was a man of great learning as well as organisation, investing in literary and cultural activities even in the midst of a campaign. (PD/CC)*

ENGINEERS

The deployment, positioning and movement of logistics, and indeed of all Napoleon's armed forces, were assisted by the considerable efforts of French Army engineers. Engineer forces were roughly divided into three types of troops. *Mineurs* (miners) provided skilled excavation work alongside units of *sapeurs* (sappers); together these men had the brawn and understanding to do the earth-moving associated with field works, road construction and building artillery emplacements, plus they could be used in assault roles during siege operations. These men were skilled and highly trained, not mere labourers. For the most manual of tasks the engineer troops would co-opt the help of units of *pioniers* (pioneers) and regular infantry. The scale and professional identity of engineer units grew over time. In the early years of the Revolutionary Wars the miners were part of the Foot Artillery, but in 1793 they were separated out to help form a dedicated Engineer Corps, alongside new battalions of sappers. By 1812 the engineer troops had grown to eight battalions of sappers and two of miners. Each army corps would receive the support of its own engineer detachment. Napoleon, a technocratic thinker, also invested in expansion of the engineer officers, with some 150 graduates a year emerging from the Mézières School of Engineering. There was also a corps of *ingenieurs-géographes* (geographical engineers), responsible for land surveying and map production. Napoleon's promotion of what became the most professional military engineering force in Europe was another factor feeding in to his military success.

SUPPLY TRAIN

Another important element of logistical organisation was the French Army's supply train, the endless lines of wagons and horses snaking through the theatre, hauling the thousands of tons of provisions and equipment. Until 1807, military transportation was actually a civilian responsibility, with the wagons driven and manned by civilian operators.

IMPROVING THE SYSTEM

Finding wagons for use in campaigns was no easy matter; the vehicles were a mix of requisitions from civilian stocks and contracted production.

Prior to Napoleon's Ulm campaign in 1805, orders were given to secure 4,650 wagons from three sources: 150 brought in from Boulogne, 3,500 requisitioned from French departments on the Rhine, and 1,000 provided by the Compagnie Breidt, a private company with a profitable military supply contract. The failures of both the Compagnie Breidt and the system of requisitioning led Napoleon in 1807 to create a militarised network in the *Train des équipages* (supply train), in addition to the civilian one, to inject a little precision into a sometimes haphazard system. The initial establishment of the supply train comprised nine battalions, six companies each, with the headquarters at Evreux in Normandy. The inexhaustible demands of war, however, meant that the organisation grew substantially, rising to 13 battalions by 1810 and 20 battalions in 1812, dropping back to nine battalions again after the Russian campaign left thousands of French wagons back on the Russian steppe.

The supply train was used in a flexible manner; its resources were allocated according to need per infantry battalion or cavalry regiment, or in more centralised fashion to transport major volumes of rations or ammunition to a division or corps.[5] Typically the wagons accompanying a battalion would carry some two to four days of supplies for the troops, while the troops themselves would personally hold about two or three days of rations on themselves. Occasionally

▲ *French logistical movements through the Gran San Bernando Pass in 1800. (PD/CC)*

wagons would be used for troop transport, with 4–5 men occupying a two-wheeled carriage, and up to 12 in a four-wheeled carriage. One famous example of this procedure occurred in 1805, when soldiers of the Imperial Guard were moved from Paris to Strasbourg by the post system, in which the movement was kept constant by changing the horses at staging posts set 10 miles (16km) apart along the entire route of travel. In this way, they were able to travel 60 miles (97km) per day. But generally, troops marched alongside their vehicles, with the space inside the wagons usually assigned to the more important movement of supplies.

5   Haythornwaite 2017: 64

◄ *This depiction of the French retreat from Moscow in 1812 captures the cruel collapse of logistics. (PD/CC)*

WAGONS AND HORSES

A perennial problem for French logistics, however well organised theoretically, was that the numbers of wagons available generally fell below the number of wagons required. In the first instance, a very high proportion of the wagon traffic was dedicated to the transportation of ammunition and artillery-related kit, not to the movement of food and clothing.

During the campaigns of 1805, for example, a total of 2,500 of the 4,500 wagons were slated for artillery service. On campaign, furthermore, the losses of wagons to mechanical failure was extremely high. Even in fine weather, with dry roads, the long distances, the weight of supplies (about 1.5 tons per four-wheeled carriage) and the constant rumbling impact on wheels and axles caused frequent breakdowns. This situation was worsened if the supply train consisted of many requisitioned civilian vehicles, often built for more delicate service.

POOR ROADS

If the weather was severe and the roads heavily rutted, the problems were dramatically increased, especially in theatres with a low number of metalled road surfaces. Poor road conditions had a significant impact on Napoleon's operations during the winter months, particularly in Poland in 1807, Austria in 1809 and Poland/Russia in 1812. The narrow wheeled wagons, fully laden, could quite easily sink up to their axles in the mud and have to be hauled manually to freedom, only to sink again minutes later. Under these conditions, progress could be measured at rates of about one mile per hour, and the numbers of horses allocated to each wagon or gun might have to be increased to maintain any sort of

▲ A model of a 'flying ambulance' used on the Napoleonic battlefield. This type of mobile treatment centre was developed by Baron Dominique Jean Larrey. (PD/CC)

▼ The Route Napoléon tested men, horses and the Emperor in 1815. (Ikonya / Shutterstock)

▲ *Soldiers of the 8th Artillery Regiment, 5th Division Dufour, pulling an authentic copy of a 4pdr cannon (Matthias Rietschel / Stringer / Getty)*

forward momentum. The two-wheeled wagons had better manoeuvrability, but they could not pull even 50 per cent of the capacity of a four-wheeled wagon, hence increasing the proportion of two-wheeled wagons also increased the numbers of horses required, and the forage needed to feed them. This calculation had particular relevance during long-distance campaigns such as that in Russia in 1812, where the logistical demands meant that the bulk of the transport was of the four-wheeled variety, but such vehicles were more prone to breakdown and getting stuck than the two-wheel wagons.

There was also the issue of the numbers of roads available to the French forces. Under movement, an army took up a

▼ *The sturdy Mérens horses of southern France were popular in the French army, especially for pulling artillery. (Alamy)*

huge amount of physical space. A full corps of 30,000 troops on the march took up about 5 miles (8km) of single road length. This distance, which imposed a severe tactical time delay between the front and rear of the column, was often not viable when a formation was required to march straight into battle. The optimal solution was to use parallel roads for the movement, splitting the corps into converging battalions. Often such roads were not available, however, meaning that a large proportion of the marching formation might have to travel cross-country, with all the accompanying increase in wear-and-tear and delays.

THE LIFE OF A MILITARY HORSE

Another crucial factor in Napoleonic logistics was the availability and health of horses. The volume of creatures required for a major campaign was simply huge. The Russian campaign stands as the most extreme example: in total, the wagon train for that campaign rose to 26 battalions, with some 9,300 wagons of all varieties. In total, 250,000 horses

were gathered for this mammoth logistical feat. Although the Russian campaign is the apogee of Napoleonic logistics, even campaigns closer to home required thousands of animals.

The life of a military horse during the Napoleonic era was usually brutal and short. During any campaign, the losses amongst horses (if we include cavalry mounts) was in the region of 30–40 per cent. The depredation resulted from exposure to the elements, poor nutrition, injury, disease and combat losses. Horses, even supply horses, were perfectly legitimate targets for enemy action; if enemy troops managed to reach French supply units, putting a musket ball, bayonet or sword blade into a horse could render an entire wagon of supplies immovable.

However, the true killer of horses was simply being exposed to conditions far harsher than nature intended them to endure. Many of the horses were requisitioned civilian animals, of breeds and types unsuited to pulling heavy loads for hours on end. At times of intense campaigning, horses were also requisitioned when they were young, exposing them more easily to musculoskeletal injuries than more seasoned horses.

Forage was a further pressing issue, both for the creatures and logistically. Horses need to be fed, and on campaign every single horse would typically require about 11–20lb (5–9kg) of food per day, all of which ideally was transported with the army. The staple foods were hay, straw and oats, and the recommended campaign diet for officer's horses was 11lb (5kg) of either hay or straw (preferably the former, which had a higher nutritional value), or 14lb (6.5kg) of oats.[6] For transport horses the total weight of food per day might be up to 20lb (9kg), on account of their additional strains. In reality, while the horses might have access to quality food of the right

▲ *Napoleon directs cannon against royalists in Paris, 1795. (Hulton-Deutsch Collection/CORBIS/Corbis via Getty Images)*

quantity during the first weeks of a campaign, harder times usually lay ahead. When proper forage ran out, the horses were frequently fed on freshly cut green vegetation, which eventually had a detrimental impact on their digestive systems and general health. Combine exhaustion and exposure to harsh weather, and the effect could be disastrous. During the Russian campaign, horses were dying at the rate of about 50 per three-quarters of a mile (one kilometre) travelled. Another problem, amongst many, for the horses of that campaign was that they faced the Russian winter shod in summer shoes, which offered no grip on the icy surfaces. Hundreds of horses therefore fell and broke legs.

The attrition amongst horses had a profound effect upon French logistics. Had the French Army not been so adept at marching stoically for many miles under heavy personal loads, Napoleon's successes might have been far more limited.

6   Crowdy 2015: 225

▶ *This dramatic depiction of French troops crossing the Berezina River in 1812 shows multiple supply wagons, and what appear to be requisitioned civilian vehicles, backed up on the eastern riverbank. (Leemage/Corbis via Getty Images)*

JOMINI ON LOGISTICS AND ORGANISATION

Antoine-Henri Jomini's *Art of War,* originally published in 1838, is an invaluable volume for understanding many aspects of Napoleonic warfare. His work includes useful sections on the practicalities and logistics of army management in the field. The following extended passage is included to illustrate the sheer amount of complex command decisions that needed to be taken:

1. The preparation of all the material necessary for setting the army in motion, or, in other words, for opening the campaign. Drawing up orders, instructions and itineraries for the assemblage of the army and its subsequent launching upon its theatre of operations.
2. Drawing up in a proper manner the orders of the general-in-chief for different enterprises, as well as plans of attack in expected battles.
3. Arranging with the chiefs of engineers and artillery the measures to be taken for the security of the posts which are to be used as depots, as well as those to be fortified in order to facilitate the operations of the army.

4. Ordering and directing reconnaissances of every kind, and procuring in this way, and by using spies, as exact information as possible of the positions and movements of the enemy.
5. Taking every precaution for the proper execution of movements ordered by the general. Arranging the march of the different columns, so that all may move in an orderly and connected manner. Ascertaining certainly that the means requisite for the ease and safety of marches are prepared. Regulating the manner and time of halts.
6. Giving proper composition to advanced guards, rearguards, flankers and all detached bodies, and preparing good instructions for their guidance. Providing all the means necessary for the performance of their duties.
7. Proscribing forms and instructions for subordinate commanders or their staff officers, relative to the different methods of drawing up the troops in columns when the enemy is at hand, as well as their formation in the most appropriate manner when the army is to engage in battle, according to the nature of the ground and the character of the enemy.
8. Indicating to advanced guards and other detachments well-chosen points of assembly in case of their attack by superior numbers, and informing them what support they may hope to receive in case of need.

▼ *This large gathering actually gives a good impression of the Napoleonic army at a stop. It was not uncommon for soldiers to sleep directly on the ground. (M. Mathews)*

▲ *A depiction of the 'Interior of a Military Chamber'. Beds were made after a half-hour airing in the morning. (Artokoloro Quint Lox Limited / Alamy)*

9. Arranging and superintending the march of trains of baggage, munitions, provisions, and ambulances, both with the columns and in their rear, in such manner that they will not interfere with the movements of the troops and will still be near at hand. Taking precautions for order and security, both on the march and when trains are halted and parked.

10. Providing for the successive arrival of convoys of supplies. Collecting all the means of transportation of the country and of the army, and regulating their use.

11. Directing the establishment of camps, and adopting regulations for their safety, good order and police.

12. Establishing and organising lines of operations and supplies, as well as lines of communications with these lines for detached bodies. Designating officers capable of organising and commanding in rear of the army; looking out for the safety of detachments and convoys, furnishing them with good instructions, and looking out also for preserving suitable means of communication of the army with its base.

13. Organising depots of convalescent, wounded and sickly men, movable hospitals and workshops for repair; providing for their safety.

14. Keeping accurate record of all detachments, either on the flanks or in the rear; keeping an eye upon their movements, and looking out for their return to the main column as soon as their service on detachment is no longer necessary; giving them, when required, some centre of action, and forming strategic reserves.

15. Organising marching battalions or companies to gather up isolated men or small detachments moving in either direction between the army and its base of operations.

16. In case of sieges, ordering and supervising the employment of the troops in the trenches, making arrangements with the chiefs of artillery and engineers as to the labours to be performed by those troops and as to their management in sorties and assaults.

17. In retreats, taking precautionary measures for preserving order; posting fresh troops to support and relieve the rear-guard; causing intelligent officers to examine and select positions where the rear-guard may advantageously halt, engage the enemy, check his pursuit and thus gain time; making provision in advance for the movement of trains, that nothing shall be left behind, and that they shall proceed in the most perfect order, taking all proper precautions to insure safety.

18. In cantonments, assigning positions to the different corps; indicating to each principal division of the army a place of assembly in case of alarm; taking measures to see that all orders, instructions, and regulations are implicitly observed.[7]

7   Jomini 1862: np

RATIONS AND FORAGING

The depressing realities of the experience of horses in the French Army easily mirrored the equally grim experience of its human beings. There was certainly no problem with obesity in Napoleonic-era forces; the majority of foot soldiers on campaign might be at the biting point of malnutrition, due to a paucity of food combined with the constant effort of marching and, occasionally, fighting.

▲ *A field kettle and stove. The kettle would be used for preparing soups and basic broths. (M. Mathews)*

▼ *A typical bean broth. Meat rations were generally limited, especially on long campaigns, and meat broths usually required about 5–6 hours of cooking. (M. Mathews)*

BREAD RATIONS

Before looking into the foraging system, we should clarify some key points about the supply demands of the French Army at the level of the individual soldier. The cornerstone of French military nutrition was bread and hard biscuit. The former sounds austere to modern ears, but the French prided themselves on baking high-quality loaves, either courtesy of regimental bakeries or from local civilian bakeries compelled to produce loaves for military consumption. Each loaf weighed about 3lb 5oz (1.5kg), and a soldier would usually be provided with two loaves every four days. In garrison duty, soldiers would also be given a ration of stale bread for crumbling up into soups.

Bread carried with it two logistical problems: 1) It was perishable; 2) It required the facilities to bake and distribute it. Again, campaign life meant that bread might be in short supply. Its substitute or supplement was hard biscuit, produced from wheat flour. Each biscuit weighed 10oz (275g), and two were issued each day on campaign, if bread wasn't forthcoming.[8] The hard biscuits were tough on the tooth – softening in liquid was recommended – but they had the great advantage of a very long shelf life of up to six years, if properly packed and stored.

MEAT AND VEGETABLES

Meat and vegetables were also part of the daily ration. In terms of meat, the staples were beef, offal (usually of dairy cattle) and mutton, although occasionally bacon was also provided. The field butcheries calculated the distribution of meat on the principle that a single cow could provide the individual meat ration of 9oz (250g) for 1,000 soldiers. The butcheries provided each company with a large block of meat that was then distributed downwards through the squads to each soldier. In terms of vegetables and carbohydrates, the daily ration for a soldier was 1oz (30g) of rice or 2oz (60g) of dried vegetables, the latter requiring much rehydration before they could be consumed. Meat was often dried, cured or smoked, to help it resist perishing under campaign conditions.

DISTRIBUTING AND OBTAINING FOOD

Napoleon by no means disregarded the needs of food logistics, as is sometimes presented. Even in the logistical disaster that was the Russian campaign, Napoleon made huge initial investments in the support network, gathering a full 24 days of supplies at the beginning of the invasion – 20 days stocked on the food wagons and four days per man. That the length

8 Crowdy 2015: 223

THE GARRISON KITCHEN

The supply and consistency of food to French soldiers was naturally very different in a barracks setting than in the field. An garrison cook would shop every morning in the local town with one of more assistants, buying sufficient food for the day from approved suppliers. The kitchens in which the food was cooked varied according to barrack facilities and circumstances. Food might be cooked en masse in large-scale kitchens serving several barracks, the food then transferred to the men via large communal mess tins into which the soldiers all dipped with their spoons, one at a time under rotation around the pot. (Another reason why disease could spread so rapidly through military accommodation.) Alternatively, an individual barracks block might have its own cooking facilities, the raw foodstuffs distributed out to each barracks for separate preparation. Unlike in modern armies, where cooking is highly centralised, in the Napoleonic French Army cooking skills were widely distributed, although chief cooks would oversee standards to ensure consistent recipes. A typical barracks meal was a meat broth, produced by boiling meat (half a pound for each litre of water) and seasonal vegetables, reducing the volume of water down over 5–6 hours then adding bread as a thickening agent and for extra nutrition.

▲ *Dried fish would be stored via a string passing through the fish's throat. (M. Mathews)*

▼ *Typical French cooking equipment. The smokey camp fires would be used to dry out meats; meats might also be half-cooked for preservation. (M. Mathews)*

of the campaign dramatically outstripped this time frame is more a tactical miscalculation than a logistical oversight. But it is ultimately true that supply train provisioning came secondary to his requirements for fast, decisive deployments. To keep soldiers within reach of food supplies, food depots were often situated along the line of advance or close to the centre of action. In October 1805, for example, Napoleon ordered the establishment of a huge logistics base at Augsburg to fuel his army's drive eastwards. The base was sufficient to hold some three million rations, or 18 days' worth of supplies.[9]

But when neither depots nor the supply train could keep up with demand, which was often, then it was left to the individual formations to forage and 'live off the land', a situation that Napoleon regarded as a normal part of military life. The problem was that Napoleon's armies were quite simply an order of magnitude greater in size than those of the past. Hundreds of thousands of men would soak up the food of an entire region, like a sponge absorbing a small pool of water.

Martin Van Creveld paints one of the clearest portraits of the insatiable nature of foraging activities, relating to the campaigns of 1805:

As they gradually turned requisitioning into a fine art, the corps ordonnateurs [authorising officers] were able to draw enormous quantities of supplies from the towns and villages on their way. Thus, for example, Soult forced Heilbronn and its surroundings – total population perhaps 15,000–16,000 – to surrender no less than 85,000 bread rations, 24,000lb. salt, 3,600 bushels of hay, 6,000 sacks of oats, 5,000 pints of wine, 800 bushels of straw and 100 four-horse wagons. Hall and its district probably had only about 8,000 inhabitants but were nevertheless made to yield 60,000 bread rations, 35,000lb. meat (seventy oxen), 4,000 pints wine, 100,000 bundles of hay and straw, 50 four-horse and 100 other carts, as well as 200 horses with harness. Even much smaller places were able to bring forward truly astounding quantities. For example, Marmont and his 12,000 men stayed for five days in the village of Pfhul (forty houses, 600 inhabitants) and 'did not lack for anything'. Bugeaud's famous question to his sister, 'judge for yourself if 10,000 men arriving in a village can easily find enough to eat', should be answered in the affirmative.[10]

Reflecting on the figures provided by Van Creveld, the volumes of produce taken are simply astonishing. The impact that these requisitions must have had on the local civilian populations were doubtless profound, especially when the soldiers might take away the bulk of a community's livestock and annual harvest. The impact would have been increased by the common practice of forcibly billeting soldiers in civilian homes, meaning that the civilians could not even protect small personal stocks of food from depredation. Accurate figures for civilian casualties during the Napoleonic Wars are impossible to obtain, but factoring in violence, starvation caused by pillaging and also, in certain theatres, scorched earth tactics, they certainly number in their hundreds of thousands, while some historians have them as high as three million.

But depending on the theatre, and certainly in winter time, foraging might yield only slim pickings for the soldiers, even pushing the daily calorie intake below starvation levels. On the first day of the battle of Eylau (7 February 1807), most French soldiers went into battle having eaten nothing for about 24 hours, such was the parlous state of both the supply train and the opportunities (both temporal and physical) to find food for 75,000 men in the winter landscape of East Prussia.

FORAGING DURING THE RUSSIAN CAMPAIGN

The Russian campaign stands as the greatest illustration of how the foraging principle could go terribly wrong in practice. A high percentage of the roughly 500,000 men who died on the campaign did so simply from starvation, their bodies already weakened by disease (especially typhus) and the cold. Science has indicated that the final death from starvation might actually have been the end point of malnutrition that began months or even years before the campaign. In 2015, the bodies of 3,296 men of the *Grande Armée* were discovered in a mass grave near Vilnius, packed into the earth at a density of seven bodies per square yard/metre. Scientists from the University of Central

▲ *In the upper echelons of the officer class, dining might remain a fine experience with silverware and linen, even in the field. (M. Mathews)*

STARVATION ON THE RUSSIAN CAMPAIGN

The following account comes from Jakob Walter (1788–1864), a German private soldier from Westphalia who served as one of the French allies during the Russian campaign:

> Thus in the evening I rode apart from the army to find in the outlying district some straw for the horse and rye for myself. I was not alone, for over a strip **ten** hours wide soldiers sought provisions because of their hunger; and, when there was nothing to be found, they could hunt up cabbage stalks here and there from under the snow, cut off some of the pulp from these, and let the core slowly thaw out in their mouths. Nevertheless, this time I had a second considerable piece of luck. I came to a village not yet burned where there were still sheaves of grain. I laid these before the horse and plucked off several heads of grain. I hulled them, laid the kernels mixed with chaff into a hand grinder which had been left in a house, and, taking turns with several other soldiers, ground some flour. Then we laid the dough, which we rolled into only fist-sized little loaves, on a bed of coals. Although the outside of the loaves burned to charcoal, the bread inside could be eaten. I got as many as fifteen such balls.
>
> For further supply, whenever I came upon sheaves of grain, I picked the heads, rubbed off the kernels, and ate them from my bread sack during the course of the day. Several times I also found hempseed, which I likewise ate raw out of my pocket; and cooked hempseed was a delicacy for me because the grains burst open and produced an oily sauce; yet since I could not get salt for cooking, it did not have its full strength.[11]

Florida conducted tests on the skeletons to gain a clearer idea of the causes of death, focusing on the levels of nitrogen isotopes in the bones. There were indications that about 25 per cent of the men died from typhus, but the majority seem to have been afflicted by starvation. In fact, the evidence hinted that the men might have been subjected to starvation on previous occasions that left them in general poor health. Other evidence from the site showed that the men suffered from serious dental issues, also an indicator of poor nutrition, plus bone damage that likely dated back to physical labour carried out during childhood. One further problem for the soldiers in the Russian campaign was that foraging parties often fell victim to predatory and roaming packs of Cossacks.

WATER

In addition to the necessity of finding food, there was also the accompanying, and at times more pressing, issue of finding potable water. A corps of 30,000 troops would require at least 13,000 gallons (60,000 litres) of drinking water per day (more under conditions of extreme exertion), and that is not including the voracious needs of the horses or the requirements of cooking.

As we have seen, the individual soldier carried about a pint (500ml) of water on his person in various types of bottle or canteen. Refills came from the supply wagon, wells or from naturally occurring water sources. Of course, unless water was boiled even the apparently cleanest water might contain harmful bacteria, which could further proliferate if it was kept stored in the canteen for any length of time. For this reason, in hot weather each soldier would also be issued with 1½fl oz (50ml) of vinegar, which was added to the water in an attempt to kill off the bacteria. This measure was not always available or effective, and dysenteric illnesses amongst the troops were a near daily occurrence. On occasions, retreating enemies would also poison wells to ensure that the advancing French had even less to drink.

A lack of consideration for water supplies could have truly dire consequences, especially in the summer months or in arid theatres. During Napoleon's Egyptian expedition in 1798, the tropical conditions conspired with a lack of clean drinking water to drive many men mad with thirst, even to the point of suicide. The thirst was rendered even worse by the fact that the main constituent of their diet in theatre were the mouth-drying biscuits, added to which were the dehydrating effects of the sun, airborne sand and dust. At one well, some 30 soldiers were crushed to death in a stampede to refill their canteens.

▼ *Supply wagons, here seen at the battle of Jemappes (6 November 1792), might be converted into improvised ambulances during times of battle. (PD/CC)*

TENTS AND BIVOUACS

There were two varieties of military tent available, at least theoretically, during the Revolutionary and Napoleonic Wars: one (11ft 6in × 8ft 6in / 3.5m × 2.6m) housed eight men, while a larger, newer variant (18ft 5in × 12ft 10in / 5.6m × 3.9m) housed 15 men (or eight cavalrymen plus saddles).

The distribution of the tents during the 1790s tended to follow class lines, with the smaller and less comfortable tents given to the general infantrymen and the officers' orderlies, while officers took the larger tents, which offered the additional capacity for items such as map tables.

A tented camp was established with a regimented order. The site was marked out prior to the arrival of the formation by a special group of soldiers assigned by the battalion commander and quartermaster. When the unit arrived, ropes marked at fixed distances with alternating red and black bands might be distributed to each battalion, with the bands indicating the distance between each tent. Typically the battalion would camp in 'ranges' of five tents aligned with one another, with each range housing a half-company. Properly organised, the tented camp would be put up quickly. The lines of tents created 'streets' running between them which soldiers might name, in much the same way that soldiers on the Western Front in World War I labelled both the frontline and supply trenches. The occupants of the tents would be logically assigned in terms of rank and position, so that the

camp layout reflected the seniority in the army. There would be assigned places for the stacking of muskets; out in the open if the weather was fine, or inside a small tent of their own if the weather was poor. Camp and cooking fires were also established at regular points, near both the soldiers' tents and the tents assigned to laundry services.

Historically, however, the French Army gravitated inexorably away from the use and distribution of tents, partly through endless shortfalls in supply, partly through operational realities (the time spent setting up and taking down a camp often did not fit in with tactical timetables) and partly through the poor quality of the tents and the insalubrious environment inside. For this reason, the French soldiers tended to prefer either sleeping outside – directly on the ground in warm weather – or in improvised huts and shelters or requisitioned barns and houses in colder climes. The experience of this type of living could vary considerably. On warm summer nights, next to a glowing campfire and with a 'mattress' made of fir boughs, a decent quality of sleep could be had, although the close proximity to the ground made parasite and insect infestations a perennial problem. Conversely, in wet and cold conditions, on campaigns through hard and spartan land, camp arrangements could

▼ *A reconstruction of a Napoleonic-era camp. Bayoneted muskets might be used as a cooking tripod (PD/CC)*

▲ *This image of an improvised shelter is far more faithful to the reality of French army camp life than a well-regulated and ordered tent camp. (Duncan Miles)*

be harrowing. There are accounts of French soldiers sleeping directly in the mud of ploughed fields, their uniforms soaked and their bodies slipping into hypothermia. Troops became adept at building improvised survival shelters from branches, boughs and leaves, cramming multiple people into such shelters to share body heat, but such measures were rarely able to prevent the terrible decline in health and hygiene.

The liberty with which the French Army moved certainly had a significant tactical advantage in terms of operational tempo, plus it had the added benefit that enemy reconnaissance troops or spies found it difficult to ascertain

▶ *Hay, straw and thick foliage was used to provide insulation both beneath the soldier and above. Wet weather was the greatest enemy of warmth. (Christine Pet-Sepers)*

▼ *Marshal Davout expelled 25,000 Hamburgers from their homes in 1813–14, to make way for French troops. (PD/CC)*

French strength – it is far easier to count individual tents and multiply that figure by average occupants, than it is to count thousands of people scattered over the ground. On the negative side, cold or wet weather had a terrible impact on the soldiers' health and the condition of equipment and uniforms.

We can say that Napoleon's army brought about a partial revolution in logistics. By his use of depots, a professional supply train and the official adoption of foraging procedures, Napoleon was indeed able to drive his armies around the continent with a speed that left many other enemy forces outmanoeuvred and breathless. In most cases, however, the logistical effort was at the biting point of collapse for the frontline soldier and, as in the case of the 1812 campaign, sometimes went terribly beyond it.

6

ON THE BATTLEFIELD: STRATEGY AND TACTICS

Napoleon possessed an advantage enjoyed by none of his opponents – a near-total single command, centred upon himself. The emperor acknowledged this explicitly: 'Unity of command is essential to the economy of time. Warfare in the field was like a siege: by directing all one's force to a single point a breach might be made, and the equilibrium of opposition destroyed.' Napoleon understood that speed and tempo – both enforced at a pace his enemies could not match – were critical to his style of warfare.

TACTICAL VISION

Because all initiatives and major commands, from grand strategy through to the movements of individual divisions and corps, came from Napoleon alone rather than a committee, Napoleon was quite simply able to execute strategic and tactical decisions faster than his enemy.

Of course, the flip side of this arrangement was that the outcome of a campaign depended largely upon the brilliance of the emperor alone; should his powers fail or weaken, as they did from 1812 onwards, or if there were simply just too many claims on his attention, then the consequences could be catastrophic. But in discussing the tactics of Napoleon's army, it is important to acknowledge that Napoleon actually had little real interest in the minutiae of frontline tactics. He left these matters to his subordinate commanders, who actually could exercise considerable latitude and innovation in their deployment of regiments and battalions. As long as they delivered on their overall directives, then Napoleon was largely content.

NAPOLEON'S CORRESPONDENCE

Attempting to define Napoleon's specific style and approach to military tactics can be a frustrating business. For although there are certainly repeated characteristics in his handling of forces on the battlefield, his focus on adaptation to circumstances means that it is hard to codify these characteristics into a single body of martial doctrine. One of the best sources for his strategic thinking can be found in the vast collection of personal and official communications that he produced, known as his *Correspondence*, and which survives to this day, including nearly 40,500 letters. From this and others sources we glean nuggets of military wisdom, such as:

'An army's effectiveness depends on its size, training, experience, and morale, and morale is worth more than any of the other factors combined.'

'Strategy is the art of making use of time and space. I am less concerned about the later than the former. Space we can recover, lost time never.'

'If you wage war, do it energetically and with severity. This is the only way to make it shorter and consequently less inhuman.'

'When you have resolved to fight a battle, collect your whole force. Dispense with nothing. A single battalion sometimes decides the day.'

'I have destroyed the enemy merely by marches.'

All such statements, combined with the actual evidence of his campaigns, give insight into Napoleon's tactical spirit. Napoleon, however, was a commander who was not slavishly wedded to theory, but would rather simply do what needed to be done to secure the intended outcome. This is what made him such a profound shock to many of the more traditionalist armies of Europe at this time. We can, however, usefully distil some overarching elements of his approach to warfare.

▼ *A re-enactment battle; note the Napoleonic eagle standard to act as a point of visual orientation. (M. Mathews)*

◢ *A French infantryman's book, listing pay, equipment issued, promotions, punishments, wounds etc. (M. Mathews)*

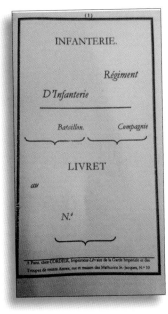

BATTLE OF BORODINO

The battle of Borodino was fought on 7 September 1812 around the village of Borodino, Russia, located some 80 miles (130km) south-west of Moscow. Napoleon had been in pursuit of the tactically retreating Russian forces since the French invasion began in late June, and it was at Borodino that the Russians, commanded by Prince Mikhail Kutuzov, decided to make a stand. Kutuzov commanded a force of about 120,000 men, including 72,000 infantry and 24,000 cavalry (the latter including some 7,000 irregular Cossacks), plus about 640 cannon. These forces were positioned over a 5-mile (8km) front, many behind scattered defensive earthworks and features; the most potent of these was the 'Great Redoubt', just to the south-west of Borodino village, and a series of arrow-shaped hill fortifications further south known as the *flèches*.

The principal Russian formations were the First Army under General Mikhail Barclay de Tolly, which held the northern part of the line, and the Second Army of Peter Bagration to the south, while the Imperial Russian Guard held the centre around the Great Redoubt. Napoleon bore down on Borodino with a total force of about 135,000 men and nearly 600 guns, but this force was seriously weakened by the grinding effort of the two-month advance. Napoleon's military imagination seems to have left him somewhat at Borodino, and he opted for a straight-out frontal assault, launched at 0600hrs on 7 September. There were some initial French gains – Borodino itself fell to Beauharnais' IV Corps; Davout and Ney (I and III

Corps respectively) pushed forward against the *flèches*; and Poniatowski claimed the village of Utitsa in the far south of the front. But from about 0700hrs the energy began to bleed out of the French assault, and casualties mounted alarmingly. A major French attempt to break the centre of the Russian line suffered terribly from artillery fire – rough terrain channelled and concentrated the French troops into a densely packed target. The Russians were also taking appalling losses. Finally a French assault by Beauharnais on the Great Redoubt, just after 1400hrs, destroyed the defenders there and claimed the position for Napoleon. Yet the exhausted French troops, who now faced two fresh cavalry corps deployed by Barclay de Tolly, were unable to exploit the breakthrough, and again the battle became mired in mostly static attrition.

Eventually Kutuzov bowed to French pressure, having taken about 40,000 casualties, and on the morning of 8 September he made professional withdrawal, ceding all the Borodino position to the *Grande Armée*. But this did not signal a clear French victory. The clash had inflicted as many as 50,000 casualties upon the French and, unlike the Russian troops, they did not have the logistical support or the means of reinforcement to make good these losses.

▼ *Louis François Lejeune's famous painting of the 'battle of Moscow' (Borodino), depicting the attack on the Shevardino Redoubt. (PD/CC)*

ARMY ORGANISATION

Part of Napoleon's tactical genius lay in the way he structured his army, particularly through the *corps d'armée* (army corps) formation that became a keynote of his operational art. Among most of the armies of Europe at this time, the largest formation was typically the regiment, with numerous regiments moving together as a single ponderous army.

Napoleonic expert Major James Wassan, US Army, has summarised some of the problems with this model:

> In Frederick's time an army had no sub-structure higher than the regiment and was therefore a pondering beast that generally moved along one route. Subdividing the army into separate regiments might allow an adversary to overwhelm the separate parts piecemeal. This concentration during movement caused the army to move slowly and allowed its opponent to determine, with relative ease, its objective. Supplying this type of army required huge depots, which tended to keep the army on a 'short leash' from its supply base. Monarchs were not willing to let these armies live off the land, and even if they were, it was impractical since a single route may not have sufficient food stuffs to support such a force.[1]

Wassan's overview illustrates just how sluggish the regimental army could be, and indicates how it could be exploited by an enemy with more energetic skills of manoeuvre or tactical flexibility.

CORPS D'ARMÉE

It was to achieve just such dynamism that Napoleon, in 1800, established the *corps d'armée* system. He divided his army into self-sustained all-arms corps, each effectively an army in miniature. This approach was not entirely new,

---

1   https://www.napoleon-series.org/military/organization/c_armycorps.html

▼ *Vernet's painting of General Kellerman commanding the French forces at Valmy, 20 September 1792. (PD/CC)*

as informal combined arms forces had been in evidence during the Revolutionary Wars. Yet Napoleon worked it into a proper operational system. A typical corps had a manpower of about 30,000 men, although the strength could vary considerably, with as few as 15,000 soldiers or as many as 70,000. The corps formation was fundamentally flexible, with battalions, regiments, brigades and divisions attached or detached according to need. The corps itself acted as the headquarters for whatever element fell under its purview (each corps had a full staff headquarters).

The largest subdivision of the corps was the division. A typical divisional model was one cavalry and two infantry divisions, each headed by a *Général de Division* with his own staff, but again the numbers of divisions present could change by circumstance. The division was in turn separated into brigades, headed by a *Général de Brigade*. The divisions themselves were, like the corps, self-contained entities, including their own artillery units and transport train. There was also artillery at the corps level, although this was usually the heavier 12pdr guns, while the infantry divisional artillery was mostly armed with 8pdrs, and cavalry division horse artillery with 6pdrs. (Divisions also had the support of the corps engineer train.) Brigades were subsequently stepped down into regiments and then battalions.

The revolutionary aspect of the *corps d'armée* was the flexibility for manoeuvre it gave Napoleon. By being self-contained with its all-arms capability, a single corps could be deployed unilaterally as an offensive or defensive body, meeting sizeable enemy threats and either defeating them in battle or having the capability to fix the enemy forces in place while other corps manoeuvred into position.

But the individual strength of a corps was only part of the reason for the impact of the *corps d'armée* system. Napoleon also innovated in the way that corps manoeuvred in relation to one another. There were several options relating to standard military practice. For example, multiple corps could move in echelon, with one wing of the formation 'refused' – i.e. held back away from the enemy and facing to the flank, forming a gap that could tempt the enemy to fill in and break his line or expose his own flank. Conversely, one flanking corps could be heavily reinforced compared to its neighbour; this structure was known as *en potencé*.

BATAILLON CARRÉ

But the most innovative and dynamic structure was the *bataillon carré*. In this structure multiple corps were arranged to form a wedge-like square, with a single or multiple corps

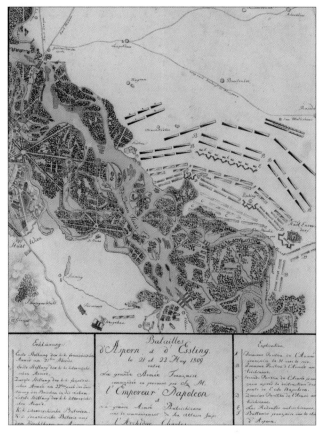

▲ *A vintage map showing the disposition of French and Austrian forces at the battle of Aspern-Essling (21–22 May 1809). (PD/CC)*

LA BATALLION CARRÉ

The bataillon carré *was a cornerstone of Napoleon's brand of manoeuvre warfare. Note that the corps formation can quickly shift to face different directions while maintaining the strength of the side facing the enemy. (Haynes)*

at each corner of the square but led by one of the corners (hence creating three lines of advance). A typical arrangement would be a lead corps flanked further back by two corps on each side, with reserve formations – such as heavy cavalry and the Imperial Guard – following up at the rear. Out in front of the line of advance was a line of light cavalry, providing screening actions and advance reconnaissance. Note that the four main corps elements of the *bataillon carré* would not be in close proximity; a general rule was that each corps should be within a day's march of the other.

The true strength of the *bataillon carré* was its multi-directionality. If, say, a corps on the flank encountered the enemy, that corps could turn and engage while the whole *bataillon carré* structure also pivoted about quickly on a new line of advance; what was a flank corps now became the lead corps of a new square. With his army thus orientated, Napoleon was then in an ideal position to concentrate his forces against weak points in the enemy's formations.

BATTLE OF JENA–AUERSTÄDT

Combined with Napoleon's abilities to deploy forces at great speed, the *bataillon carré* became an essential ingredient of many of Napoleon's post-1800 victories. A case in point is the double battle of Jena–Auerstädt, fought during the autumn of 1806. Napoleon, with his forces in southern Germany, faced

a combined Prussian–Saxon army of more than 171,000 men, massed in three armies. Their objective was to advance forward to Würzburg, but with news that Napoleon was moving his troops forward towards Saxony, they set out to intercept him, hopefully to achieve a flanking attack.

Napoleon was indeed on the move. He had massed his 180,000 troops behind the Thuringian Forest, then advanced them forward through the forest's eastern end, heading towards Leipzig. Characteristically, Napoleon was moving his troops quickly into action; his strategic aim was to defeat the Prussians in battle west of the Elbe before they could be joined in support by the Russians. Although the forest was tough terrain through which to move an entire army – Napoleon was to shrink his operational front from 124 miles (200km) to just 28 miles (45km) to make the advance – he had arranged his forces in a *bataillon carré*, three columns of two corps each column. The flexibility inherent in this organisation was crucial, as both sides found it difficult to discern the movements and dispositions of the enemy forces, despite the continual reconnaissance of light cavalry.

Some of the ambiguity lifted on 7–10 October, when French forces clashed with and defeated advanced Prussian troops at Schleiz and Saalfeld. In panicked response, the Prussians, led by the Duke of Brunswick and King Frederick

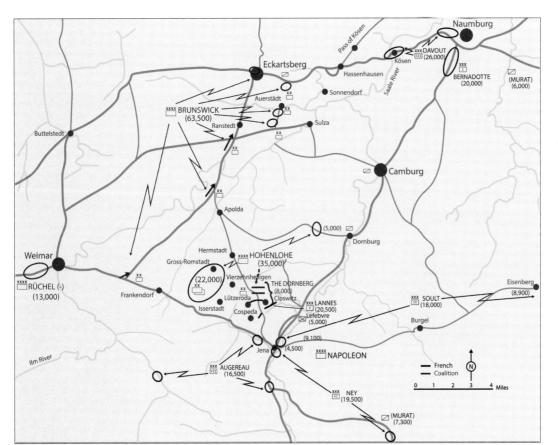

◄ *A map of the battle of Jena–Auerstädt, showing the situation at midnight on 13 October 1806. (Haynes)*

▼ *The battle of Jena–Auerstädt on the mid-morning of 14 October, with Davout clashing in the north with Brunswick's forces. (Haynes)*

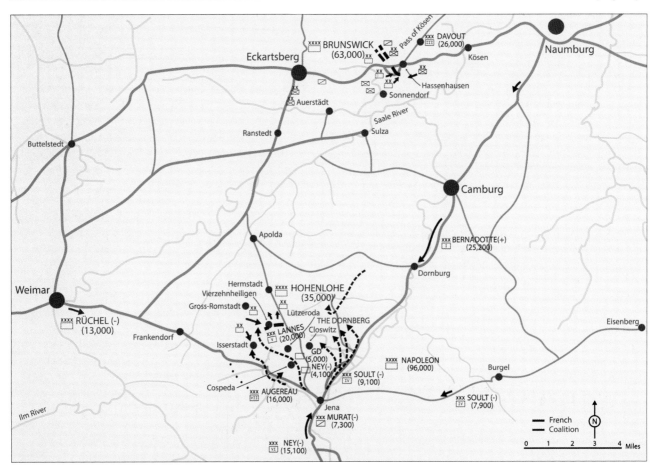

► *The battle of Jena–Auerstädt at 1400hrs on 14 October 1806. By this stage, both Prussian concentrations have been defeated and put into retreat. (Haynes)*

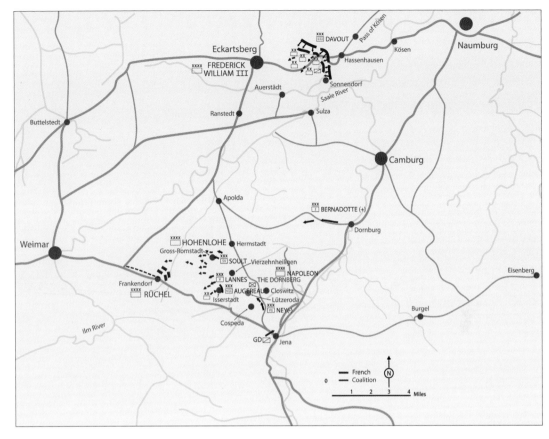

William III, now switched from an offensive to defensive mentality, based on the expectation that Napoleon was driving on Leipzig. The Prussian general Prince Hohenlohe, who had been defeated at Saalfeld, was instructed to pull his 38,000 men and 120 guns back to Jena as a blocking force, while 63,000 men under Duke Charles William Ferdinand were deployed 18 miles (29km) further north at Auerstädt, en route to a further retreat back towards Leipzig and Berlin.

On 12 October, Napoleon wheeled his *bataillon carré* to face west. Napoleon was still not totally informed about the Prussian intentions, as he believed that the main Prussian army was now concentrated at Jena, against which he directed Augereau's VII Corps, Ney's VI Corps, Lannes' V Corps and Soult's IV Corps. Further to the north, opposite Auerstädt, were Bernadotte's I Corps and Davout's III Corps, but their main role was to make a huge flanking attack against the Prussian troops at Jena. On 13 October, they were still unaware that Brunswick's army was actually advancing towards them on the roads leading north from Jena.

Attack on Jena

Napoleon unleashed his attack upon Jena on the morning of 14 October. There was much hard and bloody fighting as the French attempted to dislodge the Prussians, who responded with several counterattacks during the morning and early afternoon. There were also some French blunders, most famously Ney's unauthorised attack towards Vierzehnheiligen from the south east, which resulted in his troops being surrounded by Prussian cavalry and having to hunker down

in protective squares. Yet Napoleon's *bataillon carré* enabled him to strengthen his concentration of force against Jena, bringing into play a 42,000-strong reserve. By mid-afternoon the Prussian centre had crumbled and Hohenlohe's men were in retreat.

During the ferocious battle at Jena, further north, the large Prussian army under Brunswick eventually ran into the northern French troops of Davout, with his corps of some 26,000 men radically outnumbered by the Prussian waves. In this unequal and remarkable action, Davout was left almost entirely alone; Bernadotte, who was not on good terms with Davout, took his troops further south to Dornburg, an action that later almost earned him a court martial. Nevertheless, Davout pulled off an astonishing victory, aided by the Prussian piecemeal attacks but also by the very design of the corps: its all-arms elements meant that it could fully execute major offensive and defensive actions. Eventually the Prussian forces, deprived of their leader – Brunswick had been killed after being struck by a musket ball – lost ground to Davout's localised assaults and, on hearing of the Prussian defeat at Jena, succumbed to defeat and retreat.

The outstanding French victories at Jena–Auerstädt were not Napoleon's alone. A large measure of the credit must of course go to his talented marshals, especially Davout, who was eventually rewarded for his actions with the title Duke of Auerstädt. But what is apparent here is that Napoleon's use of the corps formations arranged in *bataillon carré* meant that his army was briskly responsive to emergencies on the immediate battlefield and the wider theatre.

COMMAND AND CONTROL

No military organisation is perfect, and the *bataillon carré* also had its share of problems and challenges. One of the most pressing, especially with the seemingly unstoppable expansion of the French Army, was that of command and control.

Napoleon was a centralising leader, taking the major tactical decisions himself and distributing them out to his marshals and generals via his aide-de-camp (ADC); in turn, the marshals and generals would have their own ADCs, to pass the orders on to smaller formation commanders. The lot of an ADC was a precarious one. He was often compelled to ride constantly around the most dangerous parts of the front, exposed to all manner of hostile fire. There were occasions, such as at the battle of Eylau in February 1807, when units had actually received orders to retreat, but the death of all messengers sent to them meant that they stayed at the front, being steadily destroyed. For such reasons, when ADCs or other couriers were deployed in particularly perilous circumstances, duplicate messages might be sent out amongst multiple riders, in case one or more of the couriers were killed.

The speed with which the ADC and other messengers transferred messages around the battlefront was limited to the speed and condition of his horse. ADCs might commonly ride a horse to its death at a gallop, but he was given the authority to requisition any suitable horse from a proximate unit to keep the delivery on track. For transferring messages over long distances, the couriers would often be arranged in a relay system, to achieve optimal speeds. Alternatively, there was also the ground breaking technological option developed by French engineer Claude Chappé.

▲ *An engraving showing Claude Chappé's ingenious telegraph system in operation. The first public demonstration was in 1791. (PD/CC)*

▼ *Napoleon surveys the battlefield at Wagram (5–6 July 1809), an engagement that cost a combined 72,000 casualties. (Leemage/Corbis via Getty Images)*

TELEGRAPH SYSTEM

Chappé's gift to humanity was the world's first telegraph system. Individually, the telegraph 'transmitter' consisted of a parallel beam, which could be revolved horizontally or vertically, with a rotating arm at each end. Each arm could be placed in one of seven positions, and these positions, combined with the movement of the main beam, meant that in total 98 separate visual combinations could be created. Six of the positions were service messages, e.g. instructions such as 'ready to transmit' or 'received', while each of the remaining 92 positions related to the vocabulary on 92 pages of a common code book. The operator of the telegraph was able to position the arms to indicate a specific word on a specific page, with a total vocabulary of 8,500 words.

The signal stations were positioned in chains across France and into the Netherlands, Germany and northern Italy, each in visual line of sight with the next in the sequence. At its peak, the system had 534 stations covering more than 3,100 miles (5,000km). The speed at which information could be transferred this way was astonishing for the time. A message could cross nearly the full length of France in a matter of 4–5 hours, although such speeds relied upon good visual conditions – fog or heavy rain could bring the system to a standstill. In such cases, the Military Telegraph Service – the unit in charge of operating Chappé's network – would have to resort to the traditional method of couriers.

FRONTLINE COMMAND AND CONTROL

At the frontline, once battle was joined, junior officers would struggle to maintain influence over the unit under their command. This was partly why formations such as column and line had been so codified and drilled in military tactics; they raised the chances that the formation would hold together through the smoke, noise and mortal chaos of action. But it was still imperative to have experienced and authoritative personnel holding a unit together. An infantry company formed up into a three-rank line, for example, would usually have senior NCOs placed along the length of the rear rank and to the sides; a sergeant on each side would often carry a small pennon; these men served to keep the company on track during its advance forward. The lieutenants were typically located towards the rear, in the most advantageous location for viewing the integrity of the line and the development of the battle. But here, too, the reach of authority was limited. Battlefield noise would dissipate verbal instructions within a few yards of their point of issue. It was for this reason that drummers and trumpeters accompanied the formations, ready to convert verbal

▼ *The centralising effect of Napoleon's personal command is clearly evoked in this painting by Henri Philippoteaux, who shows all eyes fastened on the leader during the battle of Rivoli on 14 January 1797. (PD/CC)*

◄ *Military drums had calf-skin heads, their volume susceptible to damp. (M. Mathew.*

► *Military drummers learned a defined body of rudiments. (A. Balding)*

commands into commonly understood and more audible musical motifs. Although drummers were close to the bottom of the military hierarchy, their importance in command and control was fully recognised, hence they were a prominent target for enemy marksmen or cavalry, although being positioned behind the third rank of infantry the drummers were reasonably well protected. Without his musicians, an officer would have limited capacity to influence events once the combat advance was under way.

▼ *The density and length of Napoleonic infantry lines made coordination a challenge. Prior battlefield drill was key to maintaining the formation. (A. Balding)*

SPEED AND MANOEUVRE

Napoleon certainly understood the importance of speed, both on the battlefield and during the march. In deployment, Napoleon would drive his troops with infamous severity, compelling them to cover seemingly impossible distances on foot at impressive speed. For example, at Austerlitz, Davout's corps covered some 70 miles (113km) of distance in just 48 hours to reach the battlefield.

But Napoleon combined speed with tempo – the rate at which speed can be repeated and maintained – to exceptional effect. During Napoleon's Italian campaign, for example, as soon as Napoleon had secured a victory he marched his forces on to the next; the Austrians and Piedmontese forces often simply couldn't keep pace with the tactical adjustments. This command of tempo frequently enabled Napoleon to dictate the terms of battle to his advantage. At times, of course, this desire to drive onwards could cloud his vision; the disaster of 1812 in Russia is an example.

Another key element to Napoleon's fighting approach was to focus on seeking out and destroying the enemy's armies with absolute aggression. For Napoleon, it has often been noted, war was for him not about simple absorption of territory and static sieges – which he largely avoided – but about achieving supremacy over his enemies in defining battles. Napoleon stated in 1797: 'There are in Europe

many good generals, but they see too many things at once. I see only one thing, namely the enemy's main body. I try to crush it, confident that secondary matters will then settle themselves.' In this evaluation, Napoleon had some justification – in the history of his campaigns above, it is notable how a series of major battlefield defeats could bring enemies to sue for peace. Thus Napoleon actively sought out ways of finding the main body of the enemy army, fixing it into place, advantageously manoeuvring around it, then wiping it out.

This description must not be taken as implying that Napoleon was strategically or tactically crude, in a 'just go

▼ *The battle of Borodino was not one of Napoleon's instances of creative tactical thinking. Although the largely conventional frontal assault did eventually carry the day for the French, it was at great cost in lives. (Haynes)*

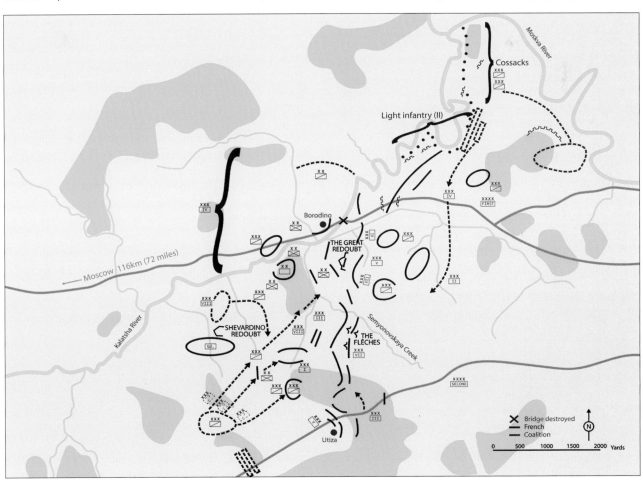

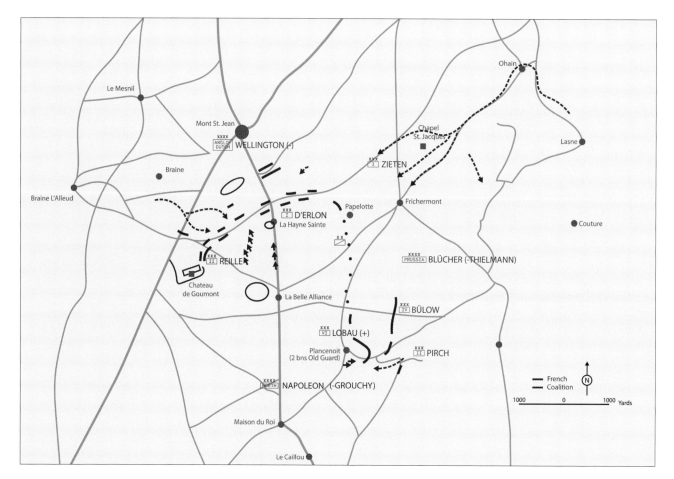

straight at 'em' sort of way. In fact, what made Napoleon so formidable was the way in which he combined aggression with judicious and fast-paced manoeuvres. Historians have given these manoeuvres various labels, but three basic types have been distinguished. All of them were expressed in movements of attack; Napoleon rarely ever adopted defensive approaches to winning battles.

STRATEGY OF THE CENTRAL POSITION

The first type of this crude taxonomy is the 'strategy of the central position'. Napoleon, by virtue of the coalitions arranged against him, would often be faced with multiple national foes from different directions. His solution was not to fight a two-front way, but to adopt a central position between two opposing armies and then fix one army in place defensively with a corps or other formation, while concentrating the bulk of his own army against the other army, defeating it in detail before turning back to face the initial foe.

As with most of Napoleon's tactics, this strategy embodied his overarching tactic of concentration of force, overwhelming the enemy at a key point with a volume of firepower and a weight of infantry and cavalry that the enemy cannot match. A good example of the strategy of the central position would be the battle of Ligny on 16 June 1815, just prior to Napoleon's defeat at the battle of Waterloo. Napoleon made a rapid advance to split the British army to the west, under

▲ The battle of Waterloo, 1930hrs on 18 June 1815. Napoleon is by now squeezed by Wellington's troops to the north and Blücher's Prussians from the south and east. (Haynes).

Wellington, from the Prussian army under Blücher to the east. Napoleon initially intended to turn and fight Wellington first, but the presence of 32,000 Prussian troops at nearby Ligny compelled a change of mind. The subsequent battle was a major defeat for the Prussians, losing 16,000 men to Napoleon's 12,000 casualties. Despite this, much of the Prussian army was able to retreat successfully and, as the French forces were too exhausted to maintain a pursuit, Blücher's army stayed in the overall fight, and would appear later at Waterloo, with decisive effect.

ADVANCE OF ENVELOPMENT

The second type of tactical manoeuvre favoured by Napoleon was the *manoeuvre sur les derrières*, or 'advance of envelopment'. The goal of this tactic was, as its name implies, to trap the enemy forces in an envelopment or pincer action. To accomplish this, a 'covering force', sufficient in strength to hold its own for some hours, would attack and grip the enemy's attention while the French main force manoeuvred itself to assault the enemy rear. To get into position, the main force would shield its movements behind terrain and cavalry screens, then at the right moment it would strike directly across the enemy's lines of communication. If all went to plan, the enemy would be trapped and destroyed. Mindful that the main force was itself vulnerable to possible rearward counter attack from enemy reserves, Napoleon would also place a *corps d'observation* behind the front, to guard against such incursions.

Napoleon used the *manoeuvre sur les derrières* to good effect at some of his most impressive victories, such as Ulm in 1805 and Friedland in 1807. At the battle of Ulm, for example, Napoleon used cavalry screens and an exceptional pace of manoeuvre (at one point the French army of 210,000 men were making 18 miles/29km per day) to cut off Baron Karl Mack von Leiberich's Austrian army between Ingolstadt and Donauwörth, separating them from their lines of retreat. Napoleon eventually squeezed Mack's main army into Ulm itself by 15 September, and Mack was driven to surrender his army five days later, as there was little hope that the Russians would ride to the rescue in a timely fashion.

STRATEGIC PENETRATION

The final category of classic Napoleonic manoeuvre was the 'strategic penetration'. This was akin to the later German *Blitzkrieg*, being a concentrated and fast-paced penetration of an enemy weak point, with the French troops driving deep into enemy territory and taking a significant position – such as a major city – which could then be turned into a 'centre of operations'. The strategic penetration depended on speed and a decisive line of advance, and if successful, the result was an enemy thrown into disarray. A good example of the strategic penetration was Napoleon's push into Russia in 1812, a campaign that took the French right to Moscow, the Russian capital itself. Yet, as this campaign demonstrates, strategic penetration was a risky business, acutely tied to the ability of logistics to keep up as the length of advance stretched. A vast country such as Russia had the land mass to absorb the advance and therefore disperse its effect.

Napoleon's most favoured strategy, one that he used more than 30 times during his military career, was the *manoeuvre sur les derrières*. This particular approach brought the crushing and conclusive outcomes Napoleon always sought. Yet he was not a rigid thinker and, looked at closely, many of his actions contain elements of several or all approaches, plus other innovations according to circumstance.

▼ *Austerlitz was one of Napoleon's seminal victories, a demonstration of how opposing forces could be broken up and defeated in turn. (Haynes)*

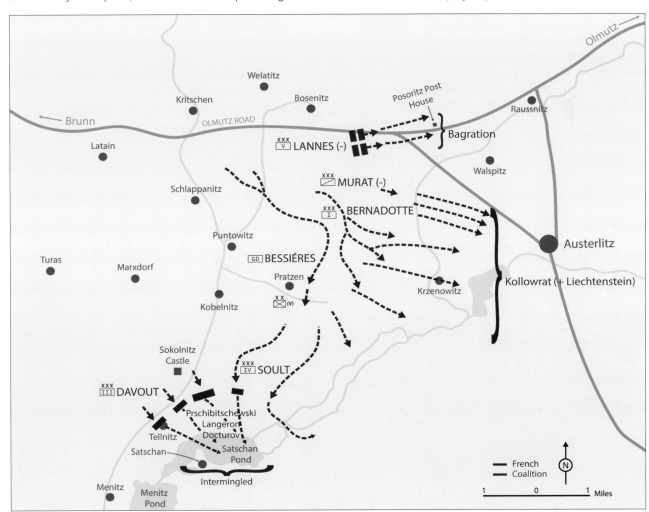

INFANTRY TACTICS

The minutiae of frontline tactics is a topic of some size and complexity, so only a reasonably detailed overview is possible here. To modern military eyes, so accustomed to unit 'fire-and-manouevre' tactics, the rules and formations of Napoleonic combat can seem bewilderingly mechanical.

Yet the organisation of men into ranks, themselves structured according to column, line or square, was the best option for managing large armies on the field of battle. The limited capacity for battlefield command and control, inaccurate weaponry (which compelled the use of mass volley fire) and frequently low levels of training amongst the soldiery meant that strict formations provided the best method for keeping battalions, regiments and divisions working to an overall tactical plan, while also concentrating firepower. There were looser and more manoeuvrable elements on the battlefield – such as light infantry skirmishers, light cavalry and horse artillery – but the overwhelming mass of the army was the regular line infantry, standing shoulder to shoulder and walking into blistering fire.

In what follows, however, we must not think that the French battalions, regiments, brigades and divisions were simply wound up like clockwork toys and made mechanical tactical movements. In fact, there was much play and improvisation at work. While we shall go on to speak of column, line and square, these formations could intermingle,

shift from one to the other repeatedly, and switch from offensive to defensive focus frequently, depending on the skill of the commander. The French Army was a formulaic force, which is one reason why it was so hard to beat.

COLUMN

In classic military thinking, the column was the formation of march or manoeuvre, while the line was that used for delivering fire upon the enemy. The rationale behind this is relatively self-evident. A body of troops arranged in a relatively narrow column has a limited front presented to the enemy, meaning that the majority of the muskets beyond the front ranks cannot be presented and fired. A line, by contrast, presents the maximum number of muskets for firing. Yet the line – often stretching over many hundreds of yards, even over miles – is difficult to maintain on the advance, especially over difficult terrain. Columns were more convenient to move at speed, being better able to adjust to the terrain, easier to reform if temporarily dispersed, faster on the march and easier to turn. Hence all infantry armies of the Napoleonic era drilled extensively in moving in column to within musket range, then deploying out into line for action, with the column either on the left, right or centre of the future line.

▼ *The battle of Jena, clearly showing the interaction between infantry lines, artillery and cavalry. (Lebrecht Music & Arts / Alamy)*

The marching column and fighting column

There are some complexities about columns that need explaining, but first we need to distinguish between the two main types of column. 'Marching columns' were those used to march troops long distances across uncontested space. They were long and thin; depending on the width of the road, the column might only be about 6–8 men across. The 'fighting column' – that used on the battlefield itself – was a very different animal. For a start, and contrary to common misconception, the frontage of a column was often wider than its depth, depending on how it was arranged. For example, the 'battalion column by division' – one of the most popular battalion column structures in battle – in its six-company organisation (two-company frontage) was about 75yds (70m) wide by 15yds (13m) deep, while a nine-company battalion (again two-company frontage) measured 50yds (46m) wide by 21yds (19m) across. Each company was arranged in three ranks of men. (Note that the term 'division' here refers to two companies, while 'platoon' was the tactical terminology for the 'company'.[2]) These dimensions would vary according to the front-to-rear intervals between the companies, of course. 'Full intervals' indicated that the distance between one company and that behind it was equivalent to the frontage of the whole column. This interval was stepped down by gradients through half-intervals and 'section' intervals down to 'closed column', in which a mere three paces separated the company ranks. If the

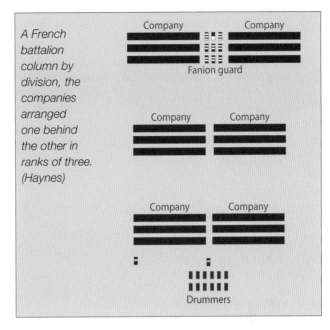

A French battalion column by division, the companies arranged one behind the other in ranks of three. (Haynes)

Company Company

Fanion guard

Company Company

Company Company

Drummers

commander did require a long, thin column of manoeuvre, then he could organise the battalion in 'battalion column by platoon', presenting a one-company frontage.

Columns at the battle of Wagram

The principle of columns could be scaled up or scaled down according to the battle, so that multiple battalions or divisions

---

2 The company was largely an administrative title. In battle, where it was necessary to have units of equal size forming the ranks, the men of unequal-sized companies would be redistributed to form equal-sized platoons, although after the battle they would return to their company command.

▼ *In this depiction of the battle of Eylau (1807) we see French infantry moving in both lines and columns. Note the cavalry column moving up in support. (PD/CC)*

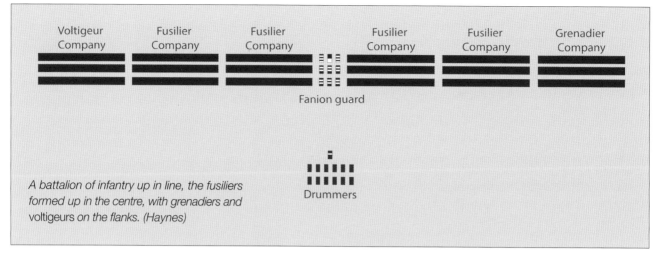

| Voltigeur Company | Fusilier Company | Fusilier Company | | Fusilier Company | Fusilier Company | Grenadier Company |

Fanion guard

Drummers

A battalion of infantry up in line, the fusiliers formed up in the centre, with grenadiers and voltigeurs on the flanks. (Haynes)

(in the conventional military sense of the term) could be formed into enormous columns of attack. One of the most famous examples of this structure is seen at the battle of Wagram on 5–6 July 1809, in which Marshal MacDonald organised three divisions of troops into something approaching a vast column. In fact, this column consisted of eight battalions in line (four-battalion frontage) forming the head of the column, with 12 other battalions arranged in column on the flanks, creating what was in effect a large, empty, three-sided box. Despite the scale and power of the column, however, it was not a success in battle. Of the roughly 10,000 troops who set off against the Austrians, as many as 8,000 were killed or wounded, mainly by Austrian artillery fire.

▼ *Napoleon reviews the ranks of his Imperial Guard during the battle of Jena, 14 October 1806. (PD/CC)*

Vulnerability on the battlefield

This action illustrates one of the key disadvantages of the column – its vulnerability to cannon fire. Because of the depth of a column, a single round shot could wipe out numerous men as it skipped through the ranks. Indeed, artillery commanders would ideally try to orientate their barrels so that round shot went into the column at an angle, to maximise the potential for destructive effect.

On the battlefield, the column was a force of momentum, with the mass of men moving quickly forward, or backward, to achieve the right positioning on the battlefield chessboard. Sometimes the visual threat of the column might be enough to put an enemy line into disorder, but the skill of the battalion commander was to maintain the column for the appropriate length of time before spreading out into line for musket fire and a bayonet charge. At Austerlitz, for example, some French infantry units were a mere 50 paces away from the Russians before deploying into line. But also, there were many French attacks in which the column was maintained up to and through the point of contact, with the commander opting to keep the momentum of his infantry in preference to the line formation.

LINE AND THE ORDRE MIXTE

Some of the advantages and disadvantages of the line have already been mentioned. This long, thin front – often stretching hundreds of yards or even miles – was an unwieldy entity to manoeuvre, but it presented the most powerful frontage of musketry. A six-company battalion arranged in line consisted of each company side by side, in three ranks of men, with a technical interval of 1ft (30cm) between each rank. *Voltigeur* and grenadier companies would hold the flank positions; similarly, in column formations the *voltigeurs* and grenadiers would be the lead units.

The three-rank line was largely the norm in the French Army throughout the Napoleonic Wars, but two-rank lines were also formed. Indeed, two-rank lines were standard for peacetime drill, and some European military leaders, such as the Austrian General Mack and Napoleon's own Marshal Ney, actually advocated two ranks as more efficient than three.

Ney, for example, believed in the efficiency of two ranks, stating in his *Military Studies*:

> The firing of two ranks, or file firing, is, with the exception of a very few movements, absolutely the only kind of firing which offers much greater advantages to infantry... Most infantry officers must have remarked the almost insurmountable difficulty they find in stopping file-firing during battle, after it has once begun, especially when the enemy is well within shot; and this firing, in spite of the command given by the field officers, resembles general discharges. It would be better, therefore, after the two first ranks have fired, to charge boldly with the bayonet, and by an act of vigour force the enemy to retreat.[3]

An important moment in the debate about two ranks or three came in October 1813, when Napoleon issued the order that 'the entire infantry of the army are to form up in two ranks instead of three, in that his Majesty regarded that the fire and the bayonet of the third rank useless.' Partly this modification was born of necessity; with his army so heavily depleted following the campaigns of 1812 and 1813, Napoleon's switch to the two-rank line was one way of maintaining the frontage of his army in battle. But the extent to which two ranks were generally adopted in action is unclear, although there certainly were localised two-rank actions in 1814 and 1815. The use of three ranks, however, seems to have remained the preferred and drilled option.

By presenting infantry line and column separately, we can wrongly gain the impression of a highly formulaic battlefield. In reality, adaptations took place frequently, both from the innovations of the particular commander and through the necessities of the battlefield. One formation, popular with

3   Ney 1833: 368

VOLLEY FIRE AND 'BATTLE FIRE'

A key distinction in French infantry musketry was that between volley fire and what has been called 'battle fire'. Volley fire was, as indicated in Chapter 2, the best way of compensating for the inveterate inaccuracy of the individual musket. The three ranks would establish an alternating system of fire, with one rank firing while another reloaded or prepared to fire, thus reducing the time gaps between instances of engagement. Volley fire, however, had its fair share of problems. Although coordinated fire was part of training, and its cadences on the battlefield marked out with commands, volley fire was extremely difficult to maintain in the heat of battle for any sustained period. The adrenaline of battle, different individual paces of reloading and the slowing effects of gun fouling meant that the synchronisation between ranks and men often broke down into 'battle fire', i.e., each man was effectively firing at his own time and pace. Typically, a commander would not want his unit to remain delivering battle fire for any sustained period of time, on account of its relative inefficiency (unless the troops were skirmishing), hence he would move them forward into a bayonet charge.

Napoleon himself, was *l'ordre mixte*, a combination of both line and column. A three-battalion *ordre mixte* featured a battalion in line in the centre, with a battalion in column at either end. The supposed virtue of the *ordre mixte* was that it combined the firepower of the line with the strength

▼ *Infantry advance in three-rank lines as Napoleon commands from a hilltop, Russia, 1812. (Heritage Image Partnership Ltd / Alamy)*

▶ *A group of re-enactors form up into a hollow square on the site of the battle of Borodino. (Ekaterina Bykova / Shutterstock)*

of movement of the column. Napoleon himself used it successfully on several occasions, such as in 1796 at the battle of Tagliamento and in 1800 at Marengo.

There were also decisions to be made about the battalions and divisions in relation to one another. For example, a common battlefield organisation was to have battalions arranged in line supported by several widely spaced battalions in column several hundred yards behind. The 'battalions of second line' would be prepared to move up to support or take over from the 'battalions of first line'. Furthermore, by having large gaps between the columns, should the first line troops be routed they had clear lines of retreat, to avoid their clashing with the columns advancing forward. Lines and columns could also be arranged in echelon (i.e. at a staggered angle); this formation offered the advantage of both making and defending against a flank attack. Echelon was applied at Marengo, when General Desaix arranged the 9th Light, 30th Line and 59th Line *demi-*

brigades in echelon, refused on the right, against advancing Austrian forces. The 9th Light and the 59th Line were also internally arranged in the *ordre mixte*.

SQUARE

The square was the universal defensive formation adopted by infantry against cavalry. On spotting the enemy cavalry sweeping towards them on the attack, an isolated or outflanked infantry line or column would quickly pull itself into a rectangular shape; in a well-drilled battalion, the manoeuvre might only take 30–60 seconds (it was quicker to form the square from column than from line). In French use, the battalion square was typically oblong in profile, with two companies on each of the long sides and a single company at each end (in a six-company battalion), but there could be variations according to terrain or a command decision. Ideally, multiple squares would be arranged in a mutually defensive arrangement, with overlapping fields of fire and

◀ *Re-enactors of the 85ème Régiment d'Infanterie de Ligne demonstrate a square; albeit in a small scale, the image serves to demonstrate the all-round presentation of muskets. (Christine Sepers)*

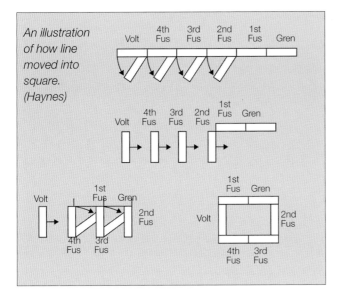

An illustration of how line moved into square. (Haynes)

artillery support in the gaps. If the squares could be arranged at oblique angles to one another, this gave each square a wider field of fire without firing into a neighbouring square.

The square provided a concentration of musket fire. This fire was usually delivered at a range of about 50–100 paces; it was best not to fire at charging cavalry at close range, as the wounded horse might fall and crash into the square, creating holes and fractures that could be exploited by the mounted troops. At close ranges, therefore, bayonets were the best method of repelling the cavalry. A single battalion in square presented some 150 bayonets on each face, which in most cases would repel the enemy. Even the much-feared lancer (see Chapter 3) had the odds stacked against him, in pure numerical terms, when tackling a unified square. If the square could position itself behind defensive terrain, or trenches, to improve the stand-off distance, so much the better.

Artillery was a key factor in the outcome of the battle between cavalry and square. The square's human density made it a tempting target for enemy artillery, which would deliver intense fire as friendly cavalry charged in, hoping to create gaps that the mounted men could exploit. Conversely, the square would ideally itself be defended by artillery, firing at the charging cavalry on their approach. Individual artillery pieces might be positioned in front of the square's corners, as these were the parts most vulnerable to being cut off. For this reason, the corners would sometimes contain concentrations of marksmen, working to kill the cavalry's officers.

Squares were not invulnerable, and much depended on the psychological constitution of the men in them. Yet they were certainly tough nuts to crack, especially if well supported by artillery, as we have seen, and also by friendly cavalry. At Ligny, for example, a heavy charge by the 6th Prussian Uhlans against a small French square of the 4th Regiment of Grenadiers of the Imperial Guard – just 13 officers and 70 men – resulted in many of the Prussian cavalry being killed by musket fire. The defenders' job was assisted by a ditch that broke up the momentum of the charge. The survivors were then forced off the field by French cuirassiers.

SKIRMISHING TACTICS

The French Army showed a particular talent for skirmishing tactics, conducted both by light and by line infantry. In battle, a company of infantry would act as a skirmish chain for its parent battalion, with the company divided into three sections. All three sections would advance in rough line ahead of the front ranks of the battalion, but the centre section was often held back 100 paces to act as a form of reserve to the two other sections. The soldiers themselves operated in pairs, with one man loading while the other man fired. They would make full use of cover and concealment, delivering accurate fire that withered the enemy ranks in preparation for the assault by the main body of infantry. The effects could be pronounced. At the battle of Jena, for example, French skirmishers placed the vast lines of Prussian infantry under fire for two hours, slaughtering large numbers of men who were relatively helpless to respond. A Prussian infantry officer, writing in 1806, noted that:

... from a great distance, the bullets of French skirmishers already reached us; they were placed formidably in the front of us, laying in the field and bushes; we were unacquainted with such tactics; the bullets appeared to come from the air. To be under such fire without seeing the enemy made a bad impression on our soldiers. Then, because of the unfamiliarity with this sort of fighting, they lost confidence in their muskets and immediately felt the superiority of the adversary. They therefore suffered, already being in a critical position, very quickly in bravery, endurance and calmness and could not wait for the time to fire themselves, which soon proved to be to our disadvantage.

▼ *A company of French light infantry skirmishing in woodland, firing their muskets at will. (PD/CC)*

CAVALRY TACTICS

Elements of cavalry tactics have already been discussed in Chapter 3. This section will look at this in more detail, explaining the typical formations adopted by French cavalry units in action, and the relative advantages and disadvantages of each. Regardless of the formation, the squadron was the basic unit of the French cavalry.

Depending on the period in history, and the combat losses endured, the strength of the squadron could vary quite considerably, from about 75 men at the lower end of the spectrum through to about 250 at greater strength. Multiple squadrons formed a regiment (see Chapter 3), and one or two regiments could constitute a brigade.

LINE

A line of literally hundreds of cavalrymen in full charge at about 35mph (56km/h), sabres drawn in the sunlight, was a sight both awe-inspiring or terrifying to behold, depending on whether the cavalry were friend or foe. Some charges stand out for the audacity of their scale. At Eylau in 1807, for example, Murat launched a cavalry charge 40 squadrons strong against the Russians, with some of the breakthroughs driving into Russian lines to a depth of 1½ miles (2.5km). The cavalry charges at the battle of Leipzig in 1813 had double that number of squadrons (French and French-allied): the action around Liebertwolkwitz was the largest clash of cavalry in European history.

▼ *Infantry was most vulnerable when cavalry caught them out in the open. Here Russian Guard cavalry seize the eagle of the 4th Line Regiment at Austerlitz. (PD/CC)*

A cavalry line, indeed most cavalry formations, was organised in two ranks, with very specific regulations decreeing that the total depth of the two ranks was to be 19ft 8in (6m) with a distance of 2ft 2in (66cm) from the tail of the front horse to the nose of the horse behind. Note that the rear line would hold about half of the formation's officers and NCOs, to prevent heavy losses on the front rank stripping the cavalry of its leaders.

In addition to its immense psychological presence, the line offered some practical tactical advantages. It was less vulnerable to artillery fire than the column, for the same reasons as the infantry, and it maximised the sheer number of cavalry attacking simultaneously. By virtue of the line's extended length, the cavalry assault could easily wrap around an infantry formation of lesser width, converting a frontal attack into flanking assaults.

A squadron of cavalry arranged in two ranks measured about 52yds (48m) across, thus, for example, a four-squadron straight line of dragoons had a frontage of more than 220yds (200m), allowing for intervals between the squadrons. The squadrons in line could also be arranged in a 'checkboard pattern', with individual squadrons alternately advanced and refused in relation to

one another, which offered more tactical flexibility than a straight line. The important point, however, was that the line was not extended too greatly. For line deployments had considerable weaknesses, ones that were magnified with the growth of the line. Long lines were difficult to manoeuvre and easy to fragment under the irregularities of pace that emerged during the advance and attack. Being thin by nature, the line could also be penetrated and broken by a concentrated enemy attack, particularly by their own cavalry. The slim depth also meant that the flanks of the line were weak and exposed.

▲ *The battle of Eylau contained one of the greatest mass cavalry charges in history, when more than 10,000 French mounted troops assaulted the Russian columns. (PD/CC)*

▼ *Napoleon takes the surrender of General Mack and the Austrians at Ulm on 20 October 1805, in which Murat's cavalry played a key role. (PD/CC)*

◢ *Arthur Wellesley, the Duke of Wellington, who unlike Napoleon had a rather critical attitude towards cavalry, relying instead on the centrality of infantry action. (PD/CC)*

WATERLOO – CAVALRY CHARGE

Captain J.H. Gronow, of the British Foot Guards, here recounts the experience of facing the French heavy cavalry at the battle of Waterloo, 18 June 1815:

About four P.M. the enemy's artillery in front of us ceased firing all of a sudden, and we saw large masses of cavalry advance: not a man present who survived could have forgotten in after life the awful grandeur of that charge. You discovered at a distance what appeared to be an overwhelming, long moving line, which, ever advancing, glittered like a stormy wave of the sea when it catches the sunlight. On they came until they got near enough, whilst the very earth seemed to vibrate beneath the thundering tramp of the mounted host. One might suppose that nothing could have resisted the shock of this terrible moving mass. They were the famous cuirassiers, almost all old soldiers, who had distinguished themselves on most of the battlefields of Europe. In an almost incredibly short period they were within twenty yards of us, shouting 'Vive l'Empereur!' The word of command, 'Prepare to receive cavalry,' had been given, every man in the front ranks knelt, and a wall bristling with steel, held together by steady hands, presented itself to the infuriated cuirassiers.

I should observe that just before this charge the duke entered by one of the angles of the square, accompanied only by one aide-de-camp; all the rest of his staff being either killed or wounded. Our commander-in-chief, as far as I could judge, appeared perfectly composed; but looked very thoughtful and pale.

The charge of the French cavalry was gallantly executed; but our well-directed fire brought men and horses down, and ere long the utmost confusion arose in their ranks. The officers were exceedingly brave, and by their gestures and fearless bearing did all in their power to encourage their men to form again and renew the attack. The duke sat unmoved, mounted on his favourite charger. I recollect his asking the Hon. Lieut.-Colonel Stanhope what o'clock it was, upon which Stanhope took out his watch, and said it was twenty minutes past four. The Duke replied, 'The battle is mine; and if the Prussians arrive soon, there will be an end of the war.'[4]

4   R.H. Gronow, quoted in 'The Battle of Waterloo, 1815,' *EyeWitness to History*, www.eyewitnesstohistory.com (2004).

COLUMN

The problems inherent in line meant that over the course of the Napoleonic Wars the balance of preference in cavalry tactics lent towards deployment in column. Columns could be assembled and ridden more quickly into battle than the intricate snaking line, and they could make faster turns and manoeuvres, as long as the correct interval (about 17½yds/16m) was maintained between squadrons, giving space for turns and halts. Like the infantry column, the cavalry equivalent was also better able to negotiate difficult or tight terrain, such as woodland, narrow valleys or even streets. The disadvantages were also basically the same – a limited frontage of weaponry and the increased vulnerability to the effects of artillery. In addition, there were the vulnerabilities of the horses themselves. Crossing rough ground at speed, while alarmed by smoke and noise, horses were prone to falling, especially when galloping over churned-up ground littered with the detritus of war. A single horse toppling could result in falls by horses to the side and behind, the whole ghastly accident snowballing out of control until the formation was shattered.

The size of cavalry column was flexible, from a few dozen light horse through to literally thousands of men and mounts crushed together from multiple divisions. The most famous example of the latter is Murat's charge of the reserve cavalry at Eylau – the rushing mass of some 10,700 cavalrymen must have shaken the earth. Cavalry typically organised themselves by regiment, and by squadrons within the regiment. The nature of the columns the regiment could produce had variable width and length, depending on how many squadrons or half-squadrons were used to form the frontage, and on the intervals applied. The simplest formation was the *colonne serré*, in which the squadrons formed a single line, one behind the other, with either full or half intervals. The cavalry could also form a half-squadron line, or by platoons.

Coordinating the cavalry column was no easy matter, especially if it were attempting to make a synchronised firing of carbines or pistols. Firing by squadron was, if it could be pulled off, highly effective, but trying to make it work with unsettled animals and the inevitable fragmentation of the formations was difficult. Ideally, the cavalry column squadrons should wheel past the enemy infantry in turn, setting up a rolling barrage of fire.

Parquin's reference (see box, right) to the danger of flanking attacks is also highly pertinent. Cavalry of both sides were always looking to find the exposed flank of the other. For this reason, intelligent commanders would always retain a reserve to the rear, ready to counteract an enemy flanking force as it massed.

◀ *Jean Louis Ernest Meissonier's detailed image of French cuirassiers about to make a charge. They are of the 12th Regiment of Cuisassiers, given that name in 1803. (PD/CC)*

ECHELON

The cavalry echelon had useful tactical applications for making flanking attacks, and for maintaining a multi-directional pressure upon the enemy. It needed skilful horsemanship and a disciplined holding of the formation to make it work. These requirements were magnified by the scale of the echelon, from a simple squadron up to divisional size. For example, a four-squadron regimental echelon would consist of the four squadrons arranged in a diagonal line, with each squadron formed either in line or column. A large brigade echelon, by contrast, might have the echelon created by staggering the two individual regiments, with each regiment formed into a battalion column.

Tactical descriptions always sound neat on paper, and polished theory often couldn't be further from the experienced reality for the frontline soldier. We do have enough first-hand battlefield accounts from the Napoleonic age to know that confusion and carnage were often the abiding memory of many soldiers. Yet ranks were held with an extraordinary tenacity, not least because the experienced soldiers in the army knew that their chances of survival were better if they fought within a united order.

COORDINATING THE COLUMN

Here is the account from a Captain Parquin, 20th *Chasseur à Cheval*, being sent into action against the Russians at Eylau:

Colonel Castex now inquired if our carbines were loaded. On receiving an affirmative answer he gave the order 'Carbines, ready' – as in campaigning we had the practice of carrying those weapons at the hooks. He next ordered the officers to fall into place in the column and then did so himself. Meanwhile the huge mass of dragoons was steadily approaching us, still at a walk, Colonel Castex regarding them perfectly unmoved. Only when the Russians had approached within 6 paces of us did his voice ring out sharply: 'Fire!' The command was carried out by our regiment as steadily as if on parade. The effect of this one volley was terrific – almost the entire front rank of the Russian dragoons was mowed down. But scarcely a single moment did the enemy waver, for almost immediately the second line took the place of the dead and wounded and the conflict became general. Were it not for Captain Kirmann's presence of mind our regiment would now be in the greatest peril, for a swarm of Cossacks rushed against our left flank ... Nevertheless more than 100 men of the 20th Chasseurs were either killed or wounded. The Russians suffered a loss of at least 300 men, for the square of the 27th Infantry Regiment poured in on them a damaging fire as they were slowly falling back.[5]

5 Parquin 1893: 67

7

THE FRENCH NAVY

It is hard to deny the French Navy was the poor relation of Napoleon's land army. Through the effects of the Revolution, low morale, inferior tactical handling and Napoleon's lack of maritime knowledge, the French Navy was never able to achieve the strategic influence that could have proved decisive in the Napoleonic Wars.

NAVAL STRENGTH

The main focus of this book is on the French land forces, which were undeniably Napoleon's principal arm of decision. This is not to say that Napoleon had only a passing interest in naval matters. At strategic level, he recognised that the Royal Navy's mastery of the waves was a critical problem for France's long-term imperial ambitions.

One of the failed attempts to redress this balance was the Continental System introduced in 1806. By placing a blockade on British imports into any French-controlled or allied state – which by 1806 effectively meant most of mainland Europe – Napoleon hoped to strip the UK of its international economic muscle, and bring it to its imperial knees. Yet, although Britain was indeed temporarily hit hard by the blockade, the strength of Britain's maritime networks, the opening of new markets (especially in the Americas) and the weak controls along many European coastlines meant that the Continental System never managed to implement the stranglehold for which Napoleon hoped. To a large degree, Napoleon's wider maritime strategy was also passive in nature. Rather than have his fleet hunt out and face the Royal Navy in critical engagements, Napoleon's military shipping acted mostly as a 'fleet in being', of sufficient size to ensure that the Royal Navy had to remain vigilant and in a high state of deployed readiness, but not actually muscular enough to take on the British in open battle for final

▼ The Battle of the Nile *by Thomas Whitcombe, showing the catastrophic destruction of* l'Orient. *(PD/CC)*

victory. The most aggressive element to his naval strategy was the distant deployment of independent frigates acting as commerce raiders to challenge British free passage on their most important trading routes.

THE STATE OF THE FRENCH FLEET

In comparison with the British Royal Navy, the French Navy in 1793 was clearly in an inferior position regarding the number of available fighting vessels. In summary, the French Navy had a fleet of 75 ships of the line plus 70 frigates; the respective numbers for the Royal Navy were 129 ships of the line and more than 100 frigates. Furthermore, the Royal Navy had not gone through the social upheaval of revolution, and therefore had a far larger and more stable human resource of experienced officers and crews. The picture for the French was actually much worse when the difference between on-paper strength and actual serviceable craft is taken into account. In fact, of the ships of the line, only 27 were actually commissioned and operational at the beginning of 1793; the others were either in the process of being fitted out or undergoing dockyard repairs.

▶ *The battle of Trafalgar was a vast engagement: 33 British ships versus 41 French and Spanish ships, the total number of vessels including 60 ships of the line. (PD/CC)*

The issue of serviceability was one that would dog the French Navy throughout the Revolutionary and Napoleonic Wars. Largely for contemporary cultural issues of discipline, the careful maintenance of seagoing vessels was often neglected by the crews and officers, resulting in a whole host of problems with seaworthiness and functionality. Badly stowed sails would rot, as would rigging lines and ropes. Woodwork become unsound – keels and hulls especially suffered from the erosion of maritime life, ranging from barnacles to the wood-piercing *Teredo navalis* (naval shipworm). A contributing factor to why Napoleon was unable to mount a successful invasion of Britain was that many of the invasion barges rotted at anchor, as they sat neglected in port.

FRENCH NAVAL LOSSES

In addition there were the consequences of losses in battle, which experienced regular peaks whenever the Royal Navy inflicted another serious blow. At Toulon in August 1793, for example, the French lost a total of 19 vessels, including four ships of the line. Just four months later, again at Toulon, the French were deprived of another nine ships of the line, plus five small vessels. And that was just in the first year of hostilities. At Aboukir Bay on 1–3 August 1798, French losses were two ships of the line sunk, nine captured and two frigates sunk. At the astonishingly imbalanced battle of Trafalgar in 1805, the French Navy lost one ship sunk and ten ships captured; their Spanish allies also suffered 11 ships captured. Taking ships of all types into account, between 1793 and 1815 the French lost some 830 vessels, captured or destroyed.

These and numerous other combat losses meant that the French Navy was never quite able to rise to threaten the Royal Navy or prise the British grip from its maritime empire. Despite this, Napoleon did direct some investment towards shipbuilding, although his ambitious plans often didn't match the eventual output. For example, after the catastrophic losses of Trafalgar, Napoleon ordered a shipbuilding programme for 150 ships of the line. The principal production facilities were at Amsterdam, Antwerp, Brest, Cherboug, Toulon and Venice, all of which had received hefty sums of money to increase their shipbuilding output.

Furthermore, the French Navy also received the collaborative contributions, at various times, from the navies of allied states, such as Spain, Portugal, Denmark, Sweden, Russia, the Kingdom of Italy, Kingdom of Naples and the Netherlands. Spain was the largest naval ally of all, having nearly 100 ships of the line and frigates in 1792.

Yet shipbuilding and alliances could never fully redress the scale of losses in battle, the problems of serviceability and the sheer size of the territory over which the French Navy would have to deploy if it were to take on Britain's naval might.

▼ *The 74-gun ship* Magnanime *is seen here towing the 110-gun ship* Commerce de Paris, *the latter launched in 1806 from Toulon. (PD/CC)*

TYPES OF WARSHIP

The vessels of the French Navy fell under the same categories as those applied to the Royal Navy and other major fleets. The most potent of a navy's ships were the 'ships of the line', which referred to those that had the size and firepower to serve in the 'line of battle' – i.e. the lines of opposing warships facing one another and slugging it out with the cannon.

The ships of the line, and indeed those below them, were further categorised according to a system of 'ratings', which had six rating categories, each according to the number of cannon (main cannon, not auxiliary types such as carronades) carried by the warship. Obviously the greater the number of guns, the physically larger the warship. Thus a 120-gun 'first-rate' ship would have cannon distributed over three decks plus the quarterdeck and forecastle, while a diminutive 'sixth-rate' 20-gun sloop would have just a single deck of firepower.

Beneath the rating system there was a whole host of other diverse minor vessels – barges, sloops, fireships, gunboats, cutters, schooners, xebecs etc. These vessels had none of the glamour of the large ships of the line, but they served in huge numbers and, through providing logistical and minor combat roles, they remained invaluable to the operational capability of the wider navy.

RATING SYSTEM

The general rating system of the ships was as follows; note that by the end of the 18th century only the first three rates were classified as having the capability to take a place in the line of battle:

First rate – These were the largest and most prestigious of the fleet vessels, hence they were often used as flagships. They carried more than 100 guns distributed over three main gun decks; the most sizeable specimens carried around 120 guns. The crew complement would be in excess of 900 men, rising to more than 1,000.

Second rate – Second-rate ships were also three-decker vessels, but carried between 90 and 98 guns and had a crew complement of about 850.

Third rate – Third-rate ships reduced the number of gun decks to two, and had 64–80 guns. Despite the now negative connotations of their name, third-raters were actually the most numerous vessels in the line of battle, and were generally quicker and more manoeuvrable than the first- and second-rate warships. Crew complement was around 750, plus or minus about 100 depending on the numbers of guns.

Fourth rate – The fourth-rate warships were also two-deckers, with 50–60 guns and a crew of about 350. The fourth-raters had a relatively shallow draft, hence were useful for operations in shallow littoral waters and for applications in logistical roles, such as troop transports.

Fifth rate – Fifth-rate warships were frigates, which mounted 32–44 guns on a single gun deck. Frigates were actually one of the most numerous and important warship types in the 19th century. Their speed, manoeuvrability and still-respectable firepower made them flexible enough for a variety of important roles, including scouting, commerce raiding and long-range patrolling, plus participation in major battles. Crew size was about 300.

Sixth rate – The sixth-rate ships were rather like diminutive frigates, with 20–28 guns and c.150 crew.

◄ *The* Wagram *was a 213ft (65m) 120-gun ship of the line, launched in 1810.*

Achille *was a Téméraire-class 74-gun French ship of the line built at Rochefort in 1803. The ship participated in the battle of Trafalgar, taking its place at the rear of the French line. During the battle, it was hit by heavy gunfire, set afire, and eventually destroyed in a magazine explosion.*

COMMERCE DE MARSEILLE

The *Commerce de Marseille* illustrates the superior military shipbuilding capability of the French during the Revolutionary and Napoleonic eras. One of 15 *Océan*-class ships built between 1788 and 1854, the *Commerce de Marseille* had no fewer than 118 cannon mounted in its three decks and on the forecastle, with the large number of weapons courtesy of the longest gundecks of any ship of the line. The armament was distributed as follows:

■ lower deck: 32 × 36pdr guns
■ middle deck: 34 × 24pdr guns
■ upper deck: 34 × 12pdr guns
■ forecastle: 18 × 8pdr guns + 6 × 36pdr carronades

With its complement of 1,079 men, the ship measured 213ft 8in (65.18m) in length, had a beam of 53ft 4in (16.24m) and a draught of 26ft 6in (8.12m); total displacement was 5,098 tonnes. Yet despite its great dimensions, the *Commerce de Marseille* still had good seagoing characteristics, courtesy of the smooth hull design. However, its size counted against it in several regards. Commissioned in 1788, it had been hugely expensive and difficult to produce – just finding sufficient

high-quality wood for the ship had been problematic. Also, its length and draught made it unsuited to docking in all but the most developed of harbours. In August 1793, the ship was captured by the British during the siege of Toulon and taken back to Britain, where it lay largely unused in Portsmouth until it was broken up in 1856.

▼ *The* Commerce de Marseille *was a cutting-edge vessel for its time, albeit in short service with the French navy. (PD/CC)*

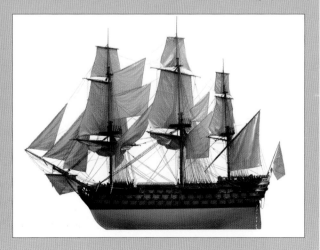

WEAPONS

The French warships were essentially platforms for their cannon, which could be carried in prodigious numbers. The greatest concentration of the cannon was naturally along the main gun decks; pointing out to the sides of the ships to deliver thunderous broadsides, the guns facing the enemy either fired simultaneously or individually as the barrel passed the point of aim.

Gun crews had few options in terms of aiming their weapons with any precision. There was almost no option for traverse – the confines of the gun deck, the nature of the cannon mount, and the barrel's projection through a narrow gun port constrained lateral movement – and elevation was limited. Despite this, the movement of the cannon barrel around the point of aim could be considerable, because of its sympathy with the roll of the ship. Gunners would learn to time their shots with a specific moment in the roll cycle, which, depending on the sea conditions, could mean target options ranging anywhere from the lower hull to upper masts. Note that the British during this period largely shifted over to a lanyard-operated flintlock ignition system for their naval cannon; flintlocks were more reliable in damp conditions, plus they removed the need for having smouldering slow matches present in confined spaces packed with gunpowder. The French adopted the artillery flintlocks in limited numbers, but largely retained the traditional method of firing.

▼ *Although a photograph of a British ship, HMS* Victory, *this image shows a typical if well-ordered gundeck of a Napoleonic-era ship of the line. Note the gun equipment stored on the roof. (PD/CC)*

TYPES AND PURPOSES OF NAVAL AMMUNITION

Round shot: Solid iron balls. Used to penetrate the ship's hull, destroy major upper-deck structures, strike at the rudder or for demasting. Sometimes round shot would be heated up in special ovens before firing. The 'hot shot' embedded itself in the wooden structures and eventually caused fires.

Chain shot: Two or more pieces of round shot connected by a length of chain. Primarily used as an anti-personnel device and for slashing down lines and rigging.

Bar shot: Used for the same purposes as chain shot, but instead of a length of chain, the round shot was connected by an iron bar. The bar was either fixed in length or (once fired) extendable, to maximise the path of destruction.

Grapeshot: Like canister, grapeshot consisted of multiple metal balls inside a canvas bag or tin case, both of which would split apart on firing to impart a massive close-range anti-personnel shotgun effect.

Lang-ridge: Like canister, but with sections of iron bars instead of metal balls.

▼ *An example of fixed bar shot, used to scythe through rigging and sail sheets. (PD/CC)*

NAVAL CANNON

The naval cannon were operated in much the same way as land artillery. The chief difference was that the cannon were mounted on wheeled trucks, which, via a system of ropes and pulleys, meant they could be drawn back inside the ship for reloading, before being pulled back out for firing. While the 12pdr was generally the largest calibre for practical field artillery, the large warships could support the 36pdr and 18pdr guns, as well as a host of lighter pieces down to 6pdr carronades and deck-mounted swivel guns. On multi-deck warships, the heaviest of the cannon would be situated on the lower decks, to keep the ship's centre of gravity as low as possible.

The 36pdrs required a gun crew of 14 and were physically exhausting to operate. They could hurl round shot to a maximum range of more than 1¾miles (3km), although in practical terms for achieving optimal penetration and a manageable trajectory, they were better applied at ranges of under 1,090yds (1,000m). At the opposite end of the scale was the short-barrel, short-range carronade, which was about half the length of a regular cannon. Because of its barrel length, and the fact that it used about half the powder charge of equivalent calibre long-barrel guns, its effective range was just a few hundred yards. Yet, as most naval battles occurred at under a 110yd (100m) range, this was not a hindrance. As well as round shot, carronades would

be used to fire a variety of unnerving anti-personnel and anti-materiel munitions, ripping apart crews, rigging and masts with intense blasts of fire.

PERSONAL WEAPONS

In addition to the main cannon armament, a warship would also be an armoury for a glinting arsenal of personal weaponry. Many naval actions would result in a boarding (see pages 157–8), in which case all manner of hand-held weapons would be put into play – sabres, straight swords, spears, pikes, axes, hammers, daggers, etc. If it could cut or deliver a blunt trauma, it would be used. Many ships would also carry an arsenal of muskets, carbines, rifles and pistols, mostly for the ship's marine contingent (if it had one), but also for officers or certain trained members of crew. The long arms would be used to good effect by soldiers positioned on elevated parts of the ship, from where they would fire down upon the enemy soldiers on the opposing decks.

There were also some types of firearms especially suited to very close-range naval combat. The blunderbuss, for example, was popular in both its pistol and long-arm forms; the flared muzzle resulted in a broad spread of shot on crowded decks. (Amongst land forces, blunderbusses were also appreciated among mounted troops.) Alternatively, but more rarely, an officer might be equipped with a multi-barrel 'volley gun', a single trigger-pull discharging all barrels at once.

CREWS AND MARITIME LIFE

The seriousness of issues surrounding crew professionalism, morale and discipline affecting the French Navy during the Napoleonic Wars can not be overstated. The social and ideological effects of the Revolution critically undermined the professionalism, knowledge and traditions of the French Navy, at the very time when France really needed the most superior crews against the British.

THE REVOLUTION AND THE OFFICER CLASS

Prior to 1789, the officer class of the French Navy was drawn from two main sources – the aristocracy through letters of appointment, and the merchant navy through those who had five years' experience at sea plus passed an entrance exam. The two types of officer often found themselves in a state of professional friction at sea, especially when the former merchant officer, who typically had a wealth of practical experience of ship-handling, felt he was being commanded by a noble with lots of book learning but little real hands-one understanding. Nevertheless, the French Navy possessed a body of officer mariners who ensured that the tight-knit worlds of operational warships stayed functional and purposeful.

That whole order, so important in maritime life, was brought crashing down by the Revolution. Hostile to anything

▼ *A Marine of the Imperial Guard. Such men were known for their versatility as soldiers, having artillery training as well as infantry and maritime skills. (PD/CC)*

that smacked of noble privilege or elitism, the civil French authorities and many lower-rank crew members and dock workers turned on the officer class, with the aggression spreading to officers of both the noble and merchant career paths. The result was a general emigration and resignation amongst the officer class. Philip Haythornwaite notes that regarding 'the most capable senior and middle-ranking officers … of those serving in 1790, perhaps as few as 25 per cent were still on active duty by June 1791.'[1] This was a disastrous development, exacerbated by the closure of several specialist naval schools, and the disbanding of the Marine Artillery corps, with its high-level expertise in naval gunnery. Sound naval knowledge is only properly acquired over years of experience at sea, and could not be easily replaced at speed. Furthermore, although the French reacted strongly against the absolute authoritarianism and brutal discipline aboard Royal Navy ships, there was no denying that such a strict rule generally made British warships bastions of order, both in battle and in peacetime.

LOW MORALE AND MUTINY

The effect of the officer purge was a precipitous collapse in discipline, morale and maintenance aboard French warships, especially during the Revolutionary years. At best, this resulted in inefficient processes or troubled and heckling crews. At worst, it brought mutiny or military defeats. The Atlantic fleet mutinied in 1790 over the introduction of a new penal code. In 1793, the Brest squadron also experienced several serious instances of mutiny, exacerbated by the fact that the lack of experienced officers to arrange supplies resulted in sailors suffering from lack of food and irregular pay. Indiscipline reached chronic levels. Sailors would sometimes simply refuse to obey orders or, worse still, refuse to fight in combat. In one instance aboard the 110-gun *Républicain* in 1793, the ship was so badly handled that her foresails were ripped off, and the subsequent breakdown of discipline meant that the officers could only corral 30 men of more than 1,000 crew to operate the ship. Desertions ran at epidemic levels. The situation for the French Navy was made worse by the fact that many experienced French mariners chose to serve aboard privateers, avoiding the maladies of state maritime service. In 1794, the Brest fleet had 26 captains but only three of them had actually held the previous rank of lieutenant. Some 50 per cent of the crews had never actually been aboard an operational warship.

---

1 Haythornwaite 2017: 162

There were efforts to reform the navy, but these were never wholly effective, and the French fleet remained forever hobbled by issues amongst crews. Despite this, the French Navy still, to its credit, remained a force that could command respect. Individual captains and commanders made a world of difference, especially on frigates roaming far and wide in foreign waters. A good example of fine leadership was that of Captain Jean Jacques Lucas, who commanded the 74-gun *Redoutable* (originally the *Suffren*) that took on Nelson's *Victory* at the battle of Trafalgar, with the highly trained French musketeers mortally wounding Nelson himself. Although Trafalgar was a battle from which the French Navy never really recovered, the fact that the French and Spanish inflicted more than 1,600 casualties upon the British showed that the French Navy could remain dangerous, although strategically contained.

OFFICERS AND MEN

As with any warships of this era, those of the French Navy were socially and professionally stratified and hierarchical, although the boundaries of authority could break down, as we have seen. At the top of the naval tree were the *amiral* (admiral), *vice-amiraux* (vice-admirals) and *contre-amirauaux* (rear-admirals), who were responsible for the leadership of entire fleets or naval forces, while the *chef de division* (equivalent to a commodore) led a naval squadron. Individual ships were commanded by a *capitaine de vaisseau* (ship of the line captain) or *capitaine de frégate* (frigate captain), the former being a more senior officer

▲ *A painting by Philip Loutherbourg shows the chaotic action on the* Glorious First of June *(1 June 1794), the battle descending into numerous piecemeal actions. (PD/CC)*

who had held at least 18 months' command as a *capitaine de frégate*. Beneath the captains, but still within the category of the ship's *État-major* (staff headquarters), were the lieutenants, ensigns, commissaries and pursers.

The men largely responsible for transferring officer commands into physical action were the *officiers-mariniers*, highly experienced 'masters' with specialisms in key areas of warship functionality. They included gunners, helmsmen, harbour pilots, shipwrights, caulkers (those who caulked, or waterproofed the ship with sealant) and sailmakers. Each type of master role was typically divided into 'master' and 'second master' personnel, and each of those categories was in turn subdivided according to first-, second- and third-class distinctions. There was a further group of specialist workers or supernumeraries, who were semi-affectionately referred to as *les fainéants* (the idlers), on account of the fact that they did not have to participate in naval watches, hence it was perceived that they had surplus time on their hands. They included carpenters, blacksmiths, armourers, coppersmiths, victuallers, cooks, bakers, butchers, apothecaries, surgeons and coopers (barrel-makers).

The majority of the ship's company, however, was composed of the regular seamen. The matelots were the most senior of these, graded as 1st, 2nd, 3rd or 4th class

▲ *The* Commerce de Paris *under construction in Toulon in 1806, the hull and gundecks completed. (PD/CC)*

according to length of service, and who acted as assistants to the artificers and performed fundamental tasks such as the furling and unfurling of sails. The lowest on the naval ladder were the ship's boys, teenagers who formed about 10 per cent of the crew. The ship's boys could graduate through 2nd class to 1st class status with experience, and then qualify as a novice, which in turn would lead to the matelot position in their late teens or early 20s, once they were strong enough to take on the role.

MARINES

French warships would include a small garrison of marines aboard, all full-time professional soldiers. The marines not only contributed skills in small-unit maritime combat (such as boarding parties and up-top musketry) and amphibious actions, but they also brought with them specialist knowledge of naval gunnery. Marines would also be used to enforce onboard discipline, if the mood was turning ugly among sections of the crew. All this expertise was threatened in the 1790s by a series of ill-considered 'reforms'. The *Corps royal des cannoniers-matelots*, the gunnery corps under the Bourbon regime, was disbanded in June 1792 and replaced by four regiments of marine infantry and two regiments of marine artillery. These regiments were themselves abolished in 1794 after some elements fought for the anti-republican rebels, and the government attempted to use army units in its place. The failures of using land army personnel for naval gunnery quickly became apparent, thus seven *demi-brigades* of marine artillery were reorganised in October 1795. This in turn became the *Artillerie de Marine* in 1803, made of four regiments. Although marines were ostensibly naval soldiers, as with modern marines they were heavily committed to land fighting, distinguishing themselves in numerous campaigns. Furthermore, groups of sailors might also be formed into units of land soldiers, particularly for use in artillery or engineering roles.

▶ *A naval marine of the Imperial Guard. Napoleon had a particularly high regard for these troops, once commenting: 'I would rather have 100 men like them than all your naval battalions.' (PD/CC)*

LIFE AT SEA

The experience of a French sailor was governed largely by well-established routines, particularly the rhythms of 'watches' – the system of dividing the 24-hour day into periods of activity, ensuring that the ship remained properly manned and operational at all times. The day was divided into six four-hour watches, with each sailor typically performing his duties for between 10 and 14 hours per day.

LIVING CONDITIONS

Actual living conditions aboard many of the French ships were akin to inhabiting an industrial slum. A by-product of the rather more relaxed discipline in the French Navy was that the ships were usually much dirtier than equivalent British craft. The resulting lack of hygiene, compounded by pools of stagnant water, animal faeces, rat and insect infestations, and sweat and body lice (laundry was usually only done twice a month), created a noisome atmosphere in the cramped and dark spaces below decks. Diseases proliferated; maladies included – depending on the deployment – dysentery, cholera, typhus, typhoid, yellow fever, malaria and bubonic plague. The loss of fresh produce through poor storage added the age-old blight of scurvy to the list of horrors.

The bulk of a sailor's daily ration was made up of bread (half a loaf), three biscuits, and a pint (500ml) of red wine or 1½ pints (750ml) of beer or cider. Distributions of salt cod, salt pork, beef, peas, beans, rice and cheese would be made at fixed intervals over the course of a ten-day week (the Revolutionary-era week was a ten-day *décade*, not our familiar seven-day week). Drinking water was stored in large scuttlebutts, but quickly became stale over the course of long voyages, whereupon it was mixed with vinegar to sanitise it. Various livestock were carried on board to provide meat, milk and eggs. For long voyages the usual allocation of livestock was six cattle and 20 chickens per 100 men.

The common sailor would have had little in the way of personal possessions on board. Those that he did have – typically a few grooming items, some playing cards, a select few mementoes of his journey – would be kept in a small sea chest, beneath his hammock. Prior to 4 February 1794, sailors generally shared hammocks, with the man coming off watch slipping into the hammock vacated by the man going on to watch. On that date, however, new regulations were issued in which each man was allocated his own personal hammock, a measure that went some way to improving hygiene and disease control.

BATTLE EXPERIENCE

Battle at sea was a brutal and explosive affair. The physical confines of a ship meant that sailors had few of the manoeuvre options available to troops on land – they simply had to survive in situ as storms of projectiles ripped through their wooden world. The effects of the projectiles on human beings were ghastly, with varying degrees of traumatic dismemberment, and the decks of the craft would become awash with blood and scattered with pieces of flesh. Even if a sailor were not

SIX-MONTH OF RATIONS FOR A MAJOR SHIP OF THE LINE	
Wine	325,415 pints (162,707l)
Biscuit	190,331lb (86,333kg)
Flour	90,807lb (41,190kg)
Salt pork	46,970lb (21,305kg)
Salt beef	3,872lb (1,756kg)
Salt cod	4,528lb (2,054kg)
Cheese	6,791lb (3,080kg)
Vegetables	6,145lb (2,787kg)
Rice	4,528lb (2,054kg)
Peas	15,523lb (7,040kg)
Beans	15,523lb (7,040kg)
Broad beans	15,523lb (7,040kg)
Oil	3,557lb (1,613kg)
Vinegar	10,069lb (4,567kg)
Salt	9,702lb (4,400kg)
Mustard	107lb (48.5kg) [2]

2 Source: Crowdy 2005: 49

struck directly by a projectile, the explosive effects of shot hitting wood produced lethal clouds of high-velocity wooden splinters, which killed or injured many in the vicinity.

Most naval combat took place at short ranges, meaning that the sailors often could clearly see their enemies opposite. Yet the gunsmoke of dozens of cannon firing enveloped the whole battle scene in a whitish-grey fog, reducing visibility to a matter of yards. Up above, in the noise and the smoke, dozens of men would cling to the masts and rigging, either firing muskets or hurling grenades down onto the opposing decks. Masts were frequently brought down by gunfire, possibly plunging the unfortunate occupants into the water – where they would typically drown or be crushed between the hulls of ships – and cluttering the upper decks with endless yards of rope and sail fabric. Below decks, the gun crews would work tirelessly, constantly repeating the patterns of loading and firing, half poisoned by the build-up of smoke in the confined space.

If the combat degenerated into a boarding action, then the two crews would fight like demons among the bodies and debris, using whatever weapons they had at hand. Those with firearms would typically only have the chance for one shot before they closed ranks with the enemy and had to fight hand-to-hand. There was little mercy in such encounters, and those who survived their first such battle would forever be changed men.

NAVAL TACTICS

The tactics of 19th-century naval warfare are a subject of some intricacy, but, in essence, the objective was simple. A commander would attempt to manoeuvre his vessel so that maximum firepower could be unleashed on his opponent's ships. Often this meant the two fleets literally sailing parallel to one another at ranges of about 110–440yds (100–400m).

DIFFERENT APPROACHES

Generally speaking, the French and the British had different approaches to gunnery targeting. The French tended to concentrate on aiming their guns at the enemy's masts, firing the cannon as the ship was on the up-roll. If the masts could be brought down, the opposing ship would lose mobility, and the French vessel could either finish it off, capture it or escape. The latter was very much part of the French tactical psyche, which aimed more at force preservation rather than the outright destruction of the enemy fleet. The British, by contrast, tended to shoot down into the enemy hull, attempting to hole the vessel below the waterline and sink it.

A superior tactical goal was that of 'crossing the T' or 'breaking the line'. In this manoeuvre, the commander would attempt to steer his ship directly past the stern of the enemy vessel. The stern would have only limited firepower – perhaps two to four guns – whereas the attacking commander would be able to unleash his full broadside. Furthermore, shot penetrating the stern would also smash along the length of the ship inside, causing far more extensive damage than it would have if fired into the side of the ship. A superior tactical outcome for a fleet commander was to have his ships pass through the enemy at right angles to the enemy's line of advance, subjecting each ship to 'raking fire' before then turning in parallel again to unleash the simultaneous broadsides.

Although gunnery was the decisive factor in a naval battle, many of the struggles were brought to an end through boarding. Sometimes boarding was compelled by the fact that the ships fought so close to one another that their masts and rigging became entangled and could not be separated. Other times a boarding was judged appropriate because an enemy ship was nearing defeat, and it was felt better to take it as a prize rather than send it to the bottom.

BATTLE OF TRAFALGAR

The battle of Trafalgar, fought on 21 October 1805, was the greatest of the naval battles of the Napoleonic Wars, and as such is a perfect case study for naval warfare tactics of this era. It came at the end of a long period of manoeuvre

▼ *The British fleet brings into Spithead six French ships captured during the Glorious First of June battle. (PD/CC)*

▲ *The French frigate* Pomone *engages the HMS* Alceste *and* Active *during the Action of 29 November 1811, in which* Alceste *was demasted by the French guns. (PD/CC)*

▼ *A 19th-century map of the ships arrayed at the battle of Cape Finisterre, fought on 22 July 1805 between Britain and a Franco-Spanish fleet. (Antiqua Print Gallery / Alamy)*

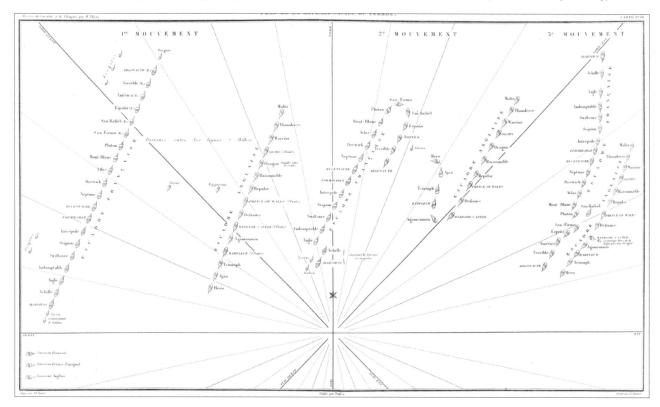

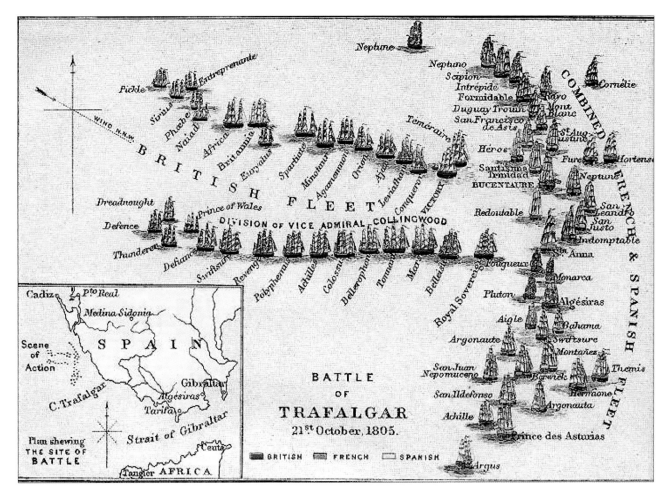

▲ *A plan of the British fleet slicing into the French column at Trafalgar. (PD/CC)*

and counter-manoeuvre by the Royal Navy and the French Combined Fleet, centred around Napoleon's desire to wrest control of the Channel away from the British in preparation for a French invasion of England. The invasion was not to be – Napoleon called it off in light of developments in the War of the Third Coalition – but Admiral Villeneuve's Combined Fleet (French and Spanish) continued to ply up and down the western European and Mediterranean coasts in support of Napoleon's land campaign, picking up troops from the Netherlands, and taking them south to Cadiz in early September. The British Mediterranean C-in-C – the great Admiral Horatio Nelson – kept his fleet searching and probing for the French, hoping for a decisive battle.

Towards the end of September, Villeneuve received his orders to set sail from Cadiz and take his contingent of troops to southern Italy. By this time, however, Nelson had garnered news of the French presence at Cadiz, and had put in place a blockading force, so Villeneuve was aware that his departure could mean a fight. In fact, Napoleon – normally a cautious man in naval affairs – was now demanding that Villeneuve indeed take on the British, and reassert a French presence in the Mediterranean. Villeneuve was naturally reluctant about this. Although his fleet was

numerically superior – 41 warships to the British 33 – the British had superiority in gunnery, ship handling, discipline and manoeuvre, especially as the French and Spanish crews were ragged from months of oceanic wandering.

On 19 October, with the wind driving in the right direction to the south west and pressure from Napoleon building, the French fleet set sail. Villeneuve was aware that Nelson, at the bridge of HMS *Victory*, was shadowing him, and he formed his fleet up into a single battle line, aiming to maximise his broadside firepower. By dawn of 21 October, the two enemies were but 20 miles (32km) apart. Nelson had by this time divided his fleet up into two parallel battle squadrons, aiming to attack the enemy directly from the west. Seeing the developing situation, Villeneuve attempted to turn his line north to run back to Cadiz, although this only succeeded in splitting up his line into two ragged and uneven columns.

Battle was finally joined around midday, when Admiral Cuthbert Collingwood, leading the larger of the British columns from his flagship *Royal Sovereign*, drove straight into the 16 ships that formed Villeneuve's rear column. For a time, Collingwood was outnumbered, as his lead ships had moved into action far faster than those following, but he was eventually reinforced and a blistering gun battle developed. Shortly after, Nelson's squadron ploughed into the centre and van of the French line, breaking through in many instances and 'crossing the T' of the French ships to devastating

▲ Victory *(left) clashes with* Redoutable *(centre) and* Temeraire *at* Trafalgar. *(PD/CC)*

▼ *Being demasted was a critical moment of danger, leaving a vessel largely static and ripe for boarding. (PD/CC)*

▲ *This engraving of Trafalgar by William Miller evokes the close-range combat of naval warfare in this period. (PD/CC)*

effect; *Victory* itself struck many hits on Villeneuve's flagship *Bucentaure* and even rammed the warship *Redoutable*. The latter responded, however, with a profound blow on the British; a French marksman, shooting from the tops, hit and mortally wounded Nelson himself.

By this time the Royal Navy's skills in gunnery were starting to claim the day. Six French and Spanish warships at the very head of Villeneuve's column, led by Admiral Pierre Dumanoir, managed to turn around and launch a counterattack against the British in mid-afternoon, but this was repelled. The battle drew to a conclusion around 5pm. (Nelson had died half an hour earlier). Nineteen French and Spanish vessels had been taken, and Villeneuve was captured; the rest of Villeneuve's vessels, battered by the gunfight, retreated with all the speed they could muster.

The battle of Trafalgar was in effect the last nail in the coffin of French Navy ambitions to control the seas. It had been costly for the Royal Navy – some 1,700 sailors had been lost. But the Combined Fleet casualties were far worse – about 3,000 – and there was no arguing that they had been emphatically outclassed by a numerically weaker enemy. Villeneuve was largely blamed for the disaster, even though Napoleon had essentially forced him to deploy his ships to sea, and he committed suicide in April 1806 after he was released by the British and returned to France.

▶ *A contemporary flyer illustrating the musket ball that killed Horatio Nelson, struck by fire while on the deck of the* Victory *at the battle of Trafalgar. (PD/CC)*

NAVAL KNOWLEDGE

Napoleon, as already noted, was not a naval man at heart. He was not disdainful of naval matters – he did make considerable financial investment in his naval war machine and infrastructure. Yet his comprehension about how maritime operations were conducted was a mix of accurate perception and a dearth of maritime experience.

The following passage, collected from Napoleon's views on the French Navy, is characteristic of his understanding of naval operations:

> Often superior in strength to the British, we have not known how to attack them and have allowed their squadrons to escape, because we have wasted time on pointless manoeuvres. [...] The French Navy is called upon to acquire superiority over the British navy. The French understand construction better and French vessels, as the British themselves admit, are all better than theirs. The guns are superior in calibre by a quarter to British pieces. That represents two great advantages.
>
> The British have more discipline. The squadrons at Toulon and on the Scheldt had adopted the same practices and customs as the British and ended up with equally strict discipline, with the difference entailed by the character of the two nations. British discipline is a discipline of slaves: it is the master faced with the slave. It is maintained solely by the practice of the most appalling terror. A similar state of things would degrade and debase the French character, which needs paternal discipline, based more on honour and feelings.
>
> In most of the battles that we have lost against the British, either we were inferior, or we were conjoined with Spanish vessels which, poorly organised and in recent times degraded, weakened our line, rather than strengthening it; or, finally, the supreme commanders, who sought battle and were advancing towards the enemy until they were face to face, then hesitated, retreated on various pretexts, and thereby jeopardised the most brave.[3]

▲ *Napoleon himself surrenders to Captain Frederick Lewis Maitland on board HMS* Bellerophon *on 15 July 1815, Napoleon's military and political career at an end. (PD/CC)*

performance was intrinsically linked to the discipline of its crews, a discipline that he decries as not in keeping with the French character. Had the French Navy emerged from the Revolution with its officer class intact, and had discipline and order been instated throughout the fleets, the naval clash between France and Britain might have been more finely balanced.

▼ *Whitcombe's depiction of the battle of the Nile in 1798. an action that asserted the Royal Navy's supremacy over the French early in Napoleon's leadership. (PD/CC)*

What is interesting about the passage above is that Napoleon clearly understands the qualities of French ships and gunnery, and appreciates that these had some superior attributes when compared to those of the British. But where his position moves onto shakier ground is his reflection on the issue of discipline. For Napoleon, the failures of the French fleets in action are the result of poor or timid manoeuvring, or the consequences of cooperating with weak allies. What he doesn't see is the fact that the British naval combat

CONCLUSION

Napoleon remains one of the most studied military commanders of all time. The output of articles and books is near constant. At military colleges worldwide, Napoleon will almost certainly have a prominent listing on the syllabus. Numerous re-enactment organisations, often based in countries that were formerly France's enemy during the period, represent assorted regiments of Napoleon's army. Few military leaders have left such an abiding impression on academic and popular culture.

◄ *A cartoon of Napoleon Bonaparte, here dressed as general-in-chief of the Italian Army. (Chronicle / Alamy)*

STRATEGIC VISION

Napoleon was truly a great military leader, a man who held sway over Europe for more than 15 years, and whose tactical confidence and dynamism brought him victory after victory. He was also a flawed man, given to hubris, anger, intolerance, strategic tunnel-vision and, later, a weakening of his tactical brilliance. Eventually his flaws manifested themselves in defeat, giving his story the pathos of a Greek tragedy.

It was the job of the French Army and Navy to execute Napoleon's overarching strategic ambitions, and it is useful to clarify for a moment exactly what they were. By the time he became emperor in 1804, Napoleon's principal objectives could be summarised as follows:

- Expand the geographical extent and international status of the French Empire, primarily by conquest.
- Defeat France's enemies on the field of battle, and create and maintain the world's greatest armed forces.
- Use France's political and military strength to isolate and enervate those powers who persisted in defying France.

Looked at in these three ways, Napoleon was a classical military imperialist in the same mould as, say, Alexander the Great, albeit with the ideological inheritance of the French Revolution. In many ways, and for many years, Napoleon was able to claim that he had achieved all or part of these goals. But there were specific faultlines and mistakes that ultimately undermined his strategic reach, and which finally brought it crashing down.

MILITARY FOCUS

First – and probably the greatest of his strategic weaknesses – was his bias for thinking of executing strategy principally through military means, accentuated by his overwhelming self-belief and grandiose vision for France. The consequences of this motivation, and his related inability to consider the needs of potential allies rather than France alone, were that he often failed to build up alliances of mutual interest that could have better served his long-term ambitions. For example, as we saw in Chapter 1, the Treaty of Tilsit in 1807 effectively made Russia a French ally, a relationship that – if it had been well maintained – could have ensured that France had a stable imperial border to the east and a more effective system for implementing the Continental System against Britain. Yet Napoleon repeatedly mismanaged his association with the tsar, especially in demanding Russian assistance for French wars but being disdainful of Russia's own military needs in its ongoing struggles in the Balkans.

The subsequent collapse of Franco-Russian relations led both to the critical weakening of the Continental System, plus the military debacle that was Napoleon's Russian campaign of 1812. We can point to Napoleon's egotistical handling of the situation in Spain and Portugal in 1808 as a further example of strategic clumsiness, or at least a belief in his own invincibility. His nepotistic re-engineering of the Spanish throne led to insurrection, and the bloody French handling of the guerrilla war in the Peninsula did nothing but create new allies for Britain, and an additional theatre of conflict that drained French resources.

The focus on military outcomes also had a patent effect on the practical management of his army in the field. His military forces were placed under near-constant pressures of campaigning and operations. Between 1804 and the battle of Waterloo in 1815, French forces fought a total of about 132 major land actions, an astonishing tempo of operations. Although this produced an army with a very high degree of combat experience, the constant action – not just fighting but endless marching, often on poor diets and hunted by disease – progressively thinned the ranks of the veterans, with an estimated 1.1 million men-at-arms killed or dying of illnesses between 1803 and 1815. Thus, by committing himself to what was in effect a war of annihilation, rather than seeking genuine diplomatic solutions when they presented themselves, Napoleon set his army on a hard and destructive path.

A BRITISH OBSESSION

Napoleon's lack of long-term comprehension also contributed to his inability to defeat his most persistent enemy – Britain. In this regard, Napoleon was strategically hobbled by his lack of a navy comparable to that of the Royal Navy, although it is by no means certain that, had he possessed such a resource, he would have used it convincingly. Instead, Napoleon attempted to contain Britain through the restrictions of the Continental System, which indeed did have an effect, including a more than 60 per cent drop in worker wages and a drop in exports to the United States from £111 million a year to £2 million a year.[4] But while Napoleon could partly control the flow of British trade into Europe (although his

▲ *Joseph Bonaparte, Napoleon's elder brother, who took the thrones of Naples, Sicily and Spain. (PD/CC)*

▼ *Josephine Bonaparte, Napoleon's first wife, had a powerful hold over Napoleon psychologically for many years until their divorce in 1810. (PD/CC)*

4   Riley, 'Napoleon as General', http://generalship.org/military-history-articles/napoleon-as-a-general.html

▲ *Much blood was split in the cause of Napoleon's wars. Here is the French Napoleonic cemetery in Acre. (PD/CC)*

restrictions were often ignored), his global reach was very limited. Britain still had a broad empire with which it could trade, and it progressively took back its commerce routes to the United States and, from 1810, with Russia – another consequence of Napoleon's failure to build a lasting alliance with the tsar. Indeed, Britain's commercial strength made that nation a principal source of bankroll for the other states that aligned themselves against France. Matthew MacLachlan, in his article 'Napoleon and Empire', sums up Napoleon's errors in relation to Britain perfectly: 'It is evident that Napoleon lost his Empire in 1814 due to personal failings, especially his grandiose self-image which led him to desire the defeat of Britain instead of constructing long-term realizable goals.'[5]

For his army, the struggle against Britain was practically expressed in the prolonged and harrowing struggle in the Peninsular War. Here was a very different form of warfare than that playing out in Central and Eastern Europe. It was an action flowing between counterinsurgency warfare and regular combat, with large numbers of French troops tied down in a theatre on the peripheries of Napoleon's ambitions. The conditions of the campaign – frequent ambushes and cruel punitive responses, a harsh landscape that often prevented conventional battle formations, hard sun and bitter winters – wore down the hundreds of thousands of troops deployed there. Nor did they feel, at times, that their sacrifice was comparatively important. When Napoleon launched the Russia campaign in 1812, some 30,000 of the Peninsular troops were withdrawn from Spain to support it, leaving those left behind stretched thin in the seemingly endless war.

THE RUSSIA CATASTROPHE

Our frequent references above to Russia bring us to Napoleon's third greatest strategic blunder, his decision to invade Russia in 1812. This failed campaign eviscerated Napoleon's *Grande Armée*, critically weakening it for future campaigns and exposing some of the limitations of Napoleonic logistics. At the level of national psychology, the defeat in Russia also demonstrated that Napoleon and his army were not invincible, a message reinforced at Leipzig the following year, and at Waterloo in 1815.

At the highest strategic levels, therefore, Napoleon's long-term ambitions did not rest on the most secure of foundations. By not moderating his imperial relations with

▼ *A monument commemorating the attack of the 21st Line Infantry Division at Waterloo. (M. Mathews)*

▶ *Infantrymen of the 76th Line Regiment reclaim their flags from an Austrian arsenal in Innsbruk in 1805, in this famous artwork by Charles Meynier. (PD/CC)*

▼ *The battle of Leipzig in October 1813 was Napoleon's first massive defeat. The map indicates the sheer weight of the Allied encirclement. (Haynes)*

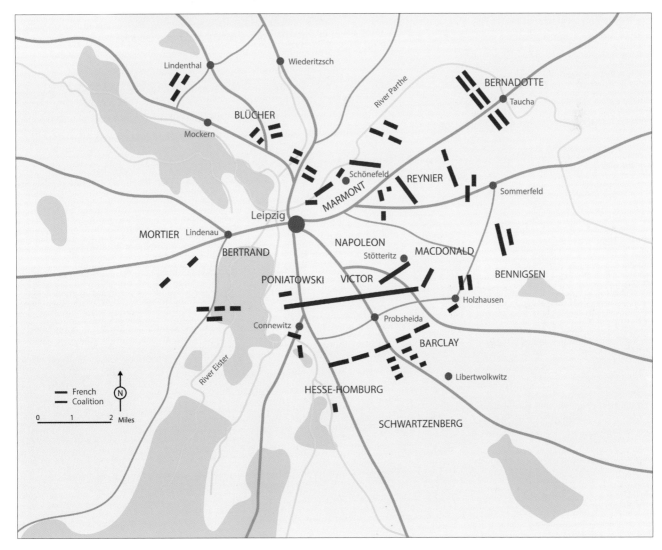

other European states, he kept the French forces committed to near unceasing war, a commitment through which attrition and time would eventually expose the emperor to battlefield defeats. This perspective, however, is largely only available through leisured hindsight. For more than a decade prior to 1812, Napoleon's military brilliance at the operational and tactical levels meant that he appeared terrifyingly unassailable to his enemies.

NAPOLEON'S ARMY

Yet, although Napoleon towers over the landscape and outcomes of the Napoleonic Wars, we must always be careful to give the French Army its independent due. From the chaos of the Revolution, the French infantry, cavalry and artillery troops wrested victories against mighty coalitions of enemy states, even before Napoleon was prominently on the scene. Once Napoleon rose to power, he had a transformative influence over the way that the army marched, moved and fought. The French Army acquired talents and motivations that, for a time, made it the greatest military force in the history of land warfare, despite its weakening under the organisational troubles of the Revolution.

Under Napoleon's influence, the French Army demonstrated an ability to deploy at speeds and tempos that few other opposing forces could match. Tactically it was highly innovative, breaking free from some of the traditional constraints of textbook warfare and exploring true combined-arms tactics with a greater emphasis on manoeuvre and concentration of force. The land army was also bolstered by improvements in its administrative system and command-and-control network, both of which enabled Napoleon to execute campaigns and battles on a scale rarely seen in history. The French Army, although frequently ragged and exhausted, also came to have a real *esprit de corps* and a pride in both its victories and its resilience. Partly this was to do with the confidence and inspiration that flowed from their supreme leader, but it was also due to the way the Napoleonic army was truly meritocratic in its system of promotion and leadership – the divisions between officers and men were clearly etched once they were in place, but they were no longer any class barriers to advancement. Credit must also be given to Napoleon's marshals and generals; his victories were partly due to his command, partly to the talents of his subordinates and also the inveterate toughness of the French soldier. Napoleon owed as much a debt of gratitude to his war machine as they did to him.

▼ *Longwood House on the island of Saint Helena was the final residence of Napoleon during his exile from 10 December 1815 until his death in Longwood on 5 May 1821. (PD/CC)*

BIBLIOGRAPHY AND FURTHER READING

'French Cavalry of the Napoleonic Wars 1805–1815.' Accessed http://www.napolun.com/mirror/napoleonistyka.atspace.com/French_Cavalry.html – 21 June 2018

Colson, Bruno (2015). *Napoleon: On War*. Oxford: Oxford University Press.

Crowdy, T.E. (2015). *Napoleon's Infantry Handbook*. Barnsley: Pen & Sword.

Crowdy, Terry (2005). *French Warship Crews 1789–1805: From the French Revolution to Trafalgar*. Oxford: Osprey Publishing.

De Bourriene, Louis Antoine Fauvelet (1905). *Memoirs of Napoleon Bonaparte*. Vol. IV. Edited by R.W. Phipps. New York: Charles Scribner's Sons.

De Saint-Hilaire, Emile Marco (2005–07). *History Anecdotal, Political and Military of the Imperial Guard*. Trans. by Greg Gorsuch. Published by The Napoleon Series, accessed https://www.napoleon-series.org/military/organization/frenchguard/sthilaire/c_sthilaire.html – 21 June 2018

Durham, Norman L. (June 2009). *The Command and Control of the Grand Armee: Napoleon as Organizational Designer* (thesis). Monterey, CA: Naval Postgraduate School.

Gavaert, Bert (2015). 'The use of the saber in the army of Napoleon'. Accessed http://hroarr.com/article/the-use-of-the-saber-in-the-army-of-napoleon-part-i/ – 21 June 2018

Haythornewaite, Philip (2017). *Napoleon's Military Machine*. Stroud: The History Press.

Haythornwaite, Philip (1983). *Napoleon's Line Infantry*. Oxford: Osprey Publishing.

Haythornwaite, Philip (1990). *The Napoleonic Source Book*. London: Guild Publishing.

Henry, Philip, 5th Earl Stanhope (1888). *Notes of Conversations with the Duke of Wellington 1831–1851*. New York: Longman, Green & Co.

Holmes, Richard (2006). *The Napoleonic Wars*. London: Carlton.

Jomini, Baron de (1862). *The Art of War*. Trans. by G.H. Mendell and W.P. Craighill. Philadelphia: J.B. Lippincott & Co.

Kiley, Kevin (2004). *Artillery of the Napoleonic Wars*. London: Greenhill.

MacLachlan, Matthew (Dec 2007). 'Napoleon and Empire.' *History Review*, Issue 59. Accessed https://www.historytoday.com/matthew-maclachlan/napoleon-and-empire – 21 June 2018

Marmont, Auguste Frederic Louis Viesse de (1862). *The Spirit of Military Institutions, or, Essential Principles of the Art of War*. Trans. by Henry Coppée. Philadelphia: J.B. Lippincott & Co.

McNab, Chris (ed.) (2009). *Armies of the Napoleonic Wars*. Oxford: Osprey Publishing.

Muir, Roy (1998). *Tactics and the Experience of Battle in the Age of Napoleon*. New Haven and London: Yale University Press.

Ney, Marshal (1833). *Military Studies by Marshal Ney*. Trans. by G.H. Caunter. London: Bull & Churton.

Nosworthy, Brent (1995). *Battle Tactics of Napoleon and His Enemies*. London: Constable.

Parquin, Charles (1893). *Napoleon's Victories: From the Personal Memoirs of Capt C. Parquin of the Imperial Guard 1803–1814*. Chicago: The Werner Company.

Pawly, Ronald (2004). *Napoleon's Imperial Headquarters (1): Organization and Personnel*. Oxford: Osprey Publishing.

Pawly, Ronald (2004b). *Napoleon's Imperial Headquarters (2): On Campaign*. Oxford: Osprey Publishing.

Pollock, Colonel John L. (2011). *Napoleon's Strategic Failures*. Carlisle Barracks, PA: US Army War College.

Pope, Stephen (1999). *The Cassell Dictionary of the Napoleonic Wars*. London: Cassell.

Riley, Jonathan (2007). 'Napoleon as a General.' Accessed http://generalship.org/military-history-articles/napoleon-as-a-general.html – 21 June 2018

Roberts, Andrew (2014). *Napoleon the Great*. London: Penguin.

Rogers, Colonel H.C.B. (1974). *Napoleon's Army*. London: Ian Allan

Smith, Digby (2000). *Napoleon's Regiments: Battle Histories of the Regiments of the French Army, 1792–1815*. London: Greenhill.

Van Creveld, Martin (2004). *Supplying War: Logistics from Wallenstein to Patton*. Cambridge: Cambridge University Press.

Walter, Jakob (1938). *A German Conscript with Napoleon: Jakob Walter's Recollections of the Campaigns of 1806–1807, 1809, and 1812–1813*. Ed. and trans. by Otto Springer. Lawrence, KS: University of Kansas

Wartenburg, Count Yorck von (1902). *Napoleon as a General*. London: Kegan Paul, Trench, Trübner & Co. Ltd.

Wassan, Major James. 'The Development of The Corps D'Armée And Its Impact on Napoleonic Warfare.' Published by The Napoleon Series, accessed at https://www.napoleon-series.org/military/organization/c_armycorps.html – 21 June 2018

Wise, Terence (1979). *Artillery Equipment of the Napoleonic Wars*. Oxford: Osprey Publishing.

INDEX